ENDANGERED ANIMALS

SPECIES FACING EXTINCTION, AND THE THREATS TO THEIR HABITATS

ENDANGERED ANIMALS

WILLI DOLDER   URSULA DOLDER-PIPPKE

Bath · New York · Singapore · Hong Kong · Cologne · Delhi · Melbourne

This is a Parragon Publishing Book

This edition published in 2009

Parragon Publishing
Queen Street House
4 Queen Street
Bath BA1 1HE, UK

Copyright © Parragon Books Ltd 2009

ISBN: 978-1-4075-5697-0

Printed in China

German edition created and produced by: ditter.projektagentur GmbH
Editor: Irina Ditter
Picture editor: Willi Dolder, CH-Kirchberg
Layout and design: Ilona Buchholz
Cartography and graphics: Burga Fillery, Milch | Design und Kommunikation
Lithography: Klaussner Medien Service GmbH

American edition produced by: Cambridge Publishing Management Ltd
Project editor: Diane Teillol
Translator: David Darrah-Morgan
Copy editor: Charlotte Kelchner
Layout: Donna Pedley
Proofreader: Karolin Thomas
Indexer: Marie Lorimer

CONTENTS

FOREWORD

Life on Earth developed over an extremely long period of time, during which species appeared and then died out according to their own genetically determined cycle of life.

This cycle changed with the emergence and spread of humans, who, through their increasing interventions in various habitats, exerted a growing influence on flora and fauna: deserts were irrigated, wetlands drained, savannas and forests cleared, land sealed with concrete and asphalt, rivers straightened, and soil, air, and water polluted with harmful substances. Consequently, numerous animal and plant species have been eradicated or are at risk of disappearing, and today, humankind itself is facing increasing problems: Earth and its atmosphere are warming, the number and severity of natural disasters are increasing, and drinking water and food are becoming scarce. Meanwhile, there is now a certain degree of awareness of the problems, and attempts are being made to reverse the trend, so that at least some of the damage feared may still possibly be averted.

In Africa, there are still some large expanses that convey an impression of pristine wilderness, such as the Masai Mara, a national park in Kenya.

A small, increasingly rare idyll: Grazing sheep in the Scottish Highlands ensure that open areas do not become overgrown.

Where too much water is retained in reservoirs, all that remains of once-raging mountain streams is a mere trickle of water.

Right: Planet Earth is surrounded by a gossamer-thin atmosphere, which humankind has been heedlessly altering for the last 200 years.

Below: The primary forests in South America, Asia, and Africa, which are essential to our climate, are disappearing at a breathtaking rate. What remains is barren wasteland.

Structure and focal points of the book

It is a fact that thousands of animal species are currently vulnerable or even threatened with eradication, so the animals described here represent merely a cross section.

The structure of the book is based on the zoological classification system, but given that there are two million scientifically described animal species, it was not possible to begin to include all classes of animals. The emphasis is on vertebrates, and the weighting given to individual classes depends primarily on how well scientifically researched they are, and secondarily on the extent of their "audience appeal." For this reason, mammals and birds are accorded the majority of the space in this book and—in contrast to the more general approach adopted in the chapters on fishes, amphibians, and reptiles—are subdivided into smaller sections, based principally on animal families. In addition, mammals and birds have been studied in greater depth, so there is more information available about their numbers and about their threat status. Furthermore, people generally feel more of an emotional link to them than to such animals as bristle worms and crawfish.

Invertebrates are also threatened

The focus on vertebrates meant that the largest class of animals, which, by virtue of their position near the base of the food web, is of enormous importance for the animal kingdom, had to be ignored: insects (Insecta) from the group of invertebrates (Invertebrata). About one million insect species so far have been scientifically recorded, but the majority of species—the number is estimated at up to 20 million—which live primarily in the huge virgin forests of South America, central Africa, and tropical Asia, are as yet unknown to science. This means that more than 99 percent of all known living organisms, and probably 99.9 percent of all as yet undiscovered organisms, belong to this class. In recent decades, monocultures and, in particular, the extensive use of insecticides, have led to

Even in Africa, where animals were once so abundant, the fauna now remains to a certain extent intact only in some of the large national parks, such as the Serengeti, Kruger, or Etosha national parks.

the extermination of billions of insects, to the extent that the situation for insects has also deteriorated. In 2007, the Red List of the International Union for Conservation of Nature and Natural Resources (IUCN), an international nature conservation organization that also manages field projects all over the world, listed 50 percent of the insect species assessed as being under threat. However, of the nearly one million species recorded, only a fraction, i.e. just under 1,300, have been assessed. The situation is similar in the case of other invertebrates, such as mollusks, crustaceans, and corals, all of which are severely threatened to a greater or lesser extent.

Outlook for fauna is poor

The authors have, in the main, based their assessment of the threat status shown here for individual orders, families, and species on the guidelines of the IUCN and its Red List of threatened animal species, but have simultaneously taken into account more recent and up-to-date studies by other nature conservation agencies and scientists. It is essential to point out that in the past 500 years, at least 1,500 species have verifiably been eradicated, and that in the medium to long term—where "long term" means about 100 years—90 percent of all vertebrate species are likely to become vulnerable or even endangered.

Above: Earth's polar regions are particularly fragile habitats for a few, extremely specialized animal species such as the polar bear, Arctic fox, and various species of seal.

Below: The disappearance of smaller animal species—shown here is the birdwing butterfly (*Ornithoptera priamus*)—often goes unnoticed.

When is a species threatened?

A species of animal is deemed to be vulnerable or threatened when its population—or populations, in cases such as that of the orangutan, where groups are geographically widely separated—is no longer of the size necessary for the survival of the species. Or, to put it another way, a species is considered vulnerable or threatened when fewer animals are being born than are dying. Causes are manifold: biotope destruction, environmental pollution, and direct persecution through hunting or poaching.

The smallest populations, lying below the critical threshold of 200–500 animals, are always particularly vulnerable. This is often the case with island populations, as well as with animals that have a small range or that are very highly specialized in their adaptation to their habitat.

For many peoples, herds of cattle and donkeys represent their only wealth. The uncontrolled increase in the numbers of these animals is a factor contributing to the destruction of vegetation cover, which is often very fragile.

Terminology used

The widely recognized *Red List of Threatened Species* was first conceived in 1963 and is published by the IUCN on an annual basis, and for this purpose has introduced a set of terminology that many other nature conservation organizations and bodies also follow—at least in part—and on which the classifications used in this book are based:

Potentially threatened—a species is not immediately threatened, but is included on the Red List. For the purposes of this book, the various preliminary threat categories differentiated by the IUCN—near threatened, lower risk, and least concern—are combined under this heading.

Vulnerable—populations have declined substantially and can no longer be considered secure unless the circumstances threatening their survival improve.

Endangered—populations, both globally and locally, are at great risk of becoming extinct and require urgent protection. Isolated groups are dying out.

Critically endangered—populations don't comprise, in most cases, more than 1,000 animals worldwide. Their survival in the wild without special protection from humans is unlikely. (This category should really be called "threatened with eradication," because it is never a case of their dying out naturally.)

Extinct in the wild—the species has been eradicated in the wild, but there are still some, mostly small, populations in captivity, some of which will be released into the wild with varying degrees of success.

Extinct—a species has been irretrievably eradicated, and there are no animals remaining in captivity.

Above: Pollution and warming of the world's oceans are threatening tropical coral reefs.

Right: Over 70 years ago, in 1936, what was probably the last Tasmanian tiger died in Hobart Zoo in Tasmania. Confirmed sightings in the wild had already ceased before that date.

With all listings of endangered animals, it is important to be clear about the fact that they merely represent an indication of the population of an animal species at the time of a study, count, estimation, or field study and, with a few exceptions, do not necessarily express a definitive state of affairs. Moreover, many population counts are often 10 or more years old and are therefore no longer particularly meaningful; regular studies founder, in most cases, because of insufficient funding.

INTRODUCTION

Since the beginning of geological time, between 500 million and 600 million species have died out, but, as far as anyone knows, one species had never wiped another, or even itself, from the face of Earth—until humans arrived.

During the Stone Age and until well into the Middle Ages, humans and animals still coexisted peacefully, for the most part. The picture altered in the sixteenth century for two reasons: first, the human population—and thus also human demand for land and food—increased exponentially, and second, the invention of firearms enabled humans to hunt wild animals in significant numbers that had previously been able to defend themselves.

As long as the animals still had enough areas in which to seek refuge, they were able to survive; however, in the ensuing centuries these areas steadily dwindled, while firearms and hunting methods became increasingly effective. From this time onward, many species were exterminated, and others teetered on the brink of eradication. In Europe, for example, the aurochs, a wild ox, disappeared at the beginning of the seventeenth century. The tarpan, a wild horse, followed toward the end of the nineteenth century, and, at the same time, bison populations in North America were decimated.

To date, humans have eradicated thousands of species, and the destruction of fauna and flora continues unchecked: every day, two to three plant and animal species disappear. The International Union for Conservation of Nature (IUCN), in its latest *Red List of Threatened Species*, listed 16,000 plant and animal species that are critically endangered to a greater or lesser extent—out of a total of 40,000 that they had assessed. Because 1.5 million species have so far been described, and innumerable species have not yet even been discovered, one can assume that these figures represent merely the tip of the iceberg.

Bushmeat

Air pollution

Soil contamination

Monocultures

THE BEGINNINGS OF LIFE

First life on Earth

Life on our planet is nearly as old as Earth itself, i.e. 4.5 billion years old. Initially, in the Hadean eon, the oceans were populated only by single-celled bacteria, and it was two billion years before the first multicellular organisms appeared. These were Coelenterata, which likewise lived in the primeval oceans. Evidence of the first vertebrates, jawless fishes, stems from the Cambrian period, approximately 540 million years ago.

Meteoric development

Evolution then speeded up massively, compared with its development up to that point: 500 million years ago, the first plants colonized dry land; 100 million years later, the first land invertebrates arrived, predominantly lower animals, arthropods such as insects, scorpions, and spiders. In the Carboniferous period—350 million years ago—the first amphibians appeared, followed by mammal-like reptiles, the forebears of modern mammals. Of the more than 1,000 known species in this latter group, not even one has survived, but they were not the only ones to die out: about 75 percent of all land animal species and 95 percent of those living in the oceans disappeared.

The mysterious disappearance of the dinosaurs

In the Triassic period, about 250 million years ago, dinosaurs and pterodactyls appeared. These animals, of which there were almost

Dinosaurs lived on Earth for almost 200 million years before they became extinct at the end of the Cretaceous period for reasons that have not been definitively explained.

1,000 genera, then ruled Earth for 200 million years. The reason for their disappearance remains unclear to the present day: the most widely held hypothesis is based on a meteorite strike near the Mexican Yucatan Peninsula, and a secondary hypothesis cites volcanic activity and eruptions around the world. Whatever the reason, 65 million years ago the dinosaurs disappeared in an amazingly short time, leaving behind small-sized descendants that went on to evolve into birds.

Eradicated or extinct?

The terms *eradicated* and *extinct* are mistakenly often used synonymously, but strictly speaking, a difference should be made between them. Only those species that have disappeared without any human interference may be described as "extinct"; all species that have been wiped from the face of Earth through the direct or indirect influence of humans should be considered to have been "eradicated."

The geological timescale below illustrates the most important evolutionary developments on Earth.

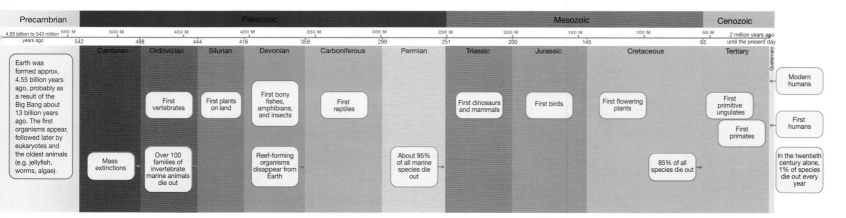

THE ADAPTABILITY OF LIVING ORGANISMS

Evolution through natural selection and genetic drift

Charles Darwin (1809–1882) published his revolutionary *Origin of the Species* in 1859 and was one of the first naturalists to recognize that a species does not remain unchanged but evolves over time and adapts to changes in living conditions. As we now know for certain, changes in the hereditary characteristics of a population—evolution—are based on the factors of genetic drift and natural selection. Whereas genetic drift, simply expressed, results in random changes in genetic makeup, natural selection is the passing on of the "best" genes for the survival of a species: the individuals that are best adapted to their living conditions have a higher chance of surviving and reproducing—and thus of passing on their "good" genetic material, while poorer genetic material gradually disappears from the population. This process is referred to as the survival of the fittest.

Genetic bottlenecks

The adaptability and longevity of a species are, in any case, limited. The disappearance of the majority of extinct animals was not due to any external influences, but to the fact that the gene pool, their genetic diversity, was exhausted and so no longer capable of reacting to new circumstances. Genetic drift also becomes less likely because the rarer variants of a gene are no longer available.

An example of this is the leopard: the African and Asiatic populations were on the brink of extinction a few tens of thousands of years ago—only a few dozen animals had survived an unknown illness or natural disaster. The remaining specimens reproduced among themselves, leading to a so-called genetic bottleneck: the leopards surviving today, of which there are between 3,000 and a maximum of 10,000, are so closely related that, due to genetic impoverishment, natural selection and genetic drift are practically no longer possible. The animals are, therefore, highly susceptible to hereditary diseases.

Right: The cheetah once passed through a particularly tight genetic bottleneck.

Below: All the Przewalski's horses surviving today can be traced back to twelve purebred specimens captured in the wild, so their gene pool is relatively small.

FACTORS IN THE ERADICATION OF ANIMALS

CHANGES IN THE WAY HUMANS LIVE

For a long time, humans were nomadic hunter-gatherers, but after the end of the last ice age, 10,000–13,000 years ago, humans began to build settlements and to become sedentary. The reasons for the change in their way of life are not known; some scientists believe that the fundamental changes in the fauna following the ice age could have been a key factor, as well as the fact that the birds and animals they hunted retreated with the ice. To survive, the former hunters had to cultivate grain and vegetables and to keep livestock, such as cattle and sheep.

Better chances of survival

Sedentarism has been the most far-reaching change in the last 100,000 years of human history. As long as humans moved around as nomads, their survival was heavily dependent on their hunting fortunes because provisions could only be laid in on a very limited scale. However, once people began to establish settlements, to plow fields and to keep livestock, their lives underwent a lasting change: it became easier to plan ahead. The building of huts and settlements and the diminishing risk of fatal hunting injuries led to a lasting improvement in their chances of survival—hunting for wild animals was not abandoned

The settlement of Skara Brae on the Orkney Islands dates from the Neolithic, the beginning of which is defined as marking the transition to sedentarism.

Proportion of immediately threatened species within a class of animals

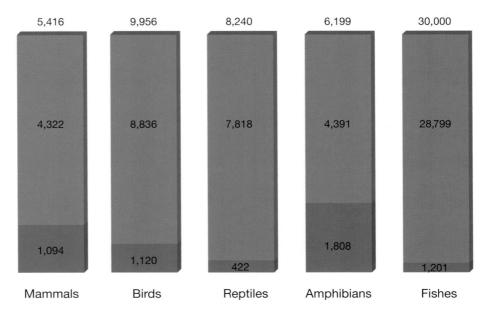

	Mammals	Birds	Reptiles	Amphibians	Fishes
Total	5,416	9,956	8,240	6,199	30,000
Not immediately threatened	4,322	8,836	7,818	4,391	28,799
Immediately threatened	1,094	1,120	422	1,808	1,201

- ▮ Species not immediately threatened
- ▮ Species immediately threatened

Distribution of immediately threatened species by individual risk category

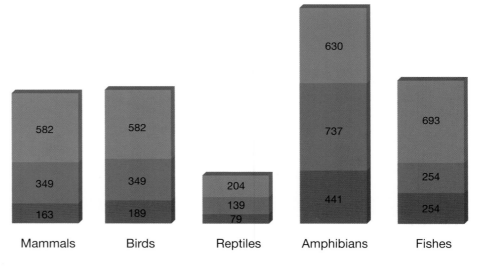

	Mammals	Birds	Reptiles	Amphibians	Fishes
Vulnerable	582	582	204	630	693
Endangered	349	349	139	737	254
Critically endangered	163	189	79	441	254

- ▮ Vulnerable species
- ▮ Endangered species
- ▮ Critically endangered species

The top chart shows the proportion of threatened species within the classes of animals, the lower chart the distribution of immediately threatened species by individual risk category. However, the figures, which are based on IUCN data, include only species that have been assessed and are of only limited information value, since it is not possible to assess all species of all classes annually.

completely at that time, but it was greatly reduced, because it was no longer essential to survival.

Humans need space

As a result of significantly improved living conditions, the human population grew, but primitive humans were not initially a danger to the fauna or to individual animal species. Only as population numbers rose into the hundreds of thousands did humans increasingly pose a threat to animals because they needed more and more land for settlements, for cultivating grain, vegetables, and fruit, and for grazing livestock. To meet this demand, new cultivable areas were created through slash-and-burn clearance, and, at the same time, both habitats and the animals living in them were destroyed. The primeval forests began to disappear—and have continued to do so through the present day—with alarming speed, as the destruction of the rainforests in South America, Asia, and Africa shows.

Biotope changes

Year after year, vast areas of forest are being destroyed and steppes and savannas are plowed up or overgrazed, i.e. loaded with more livestock than they can cope with. Other biotope changes—such as the draining of wetland areas, the straightening or damming of rivers, and the clearance of wild hedgerows and scrubland—are also harming the animals that live there. Once converted into land under

cultivation and monoculture, areas that, in their original state, provided habitats for an incredible wealth of animals and plants become desolate and species-poor.

Top: Clear-cutting of rainforest in Belize. Vast areas of forest fall victim each year to slash-and-burn clearance and deforestation.

Right: Monocultures like these corn fields in Kenya are "biological deserts" in which wild animals are unable to find a habitat or niche and are eradicated by herbicides and pesticides.

Bottom: The slash-and-burn clearance of primary forests, particularly in Southeast Asia, results in air pollution whose impact is felt even as far away as Europe.

The threat to the tropical rainforests

As recently as the 1950s, it was estimated that the tropical rainforests still covered approximately 11 percent of Earth's total land area, whereas today, the proportion amounts to only 8 percent at most—and with each piece of land disappearing, not only are plant species dying, but also animal species for whom it provides a habitat. Protection of the rainforest is therefore a key goal of many environmental organizations. The rainforests are being cleared for timber extraction, but above all, for conversion into agricultural land. This takes the form either of clear-cutting or of slash-and-burn clearance, which is particularly disastrous for the resident animals. A major problem is also posed by illegal logging—the harvesting of and trading in timber.

THE HUNTING OF ANIMALS

Hunting by humans, taken in isolation, may only extremely rarely have led to the global extermination of a species, but, particularly in combination with the destruction of areas of refuge, it has pushed a considerable number of species to the brink of eradication. This applies primarily, but not exclusively, to large mammals, such as the American and European bison, tiger, and mountain gorilla. One of the most dramatic examples of near eradication by humans is the hunting of cetaceans. As a result of hunting on a massive scale, almost all of the approximately 80 species—from the small river dolphin to the giant blue whale—are directly or indirectly threatened with eradication. In 2007, the Chinese river dolphin was the first cetacean to become eradicated in modern times and the first large mammal to become so for more than 50 years.

The problem of commercial hunting

Animals are frequently hunted for their meat, fur, or leather. As long as hunting is carried out to meet people's individual needs, it does not normally present a problem for a species, but once the emphasis is on commercial profit, the situation changes, as the example of the bison shows. Need-based hunting by the Native American peoples never posed a threat to the enormous populations, but killing of the animals by European settlers for the lucrative buffalo skins, as well as simply for pleasure, brought the species to the brink of extinction.

Illegal hunting for a range of motives

The illegal hunting of many animals for their skins or other trophies remains a problem today. In Asian countries, in particular, the body parts of a number of rare animals play an important role in traditional medicine, be it as an aphrodisiac or as a therapeutic remedy. Despite the ban, rhinoceros horns, deer antlers, and bear gallbladders are traded at high prices. The trade in bushmeat, that is, the sale of meat from wild animals, has also increased substantially in recent years.

Top: On "game farms" in southern Africa, the shooting of rhinos is once again being permitted, despite their endangered status.

Bottom left: Up until the 1950s, waste-paper receptacles and bar stools made from elephants' feet were very popular.

Bottom right: One factor contributing to the endangered status of many wild animals is the trade in bushmeat supplied to local markets in South America, Asia, and Africa—such as the head of a lowland gorilla shown here.

THE PROBLEM OF THE INTRODUCTION OF ALIEN SPECIES

Another action perpetrated by humans that can have an impact not just locally but also globally is the introduction of alien species. This is defined as the introduction by humans of nonnative species into a faunal area. These newcomers, referred to as *neozoans*, can cause severe harm to the local fauna or flora.

Rabbits, toads, and squirrels as pests

One of the best-known cases of the introduction of alien species is the introduction of the European rabbit to Australia where, in the absence of enemies, it multiplied phenomenally and caused enormous damage to the biotope. Another animal brought to Australia by humans was the cane toad (*Bufo marinus*) from South America; like the rabbit, it became a pest there. About 100 years ago, the American gray squirrel (*Sciurus carolinensis*) was introduced into the United Kingdom. Thanks to its biological advantages—greater body size, larger number

In the absence of any natural enemies, the European wild rabbits introduced into Australia for hunting were able to multiply uncontrolled and devoured the pasture of both the sheep and the indigenous wild animals.

of young, and shorter hibernation period—it has almost completely ousted the indigenous squirrel from some areas.

Starving giant tortoises on the Galapagos Islands

A further example of human carelessness can be found on the Galapagos Islands, in the Pacific Ocean off the coast of Ecuador. Settlers from mainland America and from Europe brought pigs, goats, dogs, and cats with them to the islands, which are renowned for their unique fauna. Many domestic livestock animals

Pets that were introduced by European settlers and became feral presented an enormous danger to the Galapagos giant tortoises in the past. Today, the threat from tourism is far greater.

became feral and grazed entire stretches of their new habitat bare. As a result, large numbers of giant tortoises starved to death. In addition, dogs and pigs dug up and ate clutches of tortoise eggs, as well as helping themselves to the eggs of ground-nesting sea birds, and, in doing so, brought numerous species to the brink of eradication.

ENVIRONMENTAL POLLUTION

Environmental pollution is one of the factors indirectly responsible for the eradication of many animals. Over the centuries, human activities have caused our water, soil, and air to accumulate chemical substances, many of which are extremely toxic. Pollution of one component of Earth's systems is closely linked to pollution of others because many hazardous substances easily move among the air, soil, and water. The poisoning of the environment happens in an insidious fashion, and the effects are only seldom directly visible—which may be one reason why Earth's problems are still not being taken sufficiently seriously.

Water pollution

Phosphorus and nitrogen compounds, pesticides, medicine and hormone residues, mineral oil and crude oil, nitrates, heavy metals, and other industrial wastes pollute aquatic

Above: CO_2 emissions from the 800 million motor vehicles worldwide are one of the main causes of air pollution and of the climate change that results.

environments and consequently destroy the habitats of innumerable creatures. Although water pollution has decreased in the last few years, primarily as a result of the introduction of modern sewage treatment plants in many countries, a large number of hazardous substances are still entering rivers, lakes, and seas—some from the soil, some disposed of illegally by industry. The impact of water pollution is particularly dramatically evident when large numbers of fishes die, for example, as a result of chemical spills or following tanker disasters.

Soil contamination

Soils and aquatic environments are both contaminated with very similar substances, with agriculture playing a major part in soil contamination. Although, to a certain extent, a rethink has now taken place, and increasing use is being made of biological control agents that place little or no load on ecological systems, chemicals are still deployed frequently: cultivated crops are protected with chemical

Time after time, countless animals, such as this penguin in South Africa, die as a result of pollution of the seas and coasts with oil following tanker accidents.

Although statutory provisions in the European countries ensure that fewer and fewer toxins are emitted, newly industrialized countries such as China, India, and Brazil are among the major environmental polluters.

agents against insect pests, fungi, etc., to reduce harvest losses. However, these substances are extremely harmful to the environment. Some of them even have long-term effects on humans and animals that only become apparent after years or decades. A particularly stark example is the insecticide DDT, used from the 1940s onward, which degrades only slowly and accumulates in the food chain over many years. In the 1970s, a widespread ban on the agent was introduced—first in the United States, and then in Europe—because it was recognized as a possible cause of cancers in humans. Since 2004, the use of DDT has been permitted only to combat insects that transmit diseases, such as the anopheles mosquito (malaria mosquito).

When manure enters water, ammonium nitrogen is converted into highly toxic ammonia, which, even at low concentrations, kills fishes and small living organisms.

Air pollution

Pollution of the air, which has constituted a growing problem since the industrial revolution at the end of the eighteenth century, is also causing alarm.

Since then, the situation has deteriorated drastically: large quantities of carbon dioxide (CO_2) are released through the slash-and-burn clearance of rainforests and by industries pumping waste gases into the air. Some 800 million cars contaminate the environment, millions of heating systems blow sulfur dioxide into the atmosphere, and manure spread on fields contributes methane. Toxic smog hangs over large cities. In summer, ozone levels rise far above officially permitted limits, and fine dust makes breathing difficult. Some of the pollutants fall from the air back to the soil and water. Others remain for years in the troposphere and stratosphere, where they are responsible for problems including the ozone hole and the greenhouse effect.

GLOBAL WARMING

The weather has been creating havoc for a number of years: it is bringing Europeans extremely hot summers and extremely mild winters that scarcely bring any snow. In some parts of the world, violent weather and floods are occurring as never before in the last 250 years, whereas other countries are suffering from droughts of biblical proportions. The reason for this is probably global warming and the associated rise in sea levels—a direct effect of air pollution.

Rising temperatures

Earth's average temperatures are now rising each decade by about 1.8°F (0.8°C), and tropical storms are on the increase. Those of July–August 2007 in northern India and Bangladesh destroyed the homes of 20 million people and cost tens of thousands of lives. Annual temperatures are already as high today as had been calculated by computer programs for 2050.

The greenhouse effect

Based on current knowledge, the greenhouse effect is the principal reason for Earth's warming. Methane, water vapor, and greenhouse gases (and, above all, CO_2, which enters the air as a waste gas emitted, for example, in slash-and-burn agriculture and in the burning of fossil fuels by industry, households, and vehicles) are accumulating in the atmosphere.

Although these gases allow shortwave solar radiation to penetrate the atmosphere, they prevent longwave radiation from readily escaping from Earth's surface, leading to a rise in temperature.

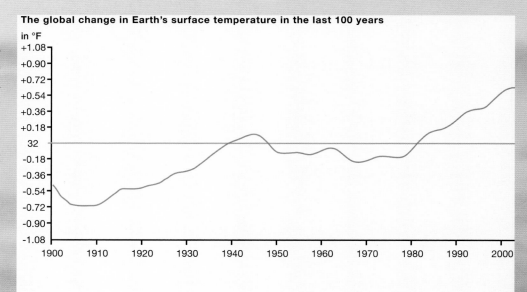

The global change in Earth's surface temperature in the last 100 years

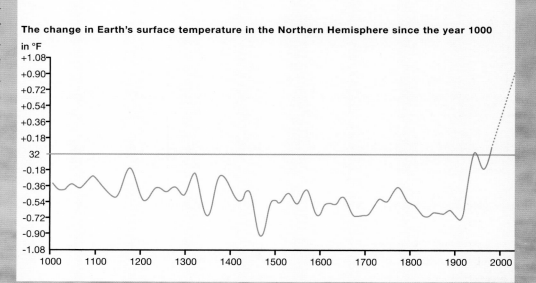

The change in Earth's surface temperature in the Northern Hemisphere since the year 1000

The changes in the temperature of Earth's surface in the last 100 and 1,000 years, respectively. The initial value (32) is the average value for the years 1961–1990. As can be seen, Earth has warmed up continuously since the start of the second industrial revolution.

Below: Polar bears are finding fewer and fewer interconnected ice floes, which they need to be able to catch seals.

Poor prognosis for the future

Being part of nature, humans will be affected just as much as the animal and plant kingdoms by the anticipated consequences of global warming. Sea levels are likely to continue to rise as a result of the melting of glaciers and polar icecaps, which will have a direct

effect on precipitation. As a consequence, storms, floods, heatwaves, droughts, and other extreme weather phenomena are expected to occur more frequently and to increase in their intensity.

In 50 to 60 years, it is highly probable that clean air and fresh water will be among the most precious commodities on Earth. Even now, lakes are drying out all over the world: Lake Chad and Lake Turkana have decreased in size by more than a third over a period of 25 years. Millions will starve because they can no longer produce enough food—first and foremost on account of a shortage of water—and millions more will die because of sharply rising temperatures. Nature as we know it is doomed unless there is a rapid rethink about the way we behave and unless appropriate action is taken at the global level.

Top: Where there is too little water runoff from dams, river biotopes are rendered desolate over extensive stretches, and the original flora and fauna are destroyed without a trace.

Center right: As a result of climate change, floods are occurring with increasing frequency, especially in the tropics. Thousands of people die in the floods, while hundreds of thousands lose everything they own.

Bottom right: The combustion of fossil fuels in industry, transport, and households releases greenhouse gases like CO_2 into the atmosphere; these gases allow shortwave solar radiation to reach Earth's surface but absorb longwave radiation emanating from the surface. This phenomenon is termed the greenhouse effect.

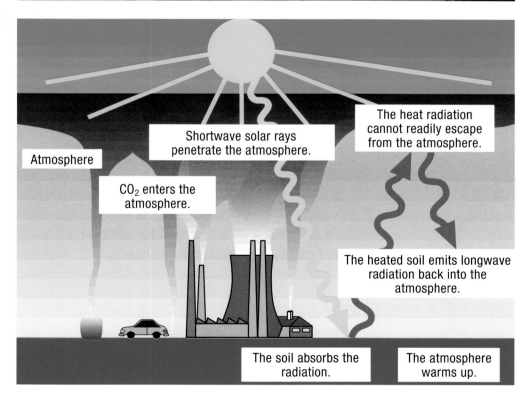

Shortwave solar rays penetrate the atmosphere.

The heat radiation cannot readily escape from the atmosphere.

Atmosphere

CO_2 enters the atmosphere.

The heated soil emits longwave radiation back into the atmosphere.

The soil absorbs the radiation.

The atmosphere warms up.

Sea horses

Rainbow trout

Stripy-tailed damselfishes

PISCES

FISHES

The taxonomy of fishes is disputed. Today, only a few taxonomists regard it as a single taxonomic class; rather, it is divided into two classes: cartilaginous fishes (Chondrichthyes) and bony fishes (Osteichthyes), which both belong to the superclass of jawed vertebrates (Gnathostomata). The small group of cartilaginous fishes includes two groups, one containing sharks and rays (Elasmobranchii), and the other, chimaeras and ratfishes (Holocephali). All other fishes, which account for about 96 percent of the total, are bony fishes.

Fishes, which are almost exclusively aquatic, are cold-blooded vertebrates with gills. To date, about 27,000 species have been identified, but every year—particularly in the oceans—numerous new ones are discovered. Fishes became widespread about 450 million years ago, in the transition between the Ordovician and Silurian periods, and occur in all aquatic environments, from ponds to polar seas. Their skeletons differ according to the class they belong to: cartilaginous fishes, as one would expect from the name, have a skeleton made of cartilage, which is extremely stable because of the calcium deposits it contains.

Fishes are very important for human nutrition. This has led to the increasingly heavy overfishing of oceans, and, to a certain extent, also lakes. Stocks of hundreds of species are now depleted and some are on the brink of collapse, not to mention whole ecosystems threatened due to the killing of bycatch, but political and economic considerations have until now prevented the adoption and above all the consistent implementation of effective protection measures. In addition to overfishing and water pollution, the trade in ornamental fishes, particularly those from the Amazon catchment area, also presents a serious problem for fish stocks.

Butterfly fish

Leopard shark

Sailfish

Lionfish

OSTEICHTHYES
BONY FISHES

Bony fishes (Osteichthyes) are the largest group of vertebrates, in terms of the numbers of both species and individuals—to date, about 26,000 different species have been identified. Their habitat is either salt water or fresh water, although some species of fish are able to live in both types of water.

FRESHWATER FISHES

Worldwide, there are just under 10,000 species of freshwater fishes living in rivers, streams, lakes, and ponds. Over half of these species belong to the superorder Ostariophysi, which includes the orders of carp-like fishes (Cypriniformes) and catfish-like fishes (Siluriformes). A few species can live both in salt water and in fresh water; the best known of these so-called peripheral freshwater fishes are the Atlantic salmon (*Salmo salar*), the common or European eel (*Anguilla anguilla*), and

Left: The annual migration of salmon to their spawning grounds is being made increasingly difficult or even prevented by the damming of rivers and by water pollution.

The brown trout (*Salmo trutta fario*) needs oxygen-rich, cool water below 68°F (20°C). Rising temperatures are increasingly restricting its habitats.

The grayling, a popular fish for eating, is even more sensitive in terms of water quality and other habitat requirements than the brown trout.

the Arctic charr (*Salvelinus alpinus*), as well as some species from the genus *Acipenser* (sturgeons). The other freshwater fishes, as far as we know, are largely nonmigratory. Where there is heavy pressure on the population, however, they will leave their birthplace.

Special habitat requirements

Except for species such as eel and carp, freshwater fishes need cool, clear, oxygen-rich water. Beyond this, however, their habitat requirements vary widely, but they tend to be very specific and many freshwater fishes have therefore only relatively small habitats.

The Arctic charr, for example, favors cold, nutrient-rich water and lives at depths of up to 250 feet (80 meters) in lakes, whereas the northern pike (*Esox lucius*) prefers shallow waters close to banks, ideally with reeds for hiding and spawning in. In contrast, rainbow trout (*Oncorhynchus mykiss*) need fast-flowing streams and rivers where the temperature rises no higher than just over 68°F (20°C), even in summer; they like sandy and pebbly beds suitable for excavating hollows for their eggs, which can number up to 1,000. The grayling (*Thymallus thymallus*), a fish much sought after by anglers for eating, lives in similar habitats, but because of its extremely exacting requirements in terms of water quality, it is particularly threatened by increasing water pollution.

Almost all freshwater fishes are vulnerable

In addition to overfishing, there are many other dangers threatening global freshwater fish stocks. The greatest of these—which affect all fishes—are water pollution caused by industry and households, which persists even in this era of modern purification plants, and global warming, which is resulting in rising average temperatures in all aquatic environments. Higher water temperatures in turn lead to a reduction of oxygen in the water, which makes it impossible for sensitive species such as the grayling to survive. Because rivers and lakes are normally much shallower than seas, freshwater fish species are even more severely affected by global warming than saltwater fish species.

River channelization, which speeds up the flow of water, construction on lake shores, and the removal of water for irrigating agricultural land also have adverse effects on species in rivers and lakes.

A further factor behind the collapse of certain fish stocks is the stocking of waters with fishes from other continents for breeding purposes: the alien species often displace the native ones or interbreed with them.

For example, the ruffe (*Gymnocephalus cernuus*) has been released into many European waters and, because it is relatively undemanding, it has spread to such an extent that it is now threatening the perch (*Perca fluviatilis*). For many species, the situation often is exacerbated by their having specific requirements in terms of habitat, which makes evading the problem impossible.

Above: Although the northern pike (*Esox lucius*) is not directly threatened, in many places it has to struggle with the destruction of its preferred habitats, in particular, reedbeds.

Below: Several sturgeon species produce caviar, which is highly sought after. However, due to—often illegal—overfishing, some populations are on the brink of collapse.

SALTWATER FISHES

About 60 percent of bony fishes live in salt water. Three-quarters of these prefer to live near the coast, the most important habitat being provided by warm coastal waters, which are home to about two-thirds of bony fishes, including many of the perch-like fishes (Perciformes) and eels (Anguilliformes). About 10 percent of fishes are found at various depths in the open ocean—these include mackerels and tunas (Scombridae) as well as anchovies and herrings (Clupeiformes)—and a further 10 percent of known saltwater fishes live in the deep sea, which is, however, still largely unreachable and unexplored.

The oceans are not indestructible

Oceans cover about 70 percent of our planet. They are full of life, providing habitats both for fishes and for crustaceans, mollusks, algae, and numerous other organisms as yet unknown. They provide millions of tons of food for people. The oceans appear to be infinitely large and infinitely deep—and indestructible. This is a disastrous misconception, as humankind will have to come to realize.

The oceans are now polluted with all kinds of waste, including heavy metals, nuclear waste, and oil. In addition, their fish stocks have been recklessly depleted due to our increasing consumption of fishes and overfishing.

Ever-improving fishing techniques

In recent decades, fishing techniques have become highly mechanized and refined. Nowadays, with shoals of herring, mackerel, Atlantic cod, sea bass, ocean perch, hake, tuna, and salmon being located by satellite or echolocation, scarcely any fish can escape the closely woven mesh of the nets.

Many species are caught on long lines, which are over 60 miles (100 km) long and can carry up to 20,000 hooks. Dragnets are also often used; these literally plow up the sea bed at depths between 300 and 3,000 feet (100 and 1,000 meters), devastating the environment of untold numbers of organisms.

Bycatch, that is, sea creatures that are not suitable for human consumption, sometimes makes up as much as 90 percent of the catch. With both longline and dragnet fishing

Above: Due to the extensive exploitation of the seas, the ocean perch (*Sebastes marinus*) is one of the species for which catch quotas need to be drastically reduced if it is to survive.

Below: Flat fishes such as the plaice are an order of bony fishes that are found on the sea bed in shallow waters all over the world.

techniques, a huge number of other fish, bird, and mammal species perish, including sharks, rays, albatrosses, petrels, dolphins, and turtles. Fishing with drift nets, which can also be over 60 miles (100 km) long and in which not only the desired herring, salmon, and tuna, but also whales, dolphins, seals, and sharks become entangled, is now banned worldwide, but it is still carried out illegally.

Catches plummeting drastically

A study has shown that three-quarters of all fish stocks worldwide are overfished, i.e. the number of fishes being taken from the oceans is greater than the number of young stock growing up to replace them. Stocks of all species are declining, sometimes, as in the cases of tunas and swordfishes, drastically.

Because fish stocks are shrinking, catches are becoming smaller: the U.S.-based Earth Policy Institute has calculated that some 90 million tons of fish are currently caught each year—in the 1980s, catches were about 50 percent larger. Other sources put the size of the annual catch at between 130 and 140 million tons, but they, too, report that this has fallen dramatically. It is now hardly worth going after some species because yields in no way match the effort and expenditure involved.

A difficult problem to solve

There is, of course, a solution to the problem of overfishing: massively reduce catch quotas for many years or even decades. However, by the time the fishing nations agree to this, it may be too late for many fish species, and possibly also for other animals for which they are the prey.

In 2007, Greenpeace proposed the establishment of large marine reserves, the equivalent of national parks for the oceans. Putting these or similar proposals into practice would appear to be absolutely essential, especially as scientific studies predict the total biological collapse of the oceans if no protection zones are established.

Below: In almost all marine fishing grounds, as here in Kalk Bay, South Africa, sections of the fishing fleets, which are now much too large, have had to be laid up.

Above: Atlantic cod are suffering both from overfishing and from climate warming, which has resulted in the fishes growing more slowly.

TUNAS AND OTHER PERCH-LIKE FISHES (PERCIFORMES)

The overwhelming majority of ocean-dwellers are small organisms, ranging in size between the length of a finger and that of an arm. However, the representatives of three families from the order of Perciformes (perch-like fishes), weighing up to a ton and measuring up to 15 feet (4.7 meters) in length, are among the giants of the ocean, making them particularly important both for the commercial fishing industry and for sport fishing. These families are the sailfishes and marlins (Istiophoridae), comprising about a dozen species, the mackerels and tunas (Scombridae), comprising six species, and the swordfishes (Xiphiidae), which consists of just one species, the swordfish (*Xiphias gladius*).

Members of these three families dwell mainly, although not exclusively, in the high seas—normally in the upper layers of water—and most of the species undertake seasonal migrations. Their streamlined bodies and enormous strength enable some of these fish species to swim at speeds between 50 and 70 mph (80 and 110 km/h).

Uncertainty regarding stock sizes

Very little is known for certain about populations of swordfish, which are extremely popular with sport anglers, or about stocks of garfish and marlin. Some species are included on the IUCN's Red List, but mainly with a comment that the data available are insufficient to enable assessment of the threat. However, it is safe to assume that, as with almost all saltwater fishes, stocks have declined sharply since the middle of the twentieth century.

Above: Together with sharks and swordfishes, sailfishes are one of the fishes most popular with sport anglers and with gourmets. Their flesh is considered a delicacy, whether smoked, grilled, or fried.

Below: Year after year, almost 5 million tons of tuna are caught worldwide. This makes them one of the most important edible fishes of all.

tuna are sold each year and made into sushi and sashimi. In 2005, 44 tons of northern bluefin tuna (*Thunnus thynnus*) were consumed in Japan—in the light of such figures, it is hardly surprising that this species has become so severely threatened. Equally intensively hunted is the yellowfin tuna (*Thunnus albacares*), which often swims in company with dolphins, with the result that both end up together in fishing nets. Because dolphins are mammals and need to breathe oxygen regularly, they drown within just a few minutes; it is estimated that between the middle of the twentieth century and the 1990s, over seven million dolphins were killed as bycatch.

Tuna massacre and drowned dolphins

For many years, the media showed pictures of the traditional tuna hunt called the *Mattanza*, in which shoals of tuna on their annual migration to their spawning grounds were caught and bloodily killed by South Italian fishers. In the meantime, however, tuna stocks have fallen so sharply that the *Mattanza* is more of a show for tourists than a commercial enterprise, especially as most tunas have often been caught by large fishing fleets before they even reach the Italian coasts.

These exceedingly tasty fishes are caught in incredible quantities all over the world, and many species have now become so rare that an International Commission for the Conservation of Atlantic Tunas (ICCAT) has been established, which 42 countries have so far joined. On the Japanese market alone, over 500,000 tons of

Above: Each morning, many tons of tuna are auctioned at the Tokyo fish market.

Below: Swordfishes are caught in the open ocean using nets up to 60 miles (100 km) long and offered for sale freshly caught.

CHONDRICHTHYES
CARTILAGINOUS FISHES

As the name suggests, the skeletons of cartilaginous fishes (Chondrichthyes) consist of cartilage rather than bones. There are about 1,000 species, the majority of which live in salt water, although some live all or some of the time in fresh water. The best-known cartilaginous fishes are sharks (Selachii) and rays (Batoidea).

An ancient group of cartilaginous fishes

Sharks and rays have been living in the world's oceans for at least 450 million years and are thus far older than the dinosaurs. A particularly astonishing fact about them is that some species have remained largely unchanged for some 60 million years. Over millions of years, about 500 shark species, and as many species of rays, have evolved. They range in size from the tiny 8-inch-long (20-centimeter-long) spined pigmy shark (*Squaliolus laticaudus*), through the manta ray (*Manta birostris*), with a span of up to 23 feet (7 meters), to the colossal whale shark (*Rhincodon typus*), the largest living fish, at over 40 feet (12 meters) in length.

Highly developed senses

Sharks, in particular, are renowned for their highly developed senses. Their eyes, for example, are considerably more sensitive to light than those of people, and are therefore suited to the murky depths, as much as 11,500 feet (3,500 meters) down, where sharks sometimes live. Furthermore, their sense of smell is extremely well developed: the olfactory bulb alone takes up over half of the brain. Consequently, sharks can smell blood at a dilution of one part per million—and can cover a large distance to find a wounded animal in a very short time.

The leopard or zebra shark is a species that is not dangerous to humans. Water pollution, bycatch, and the destruction of its habitats have led to a decline in stocks.

Right: The great white shark can weigh up to 3 tons and be over 20 feet (6 meters) long. It has been hunted intensively on account of the danger that it allegedly poses.

Below: Despite being over 40 feet (12 meters) long and weighing between 10 and 12 tons, the whale shark's diet consists only of plankton and other microorganisms.

The blue-spotted stingray (*Taeniura lymma*) is one of about 500 species of ray. With a disk diameter of no more than 3 feet (1 meter), it is one of the medium-sized species.

All sharks and many ray species are threatened

Heavy fishing of sharks in all the world's oceans, combined with habitat damage and loss from coastal development, pollution, and large-scale persecution of individual species—such as the great white shark—by sport anglers, has led to dramatic collapses in the populations of many species in the last 10 years.

The shark, which is at the top of the food chain and therefore has relatively small population sizes compared with other cartilaginous fishes, is particularly sensitive to overfishing. The problem is compounded by its low reproductive rate—it is not sexually mature until the age of at least 6 years, and sometimes as late as 30 years old—which makes any recovery of stocks practically impossible. It is thought, for example, that there are now only between 2,000 and 3,000 specimens of the great white shark remaining in the oceans between Australia and South Africa; a further 10 species are also endangered, including the sand tiger shark, basking shark (*Cetorhinus maximus*), dusky shark (*Carcharhinus obscurus*), blacktip shark, sandbar shark (*Carcharhinus plumbeus*), and Ganges shark (*Glyphis gangeticus*).

Rays are threatened by almost exactly the same factors as sharks, and with the same results. Stocks of many species of ray are falling drastically, and recovery is almost impossible because of their late age of sexual maturity and low numbers of young. Numerous species are listed as threatened on the Red List, for example, the largest ray on European coasts, the blue skate (*Dipturus batis*), as well as all sawfishes, including the following species that are listed as critically endangered: the largetooth sawfish (*Pristis microdon*), common sawfish (*Pristis pristis*), and dwarf sawfish (*Pristis clavata*).

Danger posed by sharks and rays

Although the relative risk of attack is very small, there are between 50 and 100 known shark attacks on people every year, of which about 10 percent are fatal. Incidents are most frequent on the coasts of Australia and around the southern tip of Africa, and the most frequent attacker is the great white shark (*Carcharodon carcharias*), followed by the bull shark (*Carcharhinus leucas*), the sand tiger shark (*Carcharias taurus*), and the blacktip shark (*Carcharhinus limbatus*).

There are far fewer fatalities or even accidents involving rays: up until now, only 17 fatal human encounters with these fishes are known to have occurred, and it has been shown that the rays never initiated an attack unprovoked. The best-known incident occurred in September 2006, when, while filming underwater, the Australian documentary film maker Steve Irwin was pierced in the chest—probably by accident—by the venomous barb on the tail of a stingray and died.

Alpine newt

Poison-dart frog

European tree frog

AMPHIBIA
AMPHIBIANS

Amphibians are phylogenetically the oldest land vertebrates. They colonized Earth long before birds and mammals, even before the reptiles: the first examples of primitive amphibians appeared over 350 million years ago. Over the course of their evolution, three orders have emerged: the frogs and toads (Anura), the salamanders and newts (Caudata), and the caecilians (Gymnophiona). The last species is still relatively unresearched as a result of its secluded lifestyle.

Amphibians are cold-blooded animals, meaning that their body temperature adapts to that of their surroundings. They have damp skin and can live both in water and on land. The majority of the roughly 6,000 species spend their larval stage in water and use gills to breathe during this time; however, after metamorphosis and the formation of lungs, amphibians are able to go on to land and spend lengthy periods of time there. There are fewer species in the Northern Hemisphere, but with the exception of Antarctica, they are distributed all over the world, although their habitat is limited by their dependence on the availability of fresh water.

On its Red List, the IUCN lists almost a third of amphibian species as immediately threatened. The main reason for the high level of threat is that because of the porosity of their skin, amphibians react very strongly to changes in both their aquatic and terrestrial habitats. Ultraviolet radiation due to the destruction of the ozone layer also harms them. They are thus threatened not just by habitat destruction on land but also by water pollution. The majority of vulnerable species are found in South America and the Caribbean.

Golden mantella

Harlequin poison frog

Edible frog

Giant tree frog

A LIFE IN WATER AND ON LAND

Amphibians originate from an early form of coelacanth (Crossopterygii) and were the first vertebrates to colonize dry land. To survive, most amphibians still need two biotopes: water and land. Even species that spend the entire year on dry land—for example, toads—seek out water to spawn in. The development of tadpoles takes place in water, and frogs and salamanders cannot go onto dry land until this process is complete, whereas almost all newts remain in water.

The green mantella (*Mantella viridis*) lives only at the northern tip of Madagascar and, at just 1 inch (22–25 mm) long, is one of the smallest amphibians.

The Alpine salamander (*Salamandra atra*) does not lay eggs, but gives birth to one or two fully developed live young—an adaptation to the harsh climate of the Alpine regions.

The three orders

Amphibians are generally subdivided into three orders, which are readily distinguishable by their external appearance, the shape of their bodies, and the formation of their limbs.

CAECILIANS

The worm-like caecilians are the smallest order of amphibians. About 160 species are known to date—some of these have been scientifically described on the basis of just a single specimen—but researchers assume that numerous species still remain undiscovered.

Their secluded lifestyle means that it is not known whether they are threatened; the fact that they are not often seen is not necessarily an indication that they are rare.

SALAMANDERS AND NEWTS

The order Caudata, commonly known as salamanders and newts, comprises about 500 species. They all have an elongated body and a tail, and most have four legs. They are thus well adapted to life on land, and most species spend the greater part of their time there, only returning to water to spawn. A few newts have reverted to living permanently in water.

Like the caecilians, the salamanders and newts also live highly secretive lives and are seldom encountered. The smallest species are thinner than a pencil and are only a few inches

One in three amphibians is threatened with eradication

According to an IUCN inventory, populations of about 30 percent of amphibians are threatened, and declines have been particularly intense in the Americas, Australia, and Fiji, but many species are not yet on the Red List because they are currently "only" locally threatened: it is estimated that, depending on the country concerned, between 50 and 70 percent of amphibians are vulnerable. Factors responsible for this are changes to biotopes and the poisoning of habitats with pesticides and similar toxins. Amphibians' dual habitat and the permeability of their skin exacerbate these problems.

In the 1980s, a new danger arose, principally in Australia and in South and Central America: a minute droplet fungus called the chytrid fungus (*Batrachochytrium dendrobatidis*), which affects the skin of the amphibian and kills it, probably through the production of toxins. Between 50 and 100 percent of an affected population of amphibians succumb, and no medicine or effective antidote is yet known. It is expected that numerous species of frogs, perhaps hundreds, will perish from chytridiomycosis.

(a few centimeters) long, whereas the largest can reach impressive dimensions, such as the Chinese giant salamander (*Andrias davidianus*), listed as critically endangered, which can be up to 5 feet (1.5 meters) long and weigh 45 lb (20 kg).

FROGS AND TOADS

This is the most species-rich order of amphibians, with about 5,500 species. Unlike salamanders and newts, frogs do not retain their tails when they develop into terrestrial animals; furthermore, they move with a hopping rather than a walking motion. Frogs and toads exhibit a high degree of diversity, not just in terms of numbers of species, but also as regards body size. *Eleutherodactylus iberia*, a Cuban frog with no common name, and which was not discovered until 1996, is minute and as light as a feather. In contrast, the Goliath frog (*Conraua goliath*), from Cameroon, is a real giant, with a snout-vent length of 13 inches (35 cm) and weighing 6½ lb (3 kg). This species is endangered.

Right: The blue poison frog (*Dendrobates azureus*) uses its striking warning color to show predators that it is unpalatable—or rather, highly poisonous.

Below: As with all frogs and toads, it is only the male strawberry poison-dart frog (*Oophaga pumilio*) that has a very elastic vocal sac, which makes its mating calls audible from a great distance.

Large numbers of species in the tropical belt

The majority of frogs and toads live in tropical or subtropical latitudes. The reasons for this accumulation of cold-blooded amphibians in the warm tropical belt are the constantly high temperatures and the enormous number of small creatures available as a food source. A few species can even be found in desert areas, for example, the New Holland frog (*Cyclorana novaehollandiae*), which—buried underground—can survive up to seven years of drought. Some toad species (*Bufo*) can also survive long periods of drought in deserts.

In habitats with high temperatures and corresponding levels of humidity, the number of species is extremely high. It is not unusual to find several dozen species in the space of 10 square yards (8 square meters) in the mountainous regions of Central America and in the Amazon. The marked segmentation of the landscape, by large numbers of rivers in the Amazon basin and by valleys and mountains

in Central America, has meant that as frogs and toads have evolved, countless small populations have formed. These may well be of interest to those researching evolution, but their extremely restricted geographical ranges make them highly vulnerable. Even the most minor

Above: A tropical leaf frog of the genus *Hyla* performing its nightly croaking concert, which is used to mark out its territory and attract females.

Below: The Himalayan salamander (*Tylototriton verrucosus*), like most amphibians, needs a constantly damp habitat where it can spend time in water as well as on land.

alterations in their habitat—let alone more far-reaching changes caused by settlement, logging, or fire—lead to sharp reductions in or the total collapse of populations. In Central America, this has happened more than once in the past two decades: several dozen poison-dart frog species (Dendrobatidae) and tree frog species (Hylidae) have become extinct before they had even been scientifically described.

The Palearctic region is no paradise for amphibians

Amphibians are cold-blooded animals whose body temperature and circulation are dependent on the ambient temperature. As the temperature approaches 32°F (0°C), amphibians in the northern regions of the globe enter a state of torpor: they bury themselves underground or in mud and do not return to the surface until the spring. The small number (only a few dozen) of European frog and salamander species reflects the unfavorable nature of the climate there for amphibians. The best known

are the European tree frog (*Hyla arborea*), the European common frog (*Rana temporaria*), the pool frog (*Rana lessonae*), and the edible frog (*Rana kleptospecies esculenta*), as well as the common toad (*Bufo bufo*), the natterjack toad (*Bufo calamita*), and the green toad (*Bufo viridis*). Much less known are the fire-bellied toad and the yellow-bellied toad (*Bombina bombina* and *B. variegata*), which, because of their small body size, can evade detection by even the trained eye, but are among the giants in acoustic terms.

Center right: The green tree frog (*Litoria caerulea*) lives in the rainforests of northeastern Australia and New Guinea and belongs to the largest group of tree frogs, which has 131 species in the Australian region alone.

Below right: The tiny golden mantella (*Mantella aurantiaca*), just 1 inch (25 mm) long, is found only in Madagascar. As a result of the clearing of forests, it is probably on the brink of eradication.

Above: The red-eyed tree frog (*Agalychnis callidryas*) is an excellent climber. Like many tropical frogs, it is nocturnal and spends the day well hidden in dense tangles of foliage.

Different methods of reproduction

In terms of reproduction, for amphibians there is only one basic rule: there must be water. All amphibians lay their eggs either in standing water or in swampy areas or flooded meadows. Other than this, there are few similarities between the species, even within each order. Some frogs and toads lay only five or six eggs, others, up to 10,000. Poison-dart frogs deposit their eggs initially in the water-filled urns of bromeliads or in holes in branches. Following fertilization and the hatching of the larvae, the latter are taken—often individually—to damp leaf axils and looked after there for several weeks. Sometimes the tadpoles cluster on the back of the father, who produces a secretion that feeds the young, and sometimes the female brings them food.

The southern gastric-brooding frog (*Rheobatrachus silus*), from Queensland, Australia, had a particularly remarkable method of incubating its young. It was not discovered until 1973 and became extinct for unknown reasons just nine years later.

The female swallowed the eggs and brooded them in her stomach for about eight weeks. During this time, she did not ingest any food and suppressed the production of digestive juices. Once the young had completed the larval stage, the mother unceremoniously regurgitated them into the nearest pond and left them to fend for themselves.

The skin of amphibians

Amphibians have very sensitive, permeable skin, which must always be kept moist—scales, which cut down drastically on water loss, didn't appear until reptiles arose millions of years after the first amphibians. This is achieved in three ways: through their bodily fluids, through their food, and through the water in their environment. Furthermore, excessive moisture loss can be avoided or minimized by their dwelling in a shady environment—in this way, amphibians can regulate their water balance. Levels of activity also influence the permeability of the skin: species that spend the winter in a state of torpor reduce water absorption in this way.

The fire salamander (*Salamandra salamandra*) is one of the true salamanders, and several species are distributed across Europe, North Africa, and Asia Minor.

A lethal poison in their skin

Most amphibians have venom glands in their skin and can exude a white or yellowish secretion that contains up to 30 different

Many poison-dart frogs from tropical Central and South America are at extreme risk of extinction because of their small ranges.

Road traffic, the destruction of wetlands, and poisoning with pesticides have made the European common frog, which is not under immediate threat, a rarity in many places.

toxins in the animal world. The venom of the golden poison frog (*Phyllobates terribilis*), for example, is sufficient to kill a dozen people or tens of thousands of mice, were it to be injected into the bloodstream of the victims. The pharmaceuticals industry has been trying for years to identify the up to 400 poisons occurring in the skin of poison frogs, decipher them, and use them in medicines. However, the establishment of "frog farms" is ruled out because these small amphibians lose their venomousness as soon as they are deprived of their natural prey—ants, termites, and spiders. In other words, their venom production is dependent on their diet.

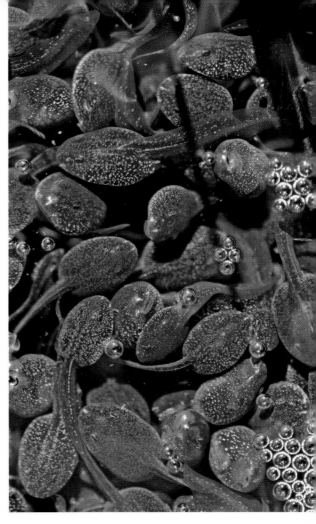

alkaloids and is extremely irritating to mucous membranes. Predators that once come into contact with a toad will never forget the experience—and will give the toad a wide berth in the future.

The poison-dart frogs (Dendrobatidae) from the tropical rainforests in South and Central America are particularly notorious for their venom. They produce one of the most potent

Right: Tadpoles, the larvae of frogs and toads, have numerous predators. It is rare that more than two or three out of every hundred reach the adult stage.

Below: As a protection against drying out, the frogspawn from which the tadpoles develop is surrounded by a layer of jelly that swells up in water.

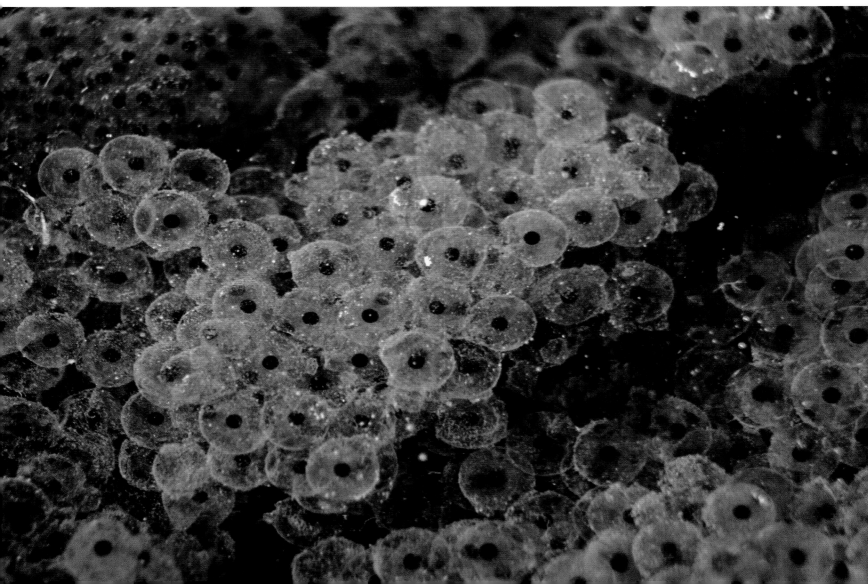

Dwarf caiman Galapagos giant tortoise Sand viper

REPTILIA

REPTILES

The class of reptiles comprises four orders: crocodiles (Crocodilia), turtles and tortoises (Testudines), tuataras (Rhynchocephalia), and scaled reptiles (Squamata). The last groups together lizards (Lacertilia), snakes (Serpentes), and the largely unknown worm lizards (Amphisbaenia).

With approximately 8,000 species worldwide, the scaled reptiles are by far the most species-rich reptile order, followed by the turtles and tortoises with an estimated 300 species. In contrast, the crocodiles number only about 25 species and the tuataras, two.

With the exception of the polar regions, reptiles are at home on all the continents, but the numbers of species and of individuals of these cold-blooded animals are many times higher in tropical areas than in cooler regions, in which many reptiles spend the winter in torpor. Reptiles are predominantly oviparous (egg-laying); only a very small number are viviparous (bearing live young). This is evidence of their relationship to birds (Aves); the two have common ancestors.

Reptiles first appeared about 300 million years ago, in the Carboniferous, and proceeded to colonize countless regions, biotopes, and niches all over the world. Changes in the environment, the conversion of natural habitats into cultivated land, global warming, and direct persecution by humans are, however, leading to an increasing number of reptiles suffering declining populations. Up to 25 percent of reptile species are to a greater or lesser extent threatened with eradication.

Seychelles giant tortoise

Land iguana

Savanna monitor

Amethystine python

CROCODILIA
CROCODILES

The order of crocodiles (Crocodilia) comprises some 23 species from the three families of true crocodiles (Crocodylidae), alligators (Alligatoridae), and gharials (Gavialidae). They all live in subtropical and tropical areas, their most northerly representatives being the American alligator (Alligator mississippiensis) in the southeastern states of the United States and the China or Chinese alligator (Alligator sinensis) in the lower reaches of the Yangtze River. Their preferred element is fresh water, but one species can also survive in brackish and salt water: the estuarine or saltwater crocodile (Crocodylus porosus). This crocodile, which measures 20 feet (6 meters) or more in length and weighs 1,100–1,300 lb (500–600 kg)—and, in exceptional cases, even as much as 2,200 lb (1,000 kg)—is the largest living reptile in the world.

Ancient animals

The origins of crocodiles can be traced back more than 200 million years. For over 100 million years, the crocodilians, the largest of which reached more than 30 feet (10 meters) in length, formed a species-rich group that had representatives, living in both salt water and fresh water, on all continents except Australia.

Modern crocodiles, that is, those that still exist today, emerged about 100 million years ago and—unlike today—were then distributed across the temperate latitudes of North America and Europe. The most ancient crocodiles are the Nile crocodile (Crocodylus niloticus) from tropical and subtropical Africa and the African slender-snouted crocodile (Crocodylus cataphractus) from West and central Africa; fossil finds show that they were already present in the early Tertiary, 65–60 million years ago.

Varied diet

Key elements in the diet of nearly all crocodiles are fishes, amphibians, small rodents, and, for some, also seabirds. Large alligators and

Far right: As impressive as the teeth of the Nile crocodile are, they are used only for holding prey, and not for cutting it up or chewing it.

crocodiles attack fairly large mammals of all kinds: they lie concealed in murky water, from which only their eyes and nostrils protrude, and wait almost motionless for prey. When wild or domestic animals come to drink, the reptiles swim silently up as close as possible to their

Sought-after skins and meat

Almost all crocodile species are threatened and appear on the IUCN's Red List. They have been hunted since earliest times, principally for their hide and meat, and also for ingredients for remedies used in traditional Chinese medicine.

As long as hunters hunted only to meet their own needs, they did no real harm to crocodile populations. This changed when commercial hunting for crocodiles started up in the middle of the nineteenth century. Crocodile hunting is now banned and the trade in crocodile products heavily restricted. To meet the demand for crocodile leather and meat, crocodile farms have been set up in many places. In some cases, farming has had a positive influence on the population, such as in Australia where it has resulted in an increase in the saltwater crocodile population as eggs have to be harvested in the wild and landowners therefore have an incentive in protecting the crocodile's habitat.

Although some species have now recovered from intensive hunting, it appears as if the hunting ban may have come too late for others—especially because the destruction of habitats by humans poses a fresh problem and is making it difficult for these ancient reptiles to survive.

Live caymans are among the goods on offer at South American markets. They end up in the cooking pots of the indigenous population.

The Yacare caiman (*Caiman yacare*) found in central South America is currently one of the less threatened crocodile species.

At 20 feet (6 meters) in length, the saltwater crocodile from the Australian/Asian region is the largest extant crocodilian species.

The gharial (*Gavialis gangeticus*), from the Indian subcontinent, is critically endangered, with fewer than 500 individuals remaining.

prey, seize it by the jaw or neck in a lightning-fast attack, pull it under water and drown it. In Kenya's Masai Mara Reserve, large specimens even eat gazelles, wildebeest, and zebra as they cross the river.

Crocodiles do not spurn carrion, either. Dead animals close to the bank, even hippopotamuses and elephants, are disposed of entirely, the spoils often having to be shared with lions, hyenas, and jackals.

Exemplary mothers

Female crocodiles become capable of reproduction at between 7 and 10 years of age. After mating—depending on the species—they build a nest or dig a hole approximately 20 inches (50 cm) deep in which they lay 20 to 60 eggs. Using the heat of fermentation and ambient heat, the clutch is incubated for between 70 and 100 days, the ambient temperature influencing the gender of the young.

Shortly before hatching, the young draw attention to themselves by chirping, whereupon the females open up the nest and carry the young in their mouths to the water, where they protect them from enemies for at least a few days, sometimes even weeks.

The mortality rate of crocodile eggs and of the hatched young is nevertheless very high: hyenas, dogs, monitor lizards, marabous, and humans all raid the nests, and there is no shortage of enemies later, in the water, either: even members of their own species will not stop short of cannibalism. Rarely do more than two or three animals from a clutch reach maturity.

Above: The African dwarf crocodile (*Osteolaemus tetraspis*), which at a length of less than 6 feet (2 meters) is one of the smallest species, occurs in a small area of West Africa.

Below: Nile crocodiles have for years been bred in farms so that their belly hide can be processed into bags, shoes, wallets, and belts.

TESTUDINES
TURTLES AND TORTOISES

Turtles, tortoises, and their ancestors have existed on Earth for almost 250 million years. They have colonized all habitats apart from the polar regions and the frozen alpine wastes and, unlike the order Crocodilia, are today still represented by an extremely large number of species: there are about 300 different species living in water and on dry land. Tortoises and turtles differ in terms of their shells. Tortoises have hard bony shells encased in a layer of horn; in turtles, rigid bones form a frame covered with a leather-like skin.

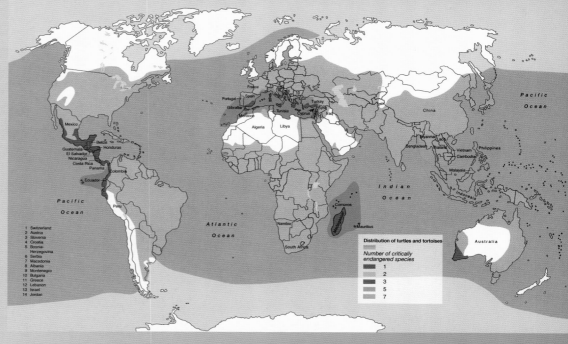

Right: Tortoises and turtles are found on all the continents except Antarctica and in all the world's oceans. The map also shows the ranges of critically endangered species, a particularly large number of which are native to Southeast Asia.

Below: Like numerous other animals in Madagascar, the beautiful radiated tortoise (*Astrochelys radiata*) is threatened by biotope destruction.

Sea turtles like the hawksbill turtle (*Eretmochelys imbricata*) come to lay their eggs on tropical sandy beaches, where they bury their clutches in warm sand.

South African star tortoises (*Psammobates*) can be seen in the semiarid biotopes of southern Africa, particularly after rain has fallen.

The Seychelles giant tortoise was virtually eradicated in the eighteenth and nineteenth centuries, but it was rescued at the last minute from total eradication.

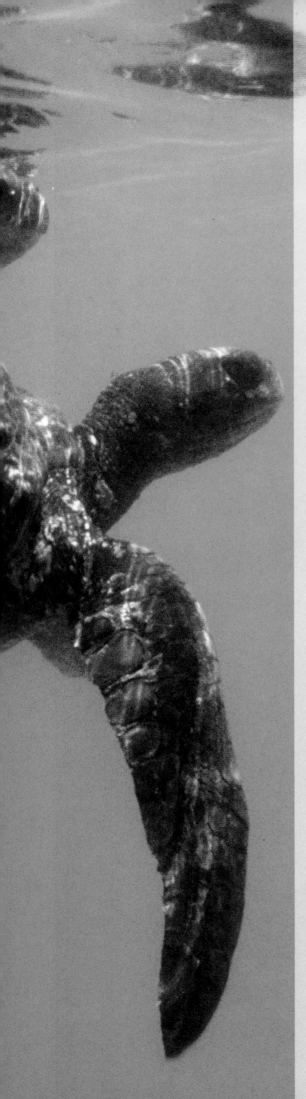

Giants and dwarves

The variety of forms exhibited by turtles and tortoises is commensurate with the large number of species. The smallest species, the speckled cape tortoise (*Homopus signatus*) is only 3½ to 4 inches (9 to 10 cm) long and weighs a little over 3½ ounces (100 g). The largest extant species, the giant tortoises of the Seychelles (*Geochelone gigantea*) and the Galapagos Islands (*Geochelone nigra*), can attain a shell length of 4 feet (1.2 meters) and a weight of over 570 lb (260 kg). The extinct Atlas tortoise (*Testudo atlas*), which lived in the Pleistocene in what is now India, was even larger. This plant-eater was 8 feet (2.5 meters) long and weighed up to 2,200 lb (1,000 kg).

Not fussy eaters

The overwhelming majority of turtles and tortoises are omnivores, feeding on both plants and small animals. The larger turtles eat aquatic birds, amphibians, reptiles, and smaller members of their own species. When eating, many species also ingest sand and small stones, which remain in the stomach and help to break up the food, because turtles have no teeth. In some omnivorous species, the composition of their diet changes primarily with the seasons and secondarily with age; for example, some species in the juvenile stage feed primarily on insects, snails, and worms, but in the adult stage, they eat plants almost exclusively.

All turtles and tortoises lay eggs

Unlike crocodiles, turtles and tortoises are not known to provide brood care. They lay their eggs in pits that they have previously dug in the ground, shovel material back over the hatching site, and leave it to the sun. The eggs are incubated by the ambient heat, and after 90 to 220 days, the young hatch. Once they have found their way from the nest to the surface, marine and freshwater turtles must immediately search out water, whereas tortoises conceal themselves in tall grass and under stones or wood. A high percentage of the young, left to fend for themselves, fall victim to their numerous enemies.

Left: Green turtles (*Chelonia mydas*) mating.

Popular in the kitchen and the terrarium

Some 130 turtle and tortoise species are listed on the IUCN's Red List as immediately threatened, with a further 50 listed as potentially threatened. Many other species have experienced population falls, some severe, in the last few years. Countless animals end up as bycatch in fishing nets or are fatally injured by ships' propellers. The main reason for the decline in numbers was and is, however, the fact that many turtles and tortoises are removed from their habitat—often illegally—and traded by the tens of thousands because they are in great demand worldwide as pets.

Turtle and tortoise meat and eggs used to be considered a delicacy in many countries and in some still are today, and this has led to populations being decimated. As early as the seventeenth century, seafarers eradicated entire populations—for example, on Mauritius and the Galapagos Islands—and even today, despite the CITES ban, meat is still being traded, turtle and tortoise egg-laying sites are being plundered, and eggs are being collected and sold by the hundreds of thousands.

Turtles and tortoises, or parts of these animals, are used as remedies in Chinese medicine to treat fevers, and they are hunted for this reason.

A further factor responsible for the threat to turtles and tortoises is the use of the horn layer of the shell for jewelry and furniture inlays. Although—or perhaps because—tortoise shell is now prohibited worldwide, it is still much in demand. Because of the high prices it commands, this trade continues to contribute to the threat to populations.

In Southeast Asia, sea turtles, which are all threatened with eradication, are still among the most prized sources of meat because they are thought to confer wisdom and health.

SQUAMATA
SCALED REPTILES

The major representatives of the highly species-rich order of scaled reptiles (Squamata) are the snakes (Serpentes), comprising approximately 3,000 species, and the lizards (Lacertilia), comprising over 4,500 species. They are found on all the continents except for Antarctica.

LIZARDS

Like the crocodiles, the lizards evolved more than 200 million years ago from ancestral reptiles and—in contrast to the dinosaurs and other prehistoric animals—survived the species extinction that occurred at the end of the Cretaceous period 65 million years ago. The suborder of lizards is enormously varied, particularly with regard to shape.

Most species are small

The Jaragua sphaero (*Sphaerodactylus ariasae*), from a tiny island in the Dominican Republic, is the smallest reptile of all: its body-tail length

Measuring 4 feet (1.5 meters) in length, the desert or gray monitor (*Varanus griseus*) is one of the larger representatives of the monitor genus.

is about 1¼ inches (30 mm) and it weighs 17-thousandths of an ounce (0.5 g). The lizard-fingered gecko (*Saurodactylus mauritanicus*) from North Africa is only marginally larger and heavier, with a length of 1½ inches (40 mm) and a weight of 7-hundredths of an ounce (2 g). Although most lizards are less than 12 inches (30 cm) in length, there are a number of veritable giants in the suborder, the most impressive of which are found in the family of monitor lizards (*Varanidae*). The Komodo dragon (*Varanus komodoensis*), with a body length of 10 feet (3 meters) and a weight of 110–220 lb (50–100 kg), is by far the largest present-day lizard.

Reproduction

Lizard species differ markedly from one another in the way in which they reproduce. For example, the number of eggs in each clutch varies greatly, ranging from a single egg up to 100 eggs. They are predominantly buried in the ground, more occasionally stuck onto rocks, trees, or the walls of houses, and incubated at ambient temperature for 70–200 days.

Above: Many small monitor species—here a green tree monitor or emerald monitor (*Varanus prasinus*)—are kept and bred successfully in zoos and by individuals.

A few species, for example, the common or viviparous lizard (*Zootoca vivipara*), give birth to live young. The young of both viviparous and oviparous (egg-laying) species are immediately left to fend for themselves.

Hundreds of lizard species are threatened

Several hundred lizard species are directly threatened with eradication. They are particularly affected by the destruction of their habitats—deserts, savannas, steppes, and above all, primeval forests—because many have only very small ranges or live on islands, which means that it is often impossible for them to escape. Hunting by humans is putting dozens of species under great pressure: the meat of many lizards is much in demand in Asia, as are the eggs. Many monitor species are hunted for their coveted skins, which are made into shoes and bags. Other species, such as the chameleons, are endangered because of the pet trade.

Defense strategies

Some lizards have, over time, developed extraordinary survival and defense strategies. Chameleons (Chamaeleonidae) can adapt their body color to blend in with the background, and many other species are capable of shedding part of their tails to distract their attackers while they flee. Horned lizards (*Phrynosoma*) have a special weapon: they spray their enemies with a torrent of foul-smelling blood from the corners of their eyes.

Above: The short-horned chameleon (*Calumma brevicornis*) is just one example of the remarkably species-rich reptilian fauna of Madagascar.

Center right: Most of the over 1,000 species of gecko are nocturnal. One of the few exceptions is the Madagascar day gecko (*Phelsuma madagascariensis*).

Below right: Chameleons, like the Parson's chameleon (*Calumma parsonii*), catch insects with their long, sticky tongues—a highly effective hunting method.

SNAKES

Snakes probably appeared about 100 million years ago in the Cretaceous period. It is assumed that they evolved from lizards. There are approximately 3,000 species of snake, and they occur in almost every conceivable habitat—in deserts, semideserts, steppes, savannas, swamps, and forests, some even in water—the greatest variety of species by far being found in tropical latitudes.

Extreme size differences

Snakes come in very different sizes. The smallest species belong to the family of blind snakes (Typhlopidae), of which there are about 200 species. These snakes live underground in the Subtropics and Tropics. Some of these, such as the Brahminy blind snake (*Rhamphotyphlops braminus*), are only 6 inches (15 cm) long. At the other end of the size scale are the boas and pythons (Boidae). The longest ever measured was a reticulated python (*Python reticulatus*), with a length of 33 feet (10 meters), closely followed by a green anaconda (*Eunectes murinus*) measuring just under 30 feet (9 meters) in length and 3½ feet (1.1 meters) in girth and weighing 485 lb (220 kg).

Effective venoms

Some 10 to 20 percent of all snakes are venomous. The venom is produced by glands that are located in the head and are connected to hollow fangs, which, in some cases, are quite long. Snakes use their venom almost exclusively to bring down or to paralyze prey animals and only rarely for defense. There are a particularly large number of venomous snakes in Africa; these also include snakes whose bite can be fatal to humans, among them the mambas (*Dendroaspis*), the adders and puff adders (*Bitis*), and the saw-scaled vipers (*Echis*). About five million people are bitten by venomous snakes each year, and approximately 150,000 die from the bite.

Brooding snakes

Most snake species excavate hollows or pits in which they lay their eggs and then abandon them; the young are incubated by the ambient temperature and hatch when the embryonic development is complete, producing miniature adults. Other species, including boas and vipers, incubate the eggs inside their bodies and bear live young that hatched out of the egg membranes while still inside the mother's body. Some pythons, as well as the bushmaster (*Lachesis muta*), incubate their clutches by coiling their bodies around the eggs.

Above: The boa constrictor (*Boa constrictor*) belongs to the boa and python family and, like all members of its family, is non-venomous.

Below: Sand racers (*Psammophis*) live in Africa, predominantly on the ground, but frequently climb into trees to sunbathe.

Ruthless persecution

For many centuries, snakes have been the subject of intense persecution, and in many regions of the world, populations have been eradicated or decimated.

They are often hunted as pests or as a danger to humans—although only a minority of snakes are venomous—but also for their meat and, above all, for their skins, which are made into shoes, bags, wallets, and belts. Some species are removed from their natural habitat, often illegally, and sold as pets, and others are used in traditional medicine, principally in Africa and Asia. Destruction of their natural habitats is also contributing to the fact that populations of numerous species are declining and are under threat.

Above: The venomous white-lipped tree viper (*Trimeresurus albolabris*) is encountered in the rainforests of Southeast Asia.

Below: Although mature emerald tree boas (*Corallus caninus*) have a leaf-green coloration, the young are chestnut-brown.

The 27 known species of rattlesnake (*Crotalus*) live exclusively in the New World—from Canada to Argentina—and all possess powerful, haemotoxic venom that can be fatal.

Green broadbill   Great white pelican   Abdim's stork

AVES

BIRDS

The class of birds, which numbers just under 10,000 different species and about 35,000 subspecies, evolved from the same ancestors as the reptiles during the Upper Triassic and early Jurassic periods, some 200 million years ago.

Birds, which, unlike reptiles, are warm-blooded, exhibit extraordinary variation in size, color, and plumage marking. Furthermore, they are unusually adaptable. They inhabit all the continents, as well as the Arctic region, and every imaginable habitat, from deserts through steppes, savannas, and prairies to forests of all descriptions, as well as high alpine regions. Their ability to fly means that birds can cover huge distances in a short time and can thus—if only temporarily—move to the areas that offer the best conditions in terms of food and nesting possibilities.

In contrast to fishes, amphibians, and reptiles, birds are exclusively oviparous, and in almost all species, the eggs are incubated by the body warmth of the parents. Only a few species rely solely on the environmental and fermentation warmth of the nest material in the nest mound to incubate their eggs. Almost all species build nests out of plants, roots, moss, feathers, and similar materials. They normally lay between 1 and 20 eggs, which are incubated either by the female alone or by both parents.

A substantial number of birds are, to a greater or lesser degree, critically endangered by human activities, including almost all parrots and raptors and many geese and cranes, as well as all species that have a very restricted range, such as those on islands.

California condors

Hyacinth macaw

Kingfisher

Capercaillie

GALLIFORMES
TURKEYS, GROUSE, PHEASANTS, AND PARTRIDGES

The 175 or so species of the pheasant family (Phasianidae) make up the largest family in the order of gamefowl (Galliformes). They are distributed across the world except in the Arctic and Antarctic and in South America, where they are extinct; the greatest diversity of species is found in Asia, followed by Africa.

Inconspicuous and iridescent species

Like most gamefowl, members of the pheasant family are medium-sized to large birds with powerful legs, which—especially in conjunction with their strong beaks—makes them ideally suited for scratching the ground in search of food. Their food is predominantly of vegetable origin and is picked up rapidly from the ground and stored in their large, expandable crops. There are some species in which both sexes are clothed in modest camouflage colors. In others, the cock birds are some of the most magnificent, iridescent, and colorful apparitions in the bird kingdom, such as the widely known Indian peafowl (*Pavo cristatus*), which boasts a magnificent fan-shaped crest of feathers and is the national bird of India.

Francolins

The largest genus of the pheasant family, with over 40 species, is the francolin (*Francolinus*), whose range extends from Africa to the Caucasus and across as far as Asia. They are all medium-sized, partridge-like birds, and males and females are similarly colored. Only

Above: The shy hazel grouse (*Bonasia bonasia*), which is threatened by the destruction of primary forests and by disturbance through tourism, has vanished from large sections of its range.

Below: The capercaillie, which is becoming increasingly rare, stays mainly on the ground. It only flies when disturbed or to reach its night roost in trees.

the cocks have spurs on their sturdy legs. Francolins are heavily hunted everywhere for their tasty meat and their eggs, which is why some species with restricted ranges are on the Red List. For example, the Djibouti francolin (*Francolinus ochropectus*), which lives only in two small areas in Djibouti, is classified as critically endangered.

The most-hunted birds

Even the adaptable phasianids have been eradicated in large parts of their original ranges, or are at least potentially threatened. Their tasty flesh and delicious eggs are their downfall—as gamefowl, the phasianids are the most hunted birds in the world. To a certain extent, they can make up for this because they have a relatively high reproductive rate—their clutches contain up to 20 eggs. However, large-scale destruction of biotopes has deprived them of their habitats, and in addition, the birds have been exposed to numerous environmental stresses, caused by logging and clear-cutting for agriculture, so populations are in some cases declining dramatically.

Specialized species are threatened

Some phasianids are very specialized and are highly demanding in terms of their habitat requirements. These include the western capercaillie (*Tetrao urogallus*), the largest representative of the Phasianidae, and indeed the largest gamefowl in Europe. The cocks attain a wingspan of 3 feet (90 cm), a weight of 9–11 lb (4–5 kg), and a height of approximately 32 inches (80 cm). These shy birds need mixed open woodland with sufficient ground vegetation, preferably consisting of blueberry bushes, because the bushes provide outstanding cover and the berries are a main source of nutrition for these food specialists. The IUCN has not yet categorized the total population of capercaillie as immediately threatened; however, the capercaillie has been eradicated in large parts of its original range, and its habitat is steadily decreasing. The long-term outlook is fairly poor because such extreme specialists will scarcely be able to survive in the face of increasing cultivation and habitat destruction.

Blyth's tragopan (*Tragopan blythii*), whose range, like that of all tragopans, is restricted to small areas in the Himalayas, is classified as vulnerable.

Above: The black grouse was formerly common in the open moor and heathland landscapes of Europe but has now been eradicated in many places through the destruction of its habitats.

Below: An African francolin: the rare Jackson's francolin (*Francolinus jacksoni*) from East Africa.

ANSERIFORMES
DUCKS, GEESE, AND SWANS

The family of Anatidae, which includes not only ducks, but also geese and swans, is, with almost 170 species, the largest and most important in the order of waterfowl (Anseriformes). With the exception of the Arctic and Antarctic, they are distributed worldwide across all climate zones.

A largely aquatic life

Anatidae live in or near water—on coasts, river banks, lakes and ponds, on moors, and indeed anywhere where water is readily accessible as they are evolutionarily adapted for swimming, floating on the water surface, and in some cases diving in shallow water. Some species spend the majority of their lives on the open ocean and only go to the mainland to breed, whereas others, including geese and swans, look for some of their food on land. Most of the water birds feed solely on plants; many species scoop their food off the water surface or dive for water plants. Small stones are often ingested during feeding, and these help to break down food in the stomach. Anatidae are monogamous breeders.

The Cape Barren goose was on the brink of eradication 50 years ago. Populations have now increased to at least 10,000–15,000 birds.

Sexual dimorphism

All Anatidae have a compact body and, in most cases, a long neck and relatively small head, as well as webbing between the three forward-pointing toes. In members of the subfamily Anserinae (swans and geese), the sexes usually look identical, but in Anatinae (ducks) there is often very pronounced sexual dimorphism. During mating and breeding, the drakes are striking in their magnificently colored plumage, but the ensuing molt is quite drastic. They often lose all their flight feathers at the same time and sometimes are even unable to fly for a while. The plumage of the male, when it grows back, is identical to the inconspicuous camouflage of the female, which provides protection from predators.

Migrant or resident?

Although waterfowl in the Tropics and Subtropics are what is known as resident birds, i.e. they spend the entire year in one location, many species from colder climatic zones are frequently migrants, moving to warmer areas in the south for the winter. Because they often have to cover thousands of miles on their migrations between summer and

The breeding grounds of the swan goose (*Anser cygnoides*) stretch from Mongolia to Siberia. With the population at less than 10,000 as a result of hunting and biotope changes, these birds are classified as endangered.

winter quarters, they are outstanding fliers with strongly developed chest muscles, and their necks are always extended when flying. These birds not only fly huge distances, but also fly at exceptional heights. The bar-headed goose (*Anser indicus*) holds the altitude record for birds: it flies over the Himalaya, has been observed above Mount Everest, and has been sighted by pilots at an altitude of 29,500 feet (9,000 meters).

Poor long-term prognosis for ducks, geese, and swans

Viewed globally, most Anatidae are not yet under immediate threat, but they are in the long term, and this is already evident in sharp declines in local populations. Reasons for these declines include environmental and water pollution, the draining of many biotopes, the straightening of rivers, and the industrial use of many aquatic environments—i.e. measures that continually restrict and reduce habitats, so that there are fewer and fewer breeding places and areas to overwinter.

Furthermore, many species are heavily hunted—legally or illegally—because their flesh is a delicacy, and their eggs are in some cases highly sought after. Geese, in particular, suffer from hunting for their feathers, which are much in demand for stuffing for bedcovers, pillows, and winter clothes.

Above: It is only thanks to intensive protection measures that the Hawaiian goose has been able to survive in captivity, and captive-bred young have subsequently been reintroduced on some Hawaiian islands.

Below: Bird species such as the whooper swan, whose summer and winter quarters are very far apart, are exposed to great danger during their migration from the Arctic regions to northern Europe.

SWANS AND GEESE

In the subfamily Anserinae (swans and geese), there are three tribes: swans (*Cygnini*), geese (*Anserini*), and cereopsis geese (*Cereopsini*). Almost all species are at least potentially threatened, and some have been or still are on the brink of eradication.

Swans

Swans are the largest and most majestic of the Anatidae family. Their populations are currently classified as being still largely secure, but they are nonetheless shrinking. One example is that of the whooper swan (*Cygnus cygnus*), which is becoming increasingly rare because of hunting, biotope destruction, and changes in vegetation due to climate change. In the past, it has already proved necessary to put some species under protection locally, for example, the trumpeter swan (*Cygnus buccinator*) from North America, which owes its name to its trumpet-like call. With a body length of 5–6 feet (1.5–1.8 meters) and a wingspan of 7 feet (2.1 meters), it is the largest swan of all. It has a totally black bill and black legs, so it is easy to distinguish from its otherwise very similar-looking relative, the whooper swan.

The trumpeter swan used to be distributed in great numbers across North America, but intensive hunting reduced stocks severely, until only isolated populations remained. Although the IUCN does not classify this bird as immediately threatened, the actual danger of the situation is evident from the fact that in the United States, protection measures, such as hunting bans and reintroduction trials, are being adopted—and these have so far met with some success.

Cape Barren goose

The Australian Cape Barren goose (*Cereopsis novaehollandiae*) is the only species in the Cereopsis genus. It is about 30 inches (75 cm) tall, making it the largest goose after the Canada goose (*Branta canadensis*). For a while, it suffered from wholesale losses of habitat, heavy hunting, and thoughtless persecution by Australian sheep farmers. In the 1960s, the Cape Barren goose was considered to be under extreme threat, but following the establishment of a strict hunting ban, numbers have recovered. However, the species remains under protection today.

For more than 10 years, the EU Commission has been funding campaigns to rescue the threatened lesser white-fronted goose (*Anser erythropus*). Hundreds of these birds fall victim to hunters during their migrations.

The trumpeter swan is an example of a successful rescue: the population rose within 15 years from 1,000 to an estimated 15,000 birds.

The population of the nene has increased over the past 50 years from just 30 remaining birds to approximately 1,000 individuals today.

Red-breasted goose

Vulnerable species of the geese genus include the strikingly marked red-breasted goose (*Branta ruficollis*), very much an ocean-dwelling bird, which breeds in northern Siberia and overwinters in central Asia. Heavy hunting, habitat loss, and in particular, the use of environmental pollutants, principally DDT, led in the 1980s to a sharp decline in the species. Today, populations are still classified as endangered and, despite protection under CITES, they are heavily hunted, especially in their winter quarters.

Nene or Hawaiian goose

Probably the rarest goose in the world, the nene (*Branta sandvicensis*) lives on the Hawaiian archipelago in the Pacific, about 1,250 miles (2,000 km) from the west coast of North America. Discoveries of fossilized bones lead us to assume that they originally occurred only on the island of Hawaii, where they lived predominantly on the lava fields and volcanic foothills from sea level up to about 8,000 feet (2,400 meters), and on the island of Maui. Today, their range covers the islands of Hawaii, Maui, and Kauai and, since 2001, also Molokai, where they have been resettled as part of a conservation program. There are about 25 different populations of varying sizes, and the smaller ones are repeatedly topped up with birds bred in captivity.

This goose has been so heavily decimated by domesticated animals introduced by humans, in particular dogs and cats, as well as by deliberate hunting, that by the middle of the twentieth century, only 30 individuals remained. Thanks to protection measures and the reintroduction program, the total population has now grown to 1,000 individuals, but the species is still listed as vulnerable.

Above right: Numerous species of goose are considered vulnerable due to heavy hunting and the destruction of their natural habitat. They include the red-breasted goose (*Branta ruficollis*).

Below right: The range of the Cape Barren goose is restricted to Australia. They are outstandingly well adapted to their habitat; for example, they drink salt water.

DUCKS

The subfamily Anatinae comprises all the various tribes of ducks, numbering over 100 species in total. Some of these are endangered and are considered to be under immediate threat, and others are experiencing huge declines in populations.

White-winged duck

The brown-and-white-colored white-winged duck (*Cairina scutulata*), one of the species that eats not just plants, but also insects, worms, fishes, and snails, lives in damp, forested areas in India and Southeast Asia.

The Laysan duck occurs only on a single Hawaiian island and despite protection measures is listed as critically endangered.

Due to large-scale biotope destruction caused by the clearing of forests and draining of wetland areas, this duck is considered to be critically endangered and is protected under CITES. Its entire population is estimated at fewer than 350 individuals.

Laysan duck

The Laysan duck (*Anas laysanensis*) is a duck species that occurs exclusively on the Hawaiian island of Laysan. Its restricted range on the 865-acre (350-hectare) island, heavy hunting, and the introduction of alien species (rabbits) caused numbers to diminish so severely that by 1912 there were only 12 birds remaining. However, through the reintroduction of captive-bred young birds onto the island, which has in the meantime been declared a bird sanctuary, as well as strict protection measures, it has been possible to increase its numbers to between 500 and 700 birds. The species is still deemed to be critically endangered.

Blue duck

Almost as rare as the Laysan duck is the blue duck (*Hymenolaimus malacorhynchos*), which lives on cold, clear, fast-flowing mountain streams in New Zealand. Habitat destruction, hunting, and the introduction of alien species soon led to the decimation of populations, but until the 1990s, the decline was not considered a cause for concern. This changed shortly after the turn of the millennium, when it was discovered that an increasing number

of territories were unoccupied and that the populations that still existed were severely fragmented. The problem is not merely that these isolated populations are more severely threatened because of changes in their habitat, including ones due to natural causes such as forest fires. The species is also heading toward what is known as a genetic bottleneck—the lack of interchange of individuals is leading to genetic depletion in the populations, making their survival difficult. The IUCN therefore lists the blue duck as endangered, and its future prospects are probably far from promising.

Madagascar teal

The small remaining populations of the Madagascar teal (*Anas bernieri*), from western Madagascar, like the majority of Malagasy fauna, is under extreme threat and is classified as endangered on the IUCN Red List. In the middle of the nineteenth century, this brownish duck still lived in large areas of western Madagascar, but now it lives exclusively in a small area of Lake Bemamba that has been allowed to remain in a relatively pristine state. In addition to loss of aquatic habitats, the Madagascar teal is vulnerable because of agricultural use of the lakeshore for rice cultivation—burning off reeds destroys breeding areas and kills nesting ducks. Furthermore, the birds are still heavily hunted in Madagascar today, because, although the entire population is estimated at only about 1,000 individuals, they are not protected.

Above: The Malagasy Madagascar teal, with a population of fewer than 1,000 individuals, is considered to be endangered, but can easily be bred in captivity, so it should be possible to prevent its eventual extinction.

Center: Heavy hunting and the destruction of wetland areas have spelled disaster for the white-winged duck. For this reason, protection of its habitats is urgently needed.

Below: In New Zealand, introduced foxes, martens, weasels, and feral cats have brought the blue duck to the brink of eradication. It is one of the rarest ducks in the world.

GRUIFORMES
BUSTARDS AND CRANES

Despite the differences in their external appearance, the large, heavy bustards (Otididae) and the long-legged, elegant cranes (Gruidae) are closely related: both families belong to the order of Gruiformes. Like all representatives of this group, they live near water in moorland and swamps, in grassland and savannas, and in open woodland. Some species are excellent swimmers, others are fast endurance runners, and yet others, in particular the cranes, are first-rate fliers and, as migratory birds, cover enormous distances.

BUSTARDS

Bustards inhabit the expansive grasslands and savannas of Africa, Eurasia, and Australia. At first glance, they look like large gamefowl, such as turkey-cocks—with which they do have some things in common. In times of danger, these shy birds seek refuge not in flight but on foot, although most of the species, with their large wings, can fly quite well.

Great bustard

The great bustard (*Otis tarda*), which stands 4½ feet (1.4 meters) tall, has a wingspan of 8½ feet (2.6 meters), and weighs 40 lb (18 kg), is a relatively large and heavy bird. Fragmented populations are distributed across the wide expanses of grassland, cultivated steppes, and arable land between Spain and Mongolia, but its future survival in densely populated Europe is in doubt. Because of its steadily declining numbers, the IUCN classifies the species as vulnerable.

Kori bustard

In terms of weight, the great bustard is surpassed by the Kori bustard (*Ardeotis kori*), the world's largest bird capable of flight. An adult male can weigh 45 lb (20 kg), although at 4¼ feet (1.3 meters) tall, it is slightly shorter than the great bustard. The two subspecies of Kori bustard live in the savannas and

Although the great bustard has an extensive range, it is threatened worldwide by intensive persecution and the destruction of its habitats.

steppes of southern and East Africa and currently appear on the Red List as only potentially threatened. However, due to their relatively small range and the progressive destruction of their habitat, it can be assumed that they will soon be under threat too.

The burning and overgrazing of savannas to create agricultural land, and hunting

present very real threats to the Kori bustard and its brood.

CRANES

The 17 species in the crane family are found almost worldwide, being absent only from South America, the Arctic, and Antarctica. Unlike herons, cranes fly with necks outstretched, not pulled back. Species living in warmer climatic zones stay in the same sites year-round, whereas species from colder regions migrate as soon as the days become shorter, the weather becomes colder, and the supply of food begins to diminish. Cranes are dietary opportunists, i.e. they eat whatever is in season—insects, small vertebrates, amphibians, and fishes, and in the fall, grains and berries.

Above: With the exception of two species, all cranes—shown here are Canada cranes—are threatened by intensive hunting as crop pests.

Below: The Siberian crane is critically endangered, and it is thought that there are at most three populations remaining.

Magnificent wings

The predominant color of these birds' plumage is a wonderful silver-gray, mostly with black and white patches or stripes; some species have bare, red areas of skin on the throat and head. All cranes are large, long-legged birds with long necks, reaching up to 5 feet (1.5 meters) in height and with wingspans of up to 8 feet (2.4 meters). In the famous crane dances, which constitute an important part of mating behavior and are accompanied by hopping, circling movements, trumpet-like calls, and display behavior, the birds show off their outspread wings in their full glory.

Many threatened crane species

The most endangered crane species include the white feathered Siberian crane (*Grus leucogeranus*), which has red eye patches, a red beak, and red legs. It is considered to be critically endangered, and there are only three isolated populations remaining, one of which, the Siberian population, may already have died out.

The white-naped crane (*Grus vipio*) lives in the marshlands of northeastern Mongolia, in neighboring China, and in the southeastern part of Russia. As with all cranes, the parent birds share the task of incubating the eggs. Populations of this bird are threatened, and it is classified on the Red List as vulnerable.

Of the six subspecies of the sandhill crane (*Grus canadensis*), whose breeding grounds stretch from the eastern tip of Siberia and the marshes and swamps of Alaska across Canada to the Midwest United States, the Mississippi sandhill crane (*Grus canadensis pulla*) and the Cuban sandhill crane (*Grus canadensis nesiotes*) face a particularly severe threat, with numbers falling year after year.

The Red List classifies the black and white feathered red-crowned crane (*Grus japonensis*) as endangered: extremely intensive hunting and large-scale loss of habitat have led to a situation where the entire population is now estimated at just under 2,500 individuals.

Above: The wattled crane (*Bugeranus carunculatus*) exists only in two very widely separated populations in Ethiopia and in southern Africa. Both have diminished considerably in the last 30 years.

Below: It is probable that there are no more than 5,000 white-naped cranes surviving in central Asia, and their numbers continue to decline.

Right: Although the red-crowned crane is considered, for example, in Japan, to be a harbinger of good fortune, humans have brought it to the brink of eradication. Today, only 800–900 breeding pairs remain.

Above: The hooded crane (*Grus monacha*) is one of the smaller and more unprepossessing species of the subfamily of true cranes. Some 8,000 birds have survived in Asia, although these are widely scattered.

Below: The South African demoiselle crane (*Anthropoides virgo*) is not yet included in those species that are immediately threatened, but its numbers are also declining alarmingly rapidly, by an estimated 5–8 percent annually.

PHOENICOPTERIFORMES
FLAMINGOS

The family of flamingos (Phoenicopteridae) comprises five extant species, which all live on highly saline lakes. With their long, thin legs, flamingos do bear a certain similarity to the wading birds, to which herons and storks belong, but they differ from these in the extreme ways in which they have adapted in terms of habitat and diet.

Variety of habitats

Flamingos inhabit a number of different continents and habitats. The smallest species, the lesser flamingo (*Phoeniconaias minor*), which occurs in eastern and southern Africa, has the largest populations. The greater flamingo (*Phoenicopterus roseus*), which, at about 4 to 4½ feet (1.2 to 1.4 meters) tall, is the largest species and the most widely distributed geographically, being found in eastern, southern, and northern Africa and in

Spain and France, as well as in India and other Asian countries. The other three species—the Chilean flamingo (*Phoenicopterus chilensis*), the Andean flamingo (*Phoenicoparrus andinus*), and the puna or James's flamingo (*Phoenicoparrus jamesi*)—live on a few Caribbean islands and in southern and southwestern South America. They are amazingly hardy; in the Andes, they are found on lakes at altitudes of up to 15,000 feet (4,500 meters).

Spectacular courtship behavior

Flamingos breed on the banks of saltwater lakes, sometimes in enormous colonies—almost a million lesser flamingos congregate on Lake Natron in Tanzania, for example. The 30-day incubation period is preceded by extraordinary mating behavior: the lesser flamingos gather in groups of 50 to 200 birds, stretch their necks upward, huddle close together, chatter, and

perform an impressive courtship dance, the purpose of which is to familiarize partners with one another and to create the right mood for the birds to breed.

Nurseries for the young

The chicks spend the first four to five days after hatching in their nests of dry mud. After that, they are gathered together in "nurseries," consisting in some cases of several hundred birds, which are supervised by several adult birds. The young birds fledge at the age of 11 to 12 weeks.

Like these lesser flamingos, the birds need to take part in group courtship displays to create the right mood for the birds to breed. If flamingo numbers fall below a certain level, the courtship display no longer takes place.

Above: The population of Andean flamingos is estimated at a few thousand, which is why the species is classified as vulnerable.

Right: Young flamingos have unprepossessing gray plumage for about a year.

Below: The various flamingo species occur on different continents. Because the Old World species have far larger ranges than those in the New World, they are considered to be at less risk.

American species are particularly vulnerable

The IUCN currently classifies only the Andean flamingo, with an estimated total population of a few thousand birds, as vulnerable, with the other four species being listed as potentially threatened. However, experts are assuming that all three American species are immediately threatened, because their populations were never very large and because they are very sensitive to environmental changes.

Even numbers of greater and lesser flamingos, which are relatively stable today, could soon decline drastically if the destruction of habitats and breeding grounds by the draining of lakes or their use for salt extraction is not halted soon. The introduction of alien species by humans—i.e. the increasingly common introduction of fishes that compete with flamingos for food—is a problem for all flamingo species.

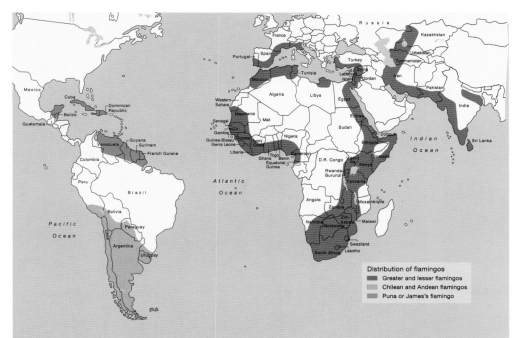

Distribution of flamingos
Greater and lesser flamingos
Chilean and Andean flamingos
Puna or James's flamingo

CICONIIFORMES
STORKS

Storks (Ciconiidae), with their long legs, long necks, and long beaks, embody the archetypal form of the order of Ciconiiformes (storks, herons, and their relatives), moving with slow, majestic strides over the ground or through water in their search for prey.

Worldwide distribution

The 6 genera and 19 species of storks can be found all over the world, except for the Arctic regions. The predominant plumage color in storks is white with black patches; their beaks are generally red, and their legs red, yellow, or black.

The stork family comprises medium-sized to large birds, the smallest representative being Abdim's stork (*Ciconia abdimii*) at 30 inches (75 cm). Its main breeding grounds lie south of the Sahara in the Sahel zone between Senegal and Somalia. The magnificent saddle-billed stork (*Ephippiorhynchus senegalensis*) is double that size, weighing up to 13 lb (6 kg) and attaining a wingspan of 8 feet (2.5 meters). It too lives in sub-Saharan Africa,

with isolated populations distributed between Senegal and Ethiopia, and can be seen as far down as South Africa.

Black stork numbers declining

The black stork (*Ciconia nigra*), whose dark-gray to black plumage gleams metallically in certain places, is a shy inhabitant of quiet riverside forests or ancient woodlands close to water. It spends the summer in its breeding grounds in Europe or Asia, and in the winter, it migrates to Africa. Due to the destruction of its habitat, the black stork, which was never particularly common, has become rare or has disappeared completely from some areas. It is thought that there are only about 20,000 breeding pairs remaining worldwide.

White storks losing their migratory behavior

Up until the 1980s, numbers of the white stork (*Ciconia ciconia*) were plummeting in large areas of Europe, due to the draining of wetlands,

rising levels of traffic, and increasing numbers of hazards on the route between breeding and winter quarters. Numerous protection measures, and in particular reintroduction programs, did produce an increase in numbers in subsequent years, but they brought in their wake an unforeseen problem. The reintroductions were generally successful—the storks built nests, incubated eggs, and raised their young—but many of the birds that had been raised by people and fed through the winter exhibited no migratory behavior. So now in some areas, it has become commonplace to see apparently freezing storks on fields covered in snow and ice, looking in vain for food; they are dependent on people to look after them.

The South American jabiru (*Jabiru mycteria*) was on the point of becoming a threatened species a few years ago, but in the meantime, populations have recovered.

All storks are suffering the effects of habitat destruction in their winter and summer quarters, in particular those caused by the draining and pollution of wetland areas.

Furthermore, some species are extremely timid and react sensitively to any disturbances, especially in their breeding grounds. The overfishing of many waters is also contributing to declining populations because there is less and less food available for the storks.

In addition, the migrations of those stork species that are migratory are affecting population sizes because they sometimes involve huge losses: young birds, in particular, are prone to colliding with utility poles, high voltage lines, and wind-power plants, often with fatal results. Many birds are also shot down during their migration.

Above: In many places, the white stork can scarcely find enough food to feed its offspring.

Right: The African saddle-billed stork is suffering from the effects of the human population explosion in sub-Saharan Africa, which has led to the cultivation of its natural biotopes—marshes and wetlands.

Below: The oriental stork is the most severely threatened stork species, next to Storm's stork, and is therefore protected in some of the countries in its range.

The most threatened stork species

The most threatened stork species are the oriental stork (*Ciconia boyciana*), also known as the oriental white stork, and Storm's stork (*Ciconia stormi*). Both are listed as endangered on the Red List, but Storm's stork, which lives only in a few small regions of Southeast Asia, is the more vulnerable species, with only between 300 and 1,000 birds remaining. The population of the oriental stork, which is native to northeastern China and southeastern Siberia, is still estimated to stand at 2,500 individuals.

CICONIIFORMES
SHOEBILLS AND NEW WORLD VULTURES

Taxonomists are still unable to agree conclusively on whether the shoebill (Balaeniceps rex) belongs to the Ciconiiformes or the Pelecaniformes; it is now generally classed with the former, where it has been allocated a family of its own (Balaenicipitidae). Moreover, studies using molecular biology have recently established that the New World vultures (Cathartidae) also belong to this order.

THE UNIQUE SHOEBILL

The unusual shoebill, which owes its name to the singular shape of its bill, inhabits the marshes of the Sudan, where it hunts for fairly large fishes, standing motionless for hours to ambush them; the moment it catches sight of prey, it stabs it at lightning speed.

The shoebill is the loner among the waders, living a mainly solitary life in its rather inaccessible territory. Even pairs that may sometimes occupy a territory together for a whole year generally keep out of each other's way, although they will collaborate to drive off invaders.

Shoebills appear on the Red List as vulnerable, but accurate estimation of their numbers is made difficult not only by their secluded lifestyle, but also by the turmoil of war in Sudan. The decline in the population is due principally to habitat destruction, but also to the civil wars.

NEW WORLD VULTURES

The best-known members of this family are the two species of condor, both of which are severely threatened by habitat destruction, intensive hunting, and the use of pesticides. There are only about 5,000 Andean condors (*Vultur gryphus*) remaining in the Andes, from Colombia down to Patagonia. The California condor (*Gymnogyps californianus*), numbering about 130 individuals, is critically endangered, but populations have already recovered considerably: at the end of the 1980s, numbers were down to just under 30, all of which were living in captivity, where they reproduced so well that, a few years later, a limited number were released. They now live in protected areas in Mexico, California, and Arizona.

Left: Although little is known about populations of the shoebill, because it lives hidden away in inaccessible swamps, it is considered a vulnerable species.

Below: The California condor was presumed to be extinct in the wild, but it has proved possible to breed it in captivity and release it into protected areas.

PELECANIFORMES
PELICANS AND CORMORANTS

The pelican family (Pelecanidae) and cormorant family (Phalacrocoracidae) belong to the order of Pelecaniformes and, like all other members, have the webbed feet (in which the toes are linked by webbing) typical of this group. Both these bird families are distributed worldwide except for the Arctic and Antarctica.

PELICANS

Pelicans are relatively large water birds: the sociable brown pelican (*Pelecanus occidentalis*), at about 3 feet (1 meter) tall, is the smallest representative of the family. The largest species is the Dalmatian pelican (*Pelecanus crispus*), which can reach a height of 6 feet (1.8 meters) and has a wingspan of up to 11½ feet (3.5 meters).

Pelicans feed on fishes. When fishing, they use their bills, which can be up to 20 inches (50 cm) long and have a capacity of just under 4 gallons (15 liters), like landing nets.

Substantial population declines

Pelicans are seen as competitors by fishers, who therefore wantonly eradicate entire colonies. In addition, water pollution and the draining of wetlands have resulted in substantial population declines. The Dalmatian pelican, in particular, is threatened globally and is listed as vulnerable on the Red List. Many species have been eradicated in some parts of their original ranges, for example, the great white pelican (*Pelecanus onocrotalus*) in Europe.

CORMORANTS

Cormorants, as might be expected, given their enormous geographical range, colonize all kinds of habitats in saltwater and freshwater environments and breed on cliffs, rocky coasts, and steep banks as well as in trees and bushes. Some species are represented worldwide, others occur only endemically, i.e. in limited areas—which is the major problem where many threatened cormorant species are concerned.

Many threatened species

Ten cormorant species are included on the Red List; like almost all water birds, they are suffering from habitat loss, water pollution, and overfishing. In addition, their colonies have long been plundered for guano (to use as fertilizer), and the birds killed. On some islands, populations are decimated by introduced dogs and cats that have run wild: for example, the Galapagos cormorant (*Phalacrocorax harrisi*), which breeds exclusively on the Galapagos islands and, with about 1,500 individuals, is classified as endangered.

Above: Hardly any other archipelago has as many endemic species as the Galapagos Islands. Most of them are under threat, including the flightless Galapagos cormorant.

Below right: Of the seven pelican species, the Dalmatian pelican of southwestern Europe and Asia is considered to be most at risk. Its global population probably stands at under 10,000 individuals.

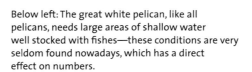

Below left: The great white pelican, like all pelicans, needs large areas of shallow water well stocked with fishes—these conditions are very seldom found nowadays, which has a direct effect on numbers.

PELECANIFORMES
GANNETS AND BOOBIES

The family of gannets and boobies (Sulidae), like the pelicans and cormorants, belongs to the order of Pelecaniformes. Most of its ten species inhabit tropical and subtropical climate zones and only come onto dry land to breed.

Clumsy only on the land

Gannets and boobies are birds of the open ocean, the wind, and the waves. They are outstanding divers and swimmers as well as being excellent, elegant fliers; with their long, narrow wings, they can glide around for hours in the wind. Boobies were given their common name because of their behavior on land, where, with their large feet and waddling gait, they appear rather awkward. Their long wings increase the effect of clumsiness because they make take-off and landing difficult; furthermore, gannets and boobies cannot take off at all when there is no wind.

Gannets and boobies are plunge divers

Gannets' and boobies' preferred method of hunting is plunge diving. From a height of 30, 60, sometimes even 300 feet (10, 20, sometimes even 100 meters), they plummet into a shoal of fishes and—from the momentum alone—can dive to depths of over 30 feet (10 meters). If they want to dive even deeper or to chase their prey, they use their wings underwater to take up the pursuit. This hunting method means that gannets and boobies frequently get caught in dragnets, where they become entangled and drown.

Two immediately threatened species

Two sulid species with extremely small ranges are included on the Red List as immediately threatened: the rare, endangered Abbott's booby (*Papasula abbotti*), which occurs only on the Christmas Islands and of which it is thought only about 3,000 breeding pairs remain, and the vulnerable Cape gannet (*Morus capensis*), which lives only off the coasts of South Africa and Namibia.

Populations of other sulid species are also on the wane; although they are not considered to be under threat globally, they frequently are at the regional level. For example, on the Galapagos Islands, the blue-footed booby (*Sula nebouxii*), which has its largest breeding grounds there, is under strict legal protection.

Right: Although there are still a few large breeding colonies of the Cape gannet on the coasts of southern Africa, the species is at risk of disappearing as a result of overfishing of the seas.

Below: The red-footed booby (*Sula sula*), the only booby species also found in trees, continually suffers a high degree of disturbance during the breeding season due to excessive tourism on the Galapagos Islands. Many young birds perish as a result.

The locally threatened blue-footed booby breeds in colonies, which provide a certain level of protection against its enemies—stray dogs and introduced red foxes and pigs.

The northern gannet has survived the intensive hunting and plundering of its colonies relatively unscathed. With about 500,000 birds worldwide, the species is not considered to be immediately threatened.

Entire colonies destroyed

In addition to habitat destruction, environmental and water pollution, and overfishing of the oceans, the principal cause of the decline in numbers of gannets and boobies has been their persecution for their meat, eggs, and feathers. At the end of the nineteenth century, the northern gannet (*Morus bassanus*) was being so heavily hunted that entire colonies were eradicated. Colonies of some species were also plundered for their guano—a very popular agricultural fertilizer from the end of the nineteenth century, consisting of the excrement of sulids and other sea birds—with numerous birds being killed and their eggs collected. Weather phenomena such as cyclones or El Niño, which in some years result in climatic variations on the coasts, negatively affect fishes stocks and thus, the food supply for gannets and boobies, from time to time causing populations to collapse.

PROCELLARIIFORMES
ALBATROSSES

Albatrosses (Diomedeidae) belong to the order of Procellariiformes, or tube-nosed seabirds, which get their name from their unusual bill: it is formed from several plates of horn and is equipped with two tubes that serve to eliminate the salt ingested with sea water. The majority of albatross species live in polar and subpolar regions of the Southern Hemisphere.

Clumsy on land, elegant in the air

All albatrosses are birds of the open ocean, spending months on end at sea and only seeking out land to mate, breed, and raise their young. Anyone who has ever observed an albatross taking off or landing will understand why these birds avoid extended stays on land: their long, slender wings drag along the ground, and in wind speeds of less than 7½ miles per hour (12 km per hour), they are incapable of taking off again. Once the albatross has managed to get its weight of up to 25 lb (12 kg) into the air, it can cover thousands of miles. It takes an enormous effort for the birds to move their gigantic wings, which have a span of up to 12½ feet (3.8 meters). Instead, whenever possible, they tend to glide without beating their wings.

Many species of albatross threatened

Populations of many albatross species are threatened, including the subspecies of the southern royal albatross (*Diomedea epomophora*) as well as the black-footed albatross (*Phoebastria nigripes*). The wandering albatross (*Diomedea exulans*), the largest representative of the albatrosses, with a wing span of up to 12½ feet (3.8 meters), is also on the Red List as vulnerable.

The outlook is much worse for the Amsterdam albatross (*Diomedea amsterdamensis*), which only breeds on the island of the same name and of which only about 130 birds remain. It is listed as critically endangered. The situation is similar for the waved albatross (*Phoebastria irrorata*): outside the breeding period, it fishes off the coasts of Peru and Ecuador, but its breeding grounds are on one particular island in the Galapagos Islands, Española. Despite protection measures, factors including disease and tourism have led to its critically endangered status.

The wandering albatross is not only an excellent long-distance flier and glider, but also a very good swimmer.

Royal albatrosses are vulnerable because so many die as a result of swallowing bait, complete with hooks, laid out by fishing fleets.

Above: The black-browed albatross (*Thalassarche melanophris*), which lives in the Southern Hemisphere around Antarctica, is considered endangered.

Below: The waved albatross, which is threatened with eradication, has a particularly small range and breeding area.

Hazards

As early as the end of the nineteenth century, whole colonies of albatrosses were exterminated for their feathers, which were very popular as filling material for cushions and bedspreads.

These days, the reasons why many albatross species are endangered are principally related to the sometimes very small size of their breeding grounds, which makes the populations extremely vulnerable to outside influences of all kinds. Under these conditions, any change in habitat—whether caused by humans or by weather phenomena—can have a lasting effect on a species. On some islands, numbers of albatrosses also declined sharply following the introduction of domesticated animals.

Further factors influencing the decline in populations are linked to longline fishing and trawling—many birds drown after becoming entangled in the lines and nets. Birds also regularly fall victim to oil pollution of oceans and beaches, plastic debris, and industrial waste. Their slow rate of reproduction—most albatross species hatch a single chick every two years—makes it hard for them to compensate for heavy losses.

SPHENISCIFORMES
PENGUINS

Penguins (Spheniscidae) are a relatively homogeneous family of birds with 6 genera and 17 species, and the only family in the eponymous order of penguins (Sphenisciformes). They have lost their ability to fly in favor of optimal adaptation to a permanent life in water; except for the breeding season, most species are found out on the open sea. Penguins are birds of the Antarctic and the Southern Hemisphere, whose main breeding grounds are on the coasts of Antarctica and on a few islands in the cool temperate zones.

Penguins look very alike

It is not difficult to recognize penguins as being birds from that order, although the differences in size and weight between the species are considerable: the smallest species is the little penguin (*Eudyptula minor*), which is only 12 inches (30 cm) tall and weighs up to 3.3 lb (1.5 kg), whereas the largest species is the emperor penguin (*Aptenodytes forsteri*), measuring up to 4 feet (1.2 meters) in height and weighing up to 90 lb (40 kg). The plumage on

Facing page: Although emperor penguins are not yet considered to be immediately threatened, their outstanding adaptation to the cold could, in the light of global warming, prove disastrous for them and exacerbate the threat they face.

The Galapagos penguin, which lives on the Galapagos Islands, as its name suggests, is one of the many species threatened in this archipelago.

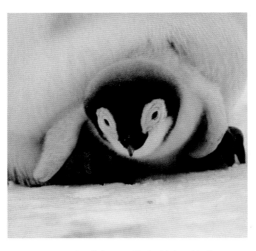

Emperor penguins bring up their chicks at between −22 and −40°F (−30 and −40°C) and use their own body temperature to keep them warm.

In the breeding season, emperor penguins walk up to 125 miles (200 km) inland, where they create colonies and hatch a single egg in just over two months.

Many dangers for penguins

Nowadays, penguins are exceedingly popular birds, enjoying a high level of public sympathy. However, this has not always been the case. The little penguin was a popular source of meat and eggs for Australian aborigines. However, for some penguin colonies, the real problems first began when the Europeans set out on the great voyages of discovery that took them to South America and South Africa—where they encountered penguins.

It did not take long for the existence of the colonies to become a real insider tip for sailors wanting to stock up their provisions with fresh eggs and meat. A little later, the whalers came along and indiscriminately slaughtered penguins to use as fuel for their stoves; sometimes penguins were also killed in huge quantities for their fat, and nesting places destroyed in the course of guano collection.

At the present time, due to the remoteness of their habitat, species that breed in Antarctica are considered to be not immediately threatened. Experience has shown, however, that this status can change very quickly—and it seems likely that it will change, because of the plethora of hazards that currently threaten them: oil spills and the pollution of the oceans with chemicals have taken their toll among all penguins; some species, including the rockhopper penguin (*Eudyptes chrysocome*), the Magellanic penguin (*Spheniscus magellanicus*), and the Humboldt penguin (*Spheniscus humboldti*), are viewed as food competitors by commercial fishers who are out to catch anchovies and sardines, and are therefore intensively hunted. In recent years, the consequences of climate change have also become increasingly noticeable: fewer shoals of fishes are present, nesting burrows are being flooded, and sometimes there is too little krill and sometimes too much.

Two species are already on the Red List as endangered: the Galapagos penguin (*Spheniscus mendiculus*), whose breeding colonies on the Galapagos Islands have been decimated by feral dogs, and the yellow-eyed penguin (*Megadyptes antipodes*), which breeds on the coasts of New Zealand, but is increasingly being driven away by major incursions into the islands' dune landscapes by people.

can catch. Diving and hunting in the ice-cold water requires huge amounts of energy. The birds not only have to cater to their immediate energy requirements, but also have to lay down a thick layer of fat for times of need. At certain stages of their lives, they have nothing to eat for weeks, sometimes even months, on end. All penguins stop eating when they are molting; many species also eat nothing during the breeding season.

The male emperor penguin, for example, loses half its body weight during the three-and-a-half-month fast while it incubates its single egg on its feet, keeps the chick warm, and feeds it with gland secretions.

the back, wings, and head is dark-gray to black, and the abdomen, the "trousers" over their short, sturdy legs, and the throat are white. Only the two great penguin species (*Aptenodytes*), the emperor penguin and the king penguin (*Aptenodytes patagonicus*), and the crested penguins (*Eudyptes*) have yellow throat and ear patches or—in the case of the members of the latter genus—yellow decorative plumage on their heads.

Masters of feast and famine

Penguins' favorite foods, depending on the species and the season, are krill, squid, and various fish species; however, they basically eat anything that swims in the ocean and that they

Above: Although it is estimated that there are still 100,000 African penguins (*Spheniscus demersus*) remaining, they are considered vulnerable because their habitat lies on busy tanker routes, where there are frequent shipping accidents resulting in major oil pollution.

Below: Emperor penguins leave the polar ocean after days spent in the water and return to their young with up to 6¹/₂ lb (3 kg) of fishes in their stomachs.

PSITTACIFORMES
PARROTS, LORIES, AND COCKATOOS

The three families of true parrots (Psittacidae), cockatoos (Cacatuidae), and lories (Loriidae) make up the parrot order (Psittaciformes). The 380 or so parrot species live mainly in tropical and subtropical regions of the Southern Hemisphere, often in lowland rainforests.

Unmistakable features

Parrots are very highly developed and have two distinguishing features: their strong beak with its sharp downward-curving tip, with which they can crack food such as nuts and

Above: On the black market, prices of several thousand dollars are paid for the extremely rare hyacinth macaw, which is much sought after by enthusiasts.

seeds, and their zygodactyl feet, with two toes pointing forward and two pointing backward, which enable them to grasp and to hold objects firmly.

The combination of these two adaptations makes parrots extremely good climbers that can move acrobatically through dense branches.

Striking differences in size

All members of the Psittaciformes can readily be recognized as such, thanks to their external similarities. They differ mainly in size, but the differences are sometimes marked: the smallest species is the 3¼-inch-long (85-mm-long) buff-faced pygmy-parrot (*Micropsitta pusio*), and the largest parrot is the hyacinth macaw (*Anodorhynchus hyacinthinus*), with a length of over 3 feet (1 meter). Their tail shapes also differ: whereas macaws, for example, have long tails, those of the cockatoos are short and rounded; the latter, unlike all other Psittaciformes, also have an erectile crest on their heads.

Gregarious birds

With a few exceptions, parrots, cockatoos, and lories are very gregarious, sociable birds.

Above: Major Mitchell's cockatoos (*Cacatua leadbeateri*) are killed by the hundreds by Australian farmers when flocks raid plantations and fields.

Below: The scarlet macaw (*Ara macao*) belongs to the genus of true macaws (*Ara*), which includes the largest and generally most colorful species in the parrot order.

They spend most of the year in groups, which sometimes fly through the forests in large formations creating a lot of noise; only during the breeding period do they live in pairs—and even then, often as part of loose colonies. Some 30,000–40,000 nests have been counted in such breeding colonies of the burrowing parakeet (*Cyanoliseus patagonus*).

Some very rare species

Of the innumerable threatened members of the order, Spix's macaw (*Cyanopsitta spixii*) is the rarest. Populations in the wild are thought to have been eradicated, and there are just under 70 birds remaining in captivity. Attempts are being made to breed from some of these. Also critically endangered is

the great green macaw (*Ara ambiguus*); the hyacinth macaw, which is now traded for huge prices by collectors, is endangered, and the kea or mountain parrot (*Nestor notabilis*) from New Zealand is considered vulnerable. Until the last species was placed under total protection in 1970, tens of thousands of keas were shot by sheep farmers every year as

The home of the burrowing parakeet is southern South America, in particular Patagonia, where it has, however, become very rare, because the local people plunder its nests on a large scale.

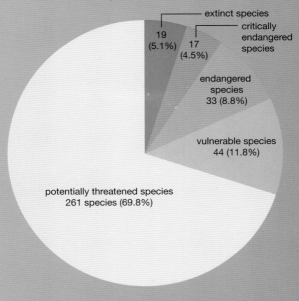

The kea or mountain parrot, which lives on the South Island of New Zealand, has been persecuted for decades as an alleged sheep-killer and consequently is now vulnerable.

Left: In Manu National Park, in Peru, various macaws and other parrot species come every day to a mineral wall, where they ingest essential minerals and fiber together with the soil.

Below: Almost all Psittaciformes are more or less severely threatened, and some species are already extinct.

Almost all parrot species are threatened

Scarcely any other of the 27 orders of birds is as greatly at risk as the parrots: almost all parrots are threatened, and according to the IUCN, at least 19 species have so far been eradicated by humans, including the well-known Carolina parakeet (*Conuropsis carolinensis*), the only parrot species native to North America. Only two Psittaciformes are not protected under CITES: the budgerigar (*Melopsittacus undulatus*) and the cockatiel (*Nymphicus hollandicus*), both of which originate from Australia and are popular as pets, and both of which are bred worldwide. Furthermore, even populations of species like the budgerigar, with its huge breeding colonies, are not considered secure because the nests are continually being thoughtlessly plundered by people.

Biotope destruction

The decline of all parrot species can, without exception, be attributed to human intervention. The principal factor to note is the destruction of biotopes: the majority of parrots live in forests and scrubland, which have been particularly hard hit by clearing by logging companies or landless settlers. Those species that live in open grassland are affected by rapid agriculturalization: where there were once "unproductive" savannas, pampas, or steppes, domesticated animals are now being raised or crops grown. The parrots are keen to partake of cultivated delicacies—often fruit and vegetables—and at harvest time, in particular, they descend on the plantations, where they can cause a considerable amount of damage. Farmers therefore do not hesitate to shoot or poison as many parrots as possible.

The problem of nest predation

In some places, nest predation plays a considerable role in the collapse of populations. In several Central and South American countries, the influence of nest predation on declining parrot numbers has been studied, with shocking results: in many areas, more than a third of parrot egg clutches are vandalized by people or the young taken from the nest. In the cases of four parrot species, including the endangered yellow-faced Amazon parrot (*Amazona xanthops*), up to 70 percent of young

alleged pests, which is why there are only a few thousand birds left in the wild today. Many representatives of the 30 or so species of Amazon parrots (*Amazona*) have also become extremely rare in the wild, because their habitats are being destroyed on a large scale. In addition, because they are popular as pets, the illegal trade in these birds is flourishing.

Threat status of parrots, lories, and cockatoos

extinct species
19 (5.1%)

critically endangered species
17 (4.5%)

endangered species
33 (8.8%)

vulnerable species
44 (11.8%)

potentially threatened species
261 species (69.8%)

The kaka (*Nestor meridionalis*) is closely related to the kea. Both subspecies, the northern and the southern, are threatened with eradication and have already disappeared from some places.

were being lost. In light of such figures, it is hardly surprising that many species cannot withstand this kind of depletion of stocks for long and that regional populations die out within a few years.

Uganda has a paradoxical attitude to nest predation: there, parrot species such as the gray parrot (*Psittacus erithacus*) and Meyer's parrot (*Poicephalus meyeri*) are often stolen from the nesting holes by young men and reared by hand. As soon as the birds can feed themselves,

they are sold overseas—quite officially and with the permission of the authorities, because, although robbing nests is illegal in this African country, selling such birds is not.

The European Union bans the import of wild birds

The bird trade in general, and the parrot trade in particular, constitutes a further significant factor in the steep fall in populations in the wild. The European Union (EU) has for many years played a leading role here: over 85 percent of all the wild birds that have been caught and traded worldwide have been imported into EU countries—at least one million birds a year. Out of the 30,000 gray parrots traded worldwide last year, 26,000 went to the EU, which was also the destination for 39,000 out of 45,000 Senegal parrots (*Poicephalus senegalus*) and 12,700 out of 14,700 orange-winged parrots (*Amazona amazonica*). Now, however, there are new laws to ensure that no more wild birds will be traded.

Birds and eggs on the black market

Rare parrot species command astronomical prices on the black market, which can reach 20,000–30,000 euros for a breeding pair. However, because it is relatively difficult to

More than half of the 30 or so different Amazon species are vulnerable, including the blue-fronted parrot (*Amazona aestiva*). Their prime misfortune is their popularity as pets.

smuggle live birds and because they often perish on the journey, the illegal trade in fertilized eggs is now gaining in popularity. In Brisbane, Australia, an incoming passenger was caught with 52 parrot eggs, which he was carrying in a jacket that he was wearing and that had made him about $12,000 (£7,000). He was arrested and sentenced to a year in jail and given a fine. However, he was just small fry: there is a flourishing black market between Australia and the islands of Southeast Asia. Smuggling rings use speedboats and small planes to bring their goods—eggs and birds—to Asian cities, from where they are distributed around the world.

Conservation organizations for parrots

In recent years, numerous conservation organizations have come into being in the United States, Europe, and the native countries of the species concerned, to save the numerous threatened parrots from eradication. Two of the most significant are the Loro Parque Foundation on the Spanish island of Tenerife and the British World Parrot Trust, which has branches in numerous countries including the United States, Canada, Australia, Germany, Italy, Spain, Belgium, Sweden, South Africa, and Japan.

Some species from the genus of caiques (*Pionites*) are particularly colorful and therefore much sought after as pets.

Their vulnerable position means that the export of many species of macaw from South America is now banned.

The Loro Parque Foundation houses the largest parrot collection in the world and breeds various species that are among the rarest of all, including Spix's macaw. In addition, it participates in field work in South America, Africa, Asia, and Australia. In contrast, the World Parrot Trust does not operate its own breeding center but restricts itself to raising funds and using them for urgent projects, because there are local breeding and protection centers in many countries that are chronically short of money and rely on financial support.

Above: The red-tailed black cockatoo (*Calyptorhynchus banksii*) from Australia, with a head-to-tail length of 24 inches (60 cm), is one of the largest parrots. It has virtually disappeared from some southern Australian states.

Right: The great green macaw lives in dense tropical rainforests and is one of the most vulnerable species of all: it is considered to be critically endangered.

FALCONIFORMES
HAWKS, EAGLES, AND RELATIVES

The hawks, eagles, and their relatives (Accipitridae) are by far the largest family in the order of raptors (Falconiformes), previously also known as birds of prey. This family comprises about 240 species that are all carnivorous and occur in a wide variety of climate zones all over the world, except Antarctica and a few islands in Oceania.

Outstanding adaptation

The powerful accipitrids, as one might expect in hunting birds, are for the most part excellent fliers and have extremely good eyesight, enabling them to make out their prey even from immense heights. Their sturdy legs have strong toes with long, sharp talons with which they can grab their victims and hold them tight. Their sharp beaks are powerful, with a greatly enlarged upper mandible with a downward-curving tip, which is ideally suited to dismembering and eviscerating prey. Most raptors catch living animals, either in the air or on the ground, such as small mammals, smaller birds, and even large insects. Some accipitrids, such as sea eagles (*Haliaeetus*), prey on fishes, and the Philippine eagle (*Pithecophaga jefferyi*) kills larger animals, such as genets and monkeys.

Threatened sea eagles

Species from the genus of sea eagles (*Haliaeetus*), which are without exception large, are particularly impressive representatives of the accipitrid family. They are threatened, at least at the local level. The widely recognized North American bald eagle (*Haliaeetus leucocephalus*), the national bird of the United States, was on the brink of eradication in the

Left: The bald eagle was on the brink of eradication in the 1960s. Thanks to intensive protection measures, populations have recovered again.

Facing page, above: Many eagle species have always been heavily persecuted because they occasionally kill poultry or young goats and sheep. They are also adversely affected by concentrations of heavy metal and pesticides in their prey.

Facing page, below: The clearing of forests and pesticide poisoning via prey now pose the greatest threat to the mighty Steller's sea-eagle (*Haliaeetus pelagicus*), which, with a total population estimated at 5,000 individuals, is considered vulnerable.

Below: Rueppell's griffon (*Gyps rueppellii*), pictured here with a dead wildebeest in the Mara river in Kenya, has disappeared from many parts of its former range, or at least become rare.

Endangered by their position in the food chain

Accipitrids are on the decline on a local and sometimes on a global level: numbers are falling inexorably, and some species have become extremely rare or have already been eradicated.

For accipitrids, habitat destruction is, in most cases, less of a determining factor in the decline of populations; far more serious is the fact that they have been heavily hunted as pests, generally by means of shooting and large-scale selective poisoning. Egg predation and trophy hunting have also contributed to the depletion of these birds.

The biggest problem for many raptors, however, is their position at the top of the food chain: their prey species are often no longer present in sufficient numbers to support them as a result of the destruction of their own habitat, and they contain accumulations of environmental toxins, such as insecticides and pesticides. These toxins are passed on to the raptors through their prey and, in addition to their lethal long-term impact on the birds' overall metabolism, they have disastrous effects on the birds' eggs and the accipitrids' ability to reproduce. Either the embryos remain underdeveloped in their shells, or the eggshells are so inadequately formed that the eggs are squashed by the parent birds during incubation.

1960s as a result of intensive hunting and the effects of the environmental contaminant DDT, but it was rescued and is now no longer considered to be immediately threatened. The same is true of its European counterpart, the white-tailed eagle (*Haliaeetus albicilla*). Pallas's fishes-eagle (*Haliaeetus leucoryphus*) lives in Asia; it was formerly common, but is now extinct in many areas and, with a total population between 2,500 and 10,000 birds, is classified as vulnerable by the IUCN. The most threatened sea eagle species is the Madagascar fishes-eagle (*Haliaeetus vociferoides*), which occurs exclusively on the west coast of the island of the same name and, due to habitat destruction there, is critically endangered; its population is estimated at fewer than 100 breeding pairs.

Above: From India to South Africa, numerous species of vulture—such as the two lappet-faced vultures pictured here—are threatened with eradication. The causes are pollution, the destruction of the environment, and a shortage of food.

Left: The Philippine eagle, with an estimated global population between 200 and 400 birds living in the wild, is one of the world's rarest bird species.

Facing page, below: Sea eagles inhabit areas rich in suitable aquatic environments in the temperate zones of Eurasia. They are gradually recovering from a sharp decline in populations in the 1980s.

Below: The destruction of forests and poisoning with herbicides and insecticides have led to the collapse of populations of the harpy eagle (*Harpia harpyja*), the largest raptor of all.

Carrion-eating Old World vultures

Although this may not be apparent at first glance, the Old World vultures (Aegypiinae) are a subfamily of the order Falconiformes. They are large to very large birds that can reach up to 3 feet (1 meter) in length and attain a wingspan of nearly 10 feet (3 meters). The members of this subfamily live in southeastern Europe, the whole of Africa, and Asia; they prefer wide open landscapes that provide good visibility, such as steppes, savannas, and semideserts. In contrast to all other raptors, Old World vultures feed predominantly on carrion. Members of the same species and family members are constantly keeping an eye on each other, so as soon as one bird spots food, they all converge on it, even from great distances.

The Asiatic Old World vultures, in particular, including the Southeast Asian white-rumped vulture (*Gyps bengalensis*) and the Indian vulture (*Gyps indicus*) from India and Pakistan, are critically endangered. However, species native to other continents are also threatened. For example, the lappet-faced vulture (*Aegypius tracheliotos*), which lives in some parts of Africa and the Middle East, is classified by the IUCN as vulnerable.

Above: Its lack of a flight response makes the Galapagos hawk, which was never particularly plentiful, easy prey for humans and for the feral dogs on the Galapagos Islands.

STRIGIFORMES
OWLS

The order of owls consists of two families, typical owls (Strigidae) and barn owls (Tytonidae), and comprises more than 130 species. Owls are nocturnal birds that live on all continents except Antarctica and have colonized a wide variety of habitats, from dry deserts through scrubland and savanna landscapes, cloud forest and rainforests, up to high mountain regions.

Very well adapted to hunting at night

All members of the order exhibit shared physical characteristics that distinguish them from other birds. They have large, forward-facing eyes, which do not just enable them to see in the twilight and in the dark, but also help with spatial perception. The eyes cannot move freely, but the head can be turned through 270 degrees, so owls have an extremely wide field of vision. The birds also have a very acute sense of hearing. The striking facial plumage of some species guides all incoming sounds toward the ears, enabling the owls to distinguish the finest nuances of sound, which helps them to track down their prey in the dark.

No nesting behavior

Owls do not build nests. Some of them live in hollows in fissured rocks or in trees, and many species nest in places built by humans, such as old walls, barns, or church towers, and thus often live in close proximity to people. At the nest site, the female usually lays her eggs directly on the surface and incubates them alone, while the male supplies her with food—predominantly large insects, small mammals, fishes, and amphibians. The young are reared by both partners.

Right: The barn owl (*Tyto alba*), which is easy to recognize because of its unusual heart-shaped facial disk, is not yet globally threatened, but it is under threat locally.

Shortage of prey and nesting places

Some owl species, such as Blakiston's fishes-owl (*Bubo blakistoni*) from Manchuria, China, or the rufous fishing-owl (*Scotopelia ussheri*) are globally endangered; many others, although they are not yet included on nature conservation organizations' international lists of threatened species, are already on the national lists because numbers have declined almost everywhere in recent decades, in some cases quite dramatically.

The problems for these birds of prey are the same everywhere: they are adversely affected by the loss of their own habitats, but even more so by the disappearance of the habitats of their prey. Cultivation of land, housing sprawl, changing of farming practices, and road building have cost many small animals their lives, so food for owls is becoming increasingly scarce.

Another exacerbating circumstance is the growing shortage of nesting places. Owls rely on breeding sites such as old attics, barns, derelict walls, or church towers where they can take up residence, and there are fewer and fewer available.

In addition to often-fatal collisions with utility poles and wind turbines, traffic in their habitat presents a huge problem for many species, because the birds cannot estimate the speed of vehicles properly. In particular, they are often hit by trains when they are eating prey animals that have been run over on the tracks—and thus become accident victims themselves.

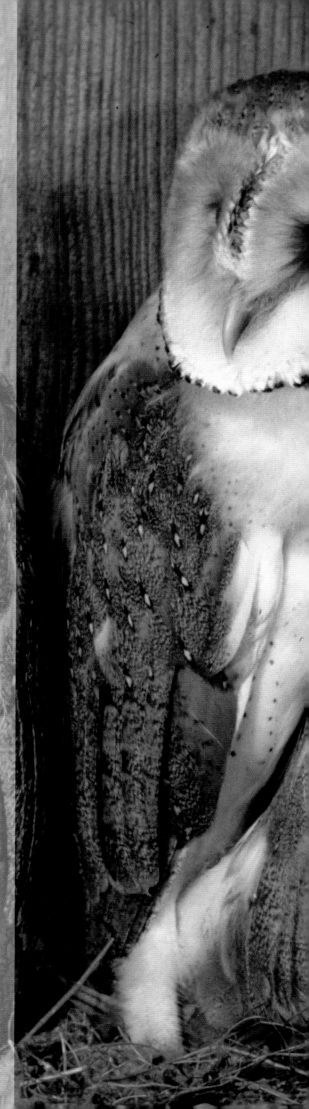

The mighty Ural owl (*Strix uralensis*), one of the largest owls of all, lives in northern forests. With the destruction of the forests and an increase in monocultures, it is vanishing from its habitat.

Blakiston's fish-owl lives in Manchuria, China, and is considered endangered. Only between 200 and 300 breeding pairs have survived the destruction of their habitat.

Thanks to costly special conservation measures, stocks of the Eurasian eagle-owl (*Bubo bubo*), which was persecuted for decades, have now recovered to a certain extent.

Due to habitat destruction, populations of the snowy owl (*Nyctea scandiaca*) have declined severely in some places and in others have disappeared totally.

CORACIIFORMES
HORNBILLS

Hornbills (Bucerotidae) belong to the order of Coraciiformes and comprise 55 species, whose unusual bills clearly differentiate them from the other families in the order. Hornbills are predominantly inhabitants of forests and woodland savannas in—tropical and subtropical Asia and Africa.

A remarkable bill

The colorful bill that gives the hornbill its name is long and downward-curving. In most species, the bill has a horny casque (helmet-like structure) that, in almost all cases, consists of light bone tissue or is hollow. In spite of this, its size alone makes the bill relatively heavy,

so the first two neck vertebrae of this bird are fused to increase stability. Pronounced neck musculature provides additional support for the head. It is thought that the "horn" serves to strengthen the long bill.

Southern ground-hornbill becoming increasingly rare

The genus *Bucorvus* (ground-hornbills) comprises two species: the Abyssinian or northern ground-hornbill (*Bucorvus abyssinicus*) and the southern ground-hornbill (*Bucorvus cafer* and *Bucorvus leadbeateri*). These are goose-sized birds that live—generally in pairs—in the savannas of

eastern and southern Africa. Although the IUCN currently classifies both species as not immediately threatened, the South African nature conservation organizations take quite a different view, at least in the case of the southern ground-hornbill. According to their studies, there are only a maximum of 500 breeding pairs remaining in southern Africa. This puts it at a critical level, meaning that the species should be classified as endangered or even as critically endangered.

The great hornbill (*Buceros bicornis*), like almost all hornbill species, needs expanses of forest with giant trees in which it can find the large nesting hollows it needs.

Above: The total population of the southern ground-hornbill is estimated at only 1,500 individuals, and the number of breeding pairs at a maximum of 500.

Below: The Visayan taractic has a relatively small geographical range, and because of the destruction of its habitat, it can no longer find suitable territories.

Hornbills on islands

As island populations, the Sulu hornbill (*Anthracoceros montani*) and the Visayan wrinkled hornbill (*Aceros waldeni*) are particularly endangered. The Sulu hornbill, which formerly inhabited three islands in the Pacific Ocean in the Sulu archipelago, part of the Philippines, now lives on the only one of the three islands that has not been completely deforested. Despite its rarity, it is still hunted. Stocks are thought to stand at considerably less than 100 breeding pairs.

The situation is similar for the Visayan wrinkled hornbill: on one of the three Philippine islands it previously inhabited, it has been eradicated; it appears on the Red List as critically endangered.

The Visayan taractic (*Penelopides panini*) has a somewhat larger range. It occurs on several islands in the Philippines and Sulawesi, but this species too is endangered.

Right: It is thought that there are now fewer than 80 breeding pairs of the Visayan wrinkled hornbill, which is considered to be critically endangered. The causes are the destruction of the forests in its habitat, as well as heavy hunting.

Hornbills being forced to retreat ever further

Hornbills are suffering hugely from the destruction of their habitats, on the one hand through logging of the rainforests, and on the other through the conversion of even the most remote semideserts into pasture land for domestic animals such as sheep and goats. Sometimes they are hunted for food and captured for sale to zoological gardens. About half of all hornbill species appear on the Red List as vulnerable, endangered, or even critically endangered, or appear on CITES, and, as shown, island populations have particularly poor chances of survival.

ALCEDINIFORMES
KINGFISHERS AND BEE-EATERS

Kingfishers (Alcedinidae) and bee-eaters (Meropidae) belong to the order of Alcediniformes. Members of both families are predominantly small, sometimes very colorful birds with similar habitat requirements. Although bee-eaters are confined to the Old World, kingfishers are found in the New World, in both North and South America.

Steep banks are essential for their survival

Bee-eaters and kingfishers live in scrubland areas as well as in forests and along the shores of rivers and lakes. The important thing is the presence of steep banks in which they can excavate nest holes so they can reproduce. The birds generally breed in colonies, often comprising several hundred individuals. Therefore, the destruction of steep banks, especially along rivers, and the excessive use of gravel pits, together with road construction and other environmental changes, are steadily extinguishing entire populations.

Iridescent kingfishers

Kingfishers inhabit large swathes of Europe, the Middle East, and Southeast Asia. In addition, they have overwintering grounds in North Africa, on the Arabian peninsula, and on the islands, large and small, of Indonesia. Despite their huge range, they are vulnerable

in densely populated areas, principally due to the regulation and straightening of streams and rivers as well as the draining of wetlands, which lead to the loss of possible breeding areas and changes in the food supply, causing the kingfishers to stop breeding or to leave their territory.

Colorful bee-eaters

Just as colorful as the kingfishers are the bee-eaters, which, in keeping with their name, really do eat bees, to whose poison they seem to be immune—although they do remove the sting before consuming the bees. In addition to eating bees, bee-eaters, like all birds in the order Alcediniformes, also eat insects, small fish, rodents, amphibians, and reptiles, depending on the bird's size and lifestyle. They beat their prey several times against a branch or another hard surface before swallowing it whole.

The bee-eater is a bird of warm regions, although with climate warming, it is advancing from southern and southeastern Europe in a northwesterly direction, and for some years it has been breeding in increasing numbers in Germany and Poland. The bee-eater normally

Right: Bee-eaters have very striking plumage and are one of the most colorful birds in Europe. Due to climate change, it has for some years even been possible to see—them north of the Alps.

One of the most beautiful birds in eastern and southern Africa is the northern carmine bee-eater (*Merops nubicus*), which nests in large colonies on steep banks near rivers during the breeding season.

To survive, the kingfisher needs natural, unspoiled rivers with clear water and a good supply of fishes.

lays between four and six eggs, which are incubated by both partners; in climatically favorable areas, they often hatch a second brood and, not infrequently, even a third in one year.

Kingfishers and bee-eaters making a comeback

The destruction of their habitats has led to difficulties for numerous kingfishers and bee-eaters. Although it appears that many species are not yet immediately threatened or are no longer immediately threatened, they are, at least locally, under strict protection because populations are declining, sometimes sharply. For example, bee-eater numbers are decreasing in many European countries. Kingfisher populations have always been relatively small, and, although they have recovered to some extent, they are not yet considered to be completely secure again. These birds are probably at least in part dependent on their protection status in individual countries.

Because the decline of many species is, to a considerable extent, caused by the loss of nesting opportunities, nature conservation organizations have started to provide the birds with artificial nesting sites, to restore streams to a natural state, and to preserve old gravel pits. In many places, these efforts have led to both kingfishers and bee-eaters returning to old breeding grounds and successfully rearing young there.

The red-bearded bee-eater (*Nyctyornis amictus*), which, in contrast to many other bee-eaters, does not form colonies, even during the breeding period, originates from the Indo-Pacific region.

UPUPIFORMES
HOOPOES

The Eurasian hoopoe (Upupu epops) is the only representative of the hoopoe family (Upupidae), which belongs to the order of Upupiformes (hoopoes, wood-hoopoes, and scimitarbills). It occurs only in the Old World, where it does, however, have an enormous range, stretching from Europe across large parts of Asia and Africa south of the Sahara.

Flight from the cold

The hoopoe is about 12 inches (30 cm) long and is easily recognizable by its long, slender, slightly curving bill and its characteristic erectile crest.

In cooler regions, hoopoes are summer birds that migrate in the fall to eastern and northeastern Africa. They do not return to their breeding grounds until the end of March or beginning of April. They do not build nests, but raise their young in hollows in old willows, olive trees, and fruit trees, as well as in cracks in walls, abandoned woodpecker holes, and even nest boxes. The birds live in a monogamous partnership for one breeding season only and then pair up afresh the following year.

Left: The destruction of natural habitats, pesticide residues in their food, and fluctuations in climate have caused a collapse in hoopoe populations throughout Europe.

Below: Artificial nesting aids, such as nest boxes, ensure the survival of the hoopoe in places where ancient tree stands have fallen victim to the chainsaw.

Decline in populations for unknown reasons

Although the hoopoe is still relatively common on the African continent, it is becoming increasingly rare in Europe and has disappeared from many of its former habitats. Particularly sharp declines in populations have been recorded in the United Kingdom, Germany, southern Scandinavia, Greece, and Turkey. In the Benelux countries, the hoopoe has now been eradicated.

The precise reasons for the population collapses are not known, especially because the hoopoe is not an exoanthropic species, but is generally extremely adaptable. It is thought that biotope changes constitute one of the factors behind its disappearance, but the principal reason is probably widescale spraying with pesticides, which destroys some of its food and poisons those hoopoes that remain. It is also suspected that the species is very sensitive to changes in climate.

PICIFORMES
WOODPECKERS

Woodpeckers (Picidae) are a family in the order of Piciformes, comprising over 200 species. They are distributed in forested areas over most of the world, but are not found in Madagascar, Australia, New Zealand, and some Pacific islands.

Woodpeckers can be heard from a long way off

Many species of woodpecker can be clearly identified from the way in which they hold on to a tree with their powerful claws and tap at it with their bills, supporting themselves with their tail feathers. However, by the time you spot a woodpecker, you will usually already have heard the loud, characteristic tapping, which serves to flush insects out of the tree trunk into the open, where they are then easy prey for the hungry bird.

Left: Like most hollow-nesters, the black woodpecker (*Dryocopus martius*) relies on old trees, in which it can create a hollow and rear its young.

Below: Populations of the red-headed woodpecker are declining sharply everywhere due to increasing levels of traffic and the destruction of its habitats.

Populations declining despite great adaptability

Thanks to their great adaptability, woodpeckers have until now coped quite well with environmental pollution, climate change, and even the destruction of their habitats. Many of the species now listed by the IUCN—which in any case make up only about 15 percent of all species—are not considered to be immediately threatened. Nevertheless, populations of some species, such as the Arabian woodpecker (*Dendrocopos dorae*), the red-headed woodpecker (*Melanerpes erythrocephalus*), the South African Knysna woodpecker (*Campethera notata*), and the Guadeloupe woodpecker (*Melanerpes herminieri*) are threatened. Two species, the ivory-billed woodpecker (*Campephilus principalis*) and the imperial woodpecker (*Campephilus imperialis*), both from North America, are thought to be extinct because they have not been sighted for a long time. Where most species are concerned, the threat status is not known, but it must be assumed that other species are vulnerable or even threatened with eradication.

CUCULIFORMES
CUCKOOS

The family of cuckoos (Cuculidae) comprises about 140 species, which are distributed across both the Old and New Worlds. Together with the hoatzins (Opisthocomidae), they form the order of Cuculiformes.

Cuckoos are brood parasites

Although cuckoos are famed mainly for their brood parasitism, most species build their own nests, incubate the eggs themselves, and bring up their own young. Only about a third of cuckoo species are actually brood parasites that lay their eggs in the nests of host birds such as warblers, reed warblers, or wagtails which then raise them as their own young—species whose eggs are deceptively similar to those of cuckoos in size, color, and markings.

Generally, the female cuckoos proceed very cautiously: they first remove one of the eggs belonging to the "foster parents" from the nest before laying one of their own in it. As a rule, the newly hatched cuckoo later throws

the hosts' eggs or chicks out of the nest to secure for itself the full attention of its adoptive parents. This ruthlessness is necessary because the fully fledged cuckoos do not leave the nest until they have reached four or five times the weight of their foster parents.

Cuckoos no longer able to find host birds
Population numbers of many cuckoos have fallen by more than 50 percent since the 1960s, particularly those of the European species. Almost all countries in central and western Europe are reporting dwindling populations and rare sightings, linked to the destruction of open deciduous forests—their preferred habitat—and to a massive decline in host species.

Cuckoos are now seen only in passage in numerous areas, not just in Europe, but also throughout the world. In many places, they have vanished completely.

Top: A reed warbler feeds its "stepchild," a newly fledged cuckoo, which is many times larger than the warbler itself.

Center: The decline in populations of many small bird species also places a question mark over the survival of the cuckoo as a brood parasite.

PASSERIFORMES
PASSERINES

Of the just under 10,000 species that make up the class of birds, 60 percent belong to the order of Passeriformes (passerines or perching birds), which is in turn divided into the suborders of Tyranni (suboscines) and Passeri (oscines or songbirds), the latter including such well-known bird families as Paridae (tits), Alaudidae (larks), Hirundinidae (swallows), and Sturnidae (starlings and mynahs). All passerines are small to medium-sized and are distributed worldwide; the only places they do not occur—at least as breeding birds—are the extreme Arctic regions.

Very adaptable birds

Many passerines are exceptionally adaptable, which is why they can be found in all climate and vegetation zones, from high in the Arctic Circle to the middle of the Amazon jungle, where the greatest abundance of species has evolved. One peculiarity of many species in the Northern Hemisphere is their marked migratory behavior: in particular, those species that feed predominantly on insects are forced to fly south in the fall to sunnier climes. Some spend the winter months in the Mediterranean, others in Africa. Migration requires immense physical effort—the birds lose up to half their body weight on the three- to four-week flight.

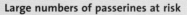

In some winters, Bohemian waxwings (*Bombycilla garrulus*), which live in the tundra of the Northern Hemisphere, turn up in central Europe on their search for rowan berries, their main food source.

Large numbers of passerines at risk

Scientists estimate that up to 20 percent of passerine populations are currently threatened. At least another 20 percent are on the brink of becoming endangered, and it is assumed that it is only a question of a few years until another 20 to 30 percent fall into this category. Island populations, from the Seychelles through Madagascar to the Southeast Asian and Australasian archipelagos, are in particular danger of eradication because, in most cases, they cannot escape the destruction of their habitats by moving to a different area.

Passerines are suffering immense population losses because of southern Europeans and Belgians who use the fall bird migrations to shoot down or catch millions of birds in nets, with glue traps, or by means of decoys. Redstarts (genus *Phoenicurus*), pied flycatchers (*Fidecula hypoleuca*), wrynecks (genus *Jynx*), yellowhammers (*Emberiza citrinella*), warblers, shrikes, and dozens of other species are on the decline everywhere because of this, and, like birds of paradise, lyrebirds (genus *Menura*), and fruiteaters (genus *Pipreola*), face an uncertain future. For many passerine species, very little hope remains.

In the spring, they head northward back to their breeding grounds. However, global warming has meant that a number of species now no longer migrate to their former winter quarters, but stay in or around their breeding areas, or else they return to their summer quarters up to four weeks earlier.

Passerines also affected by environmental changes

Despite their adaptability, passerines are suffering from the effects of environmental pollution and of changes made by humans to the natural biotope: tall orchard trees are making way for dwarf varieties, rivers are being straightened and wetlands drained, and the copses that used to edge fields have been removed. Whole forests are being felled, meadows built upon, and habitats transected by roads and railroads. For many birds, this means that the very basis of their survival is disappearing; they can find neither sufficient food, places in which to hide, nor even nesting sites. Consequently, they are migrating to regions where the environment is still relatively intact, but because these are becoming increasingly rare, the numbers of birds are being steadily depleted.

The fate of the Bali starling

The snow-white Bali starling (*Leucopsar rothschildi*), with its blue eye-ring, was first scientifically described in 1912 and occurs only in a very small range on Bali, in what is now the Bali Barat National Park. Less than one hundred years after it was first described, the Bali starling is considered to be critically endangered in the wild. Numbers have fallen to below 100 individuals today, with a low of just nine individuals recorded in February 2001.

In addition to habitat destruction, poaching for the animal trade is a principal cause of the collapse in populations: in Asia, the Bali starling is in great demand as a cage bird, with prices of up to $2,000 (£1,100) per bird sometimes being paid on the black market, although the Indonesian government has banned the keeping of these birds and punishes offenses by confiscating the birds and imposing large fines.

Several hundred specimens of this bird species are now kept in zoological gardens all over the world that have initiated a conservation breeding program. Over the years, stocks in captivity have risen to nearly 1,000 birds, and attempts are now being made to finance a reintroduction project to save the bird in the wild as well.

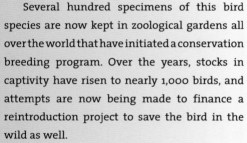

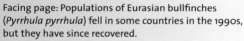

Facing page: Populations of Eurasian bullfinches (*Pyrrhula pyrrhula*) fell in some countries in the 1990s, but they have since recovered.

Left: Although there are now well under 100 specimens of the Bali starling living in the wild, stocks in zoological gardens, where this rare bird has been successfully bred in captivity, stand at 10 times that number.

Below: Bearded parrotbills (*Panurus biarmicus*) require extensive reedbeds and have disappeared from areas where there are none to be found.

STRUTHIONIFORMES
KIWIS AND CASSOWARIES

Kiwis (Apterygidae) and cassowaries (Casuaridae) belong to the Struthioniformes or ratites. These are excellent at running, but, although they have feathers and rudimentary wings, like ostriches, they cannot fly.

Left: Little is known about stocks of the southern cassowary (*Casuarius casuarius*), which is classified as vulnerable—numbers are estimated at between 1,000 and 15,000 birds.

Below: The three species of cassowary—shown here is a dwarf cassowary (*Casuarius bennetti*)—are the world's largest bird species after the African ostrich and the Australian emu.

CASSOWARIES

Cassowaries (*Casuarius* spp.) live in the tropical rainforests of northeastern Australia and New Guinea, where, despite the fact that they are up to 5½ feet (1.7 meters) tall and weigh up to 130 lb (60 kg), they are very shy and elusive and their behavior is therefore not very well known. They are among the largest living birds after ostriches and emus.

They are easily distinguished from other ratites by the helmet-like horny casque on their bare heads. All species have wattles in brilliant red or blue, but these are less pronounced in young birds.

Little is known about population sizes

Two of the three species of cassowary are classified as vulnerable on the Red List, although, due to their secluded way of life, no precise population figures are known. Cassowaries were formerly hunted by the indigenous peoples for their feathers and their meat, and their claws were sometimes used as arrow tips. Nowadays, due to the logging of the forests in their habitats, it must be assumed that not only their ranges but also their populations are shrinking. Furthermore, clutches of eggs are often plundered by feral dogs and pigs, and many cassowaries fall victim to increasing traffic in their habitats.

KIWIS

By far the smallest ratite is the kiwi, the three species of which are found in the dense rainforests of New Zealand. The kiwi is roughly the size of a chicken although its eggs are about six times the size of a chicken's egg and weigh about one pound (450 g). It has a beak that is up to 8 inches (20 cm) long, slightly downward-curving and tactile, with the nostrils located at the tip. It uses this beak to probe for worms and insect larvae in the humus-rich soil of its habitat. Kiwis are distinguishable from other ratites not only by their size, but also by their diet: the proportion of meat in their diet is far greater than it is in that of the other families, which are predominantly plant-eaters.

They are monogamous birds and a male and female kiwi tend to live their whole lives together. They usually lay only one egg per mating season.

Below: The kiwi is threatened by habitat destruction and by feral dogs and cats, as well as by introduced predators such as foxes.

Kiwis are nocturnal birds; they spend the day sleeping in hollows and do not emerge until sunset. Thanks to their good hearing and sense of smell, they can find their way around even in total darkness.

All kiwis are threatened

All three kiwi species are listed on the Red List as vulnerable, and one subspecies as endangered. New Zealand's national bird was intensively hunted as a source of meat and feathers for centuries, first by the Maoris, then later by European settlers. At the beginning of the twentieth century, hunting them was banned, and soon afterward the birds were placed under strict protection.

However, new factors have threatened and still do threaten populations: extensive biotope destruction and, in particular, introduced domestic and wild animals such as foxes, martens, dogs, cats, and wild pigs are making life difficult for the kiwi in the most literal sense. Experts estimate that over 90 percent of young birds are killed by predators.

Above: With its long, tweezer-like beak, the nocturnal kiwi probes for food on the forest floor.

Below: The ranges of both kiwis and cassowaries are very small, which is why they are particularly severely affected by habitat destruction.

African elephants

Polar bears

Bighorn sheep

MAMMALIA

MAMMALS

Mammals, the class to which humans belong, are divided into three subclasses: monotremes (Protheria), marsupials (Metatheria), and higher mammals (Eutheria). The monotremes include the egg-laying echidnas (Tachyglossidae) and platypuses (Ornithorhyncidae), which do not have teats but secrete milk through an area of glands. The young lick the milk off the mother. The marsupials include the kangaroos, koalas, marsupial carnivores (Dasyuridae), and the already extinct Tasmanian wolf (*Thylacinus cynocephalus*) from Australasia, as well as the opossums (Didelphimorphia), which occur in the Americas. Most mammal species, however, belong to the class of higher mammals.

The highly diverse mammals, whose almost 6,000 different species have colonized all the continents, the Arctic, and the world's oceans, differ from other classes in having a coat of hair and possessing the ability to produce milk—although they do so only when young are expected or have been born. The number of teats ranges between two and two dozens, and the nursing period ranges between a few days and two years or more.

The class of mammals includes numerous species, among them such well-known species as the elephant, tiger, panda, and giraffe, which are threatened—by the destruction and transformation of habitats, environmental pollution, and hunting and poaching. In addition, many of the (usually large) mammalian predators are near the top of the food chain and, therefore, also suffer if the populations of their prey animals are decimated because they can then no longer find sufficient food.

According to the International Union for Conservation of Nature and Natural Resources (IUCN), more than 70 mammalian species have been eradicated over the last few centuries—and it now looks as if many more will soon follow.

Zebras

Guanacos

White rhinoceroses

Mountain gorilla

PLATYPUSES AND ECHIDNAS

The order of monotremes (Monotremata) includes the platypuses (Ornithorhyncidae) and echidnas (Tachyglossidae), very primitive mammals that lay eggs but nonetheless—in contrast to reptiles and birds—feed their young with milk from the mother.

PLATYPUSES

The platypus (*Ornithorhynchus anatinus*), which lives in burrows on river banks in eastern Australia and Tasmania, reaches a weight of 1½ to almost 5 lb (0.7 to 2.2 kg), with a tail length of 6 inches (15 cm) and a snout-vent length of about 20 inches (50 cm). When the skin of one of these curious animals was first received at the British Museum in London in 1798, the pelt with a beaver's tail and duck's bill was taken to be a poor joke perpetrated by Chinese taxidermists.

Two weeks after mating, the female platypus usually lays two eggs, which are approximately the size of sparrow's eggs and are incubated for 7–10 days before the 1-inch-long (2.5-cm-long) naked young hatch.

Abundant but nonetheless vulnerable

Although platypuses are still quite common at the local level, water pollution, river straightening, and the spread of humans now mean that these shy animals have become rare in some areas and disappeared completely from others. Their habitat, which is restricted to Australia, is a further reason why the animals are considered vulnerable and protected accordingly—zoological gardens may keep the egg-laying mammals only with special permission, and private individuals may not do so at all.

ECHIDNAS

Echidnas are truly solitary animals that are predominantly nocturnal. Several species are known, including the short-beaked echidna (*Tachyglossus aculeatus*) and the long-beaked echidnas (*Zaglossus* spp.). For the latter, a 1982 estimate put the number of individuals at 30,000. All long-beaked echidnas live in a small area on the island of New Guinea. For this reason, and because the animal is hunted for food, it is classified by the IUCN as endangered.

Although platypuses are abundant at the local level, they are considered to be vulnerable due to the high demands being placed on their already limited habitat, and they are protected accordingly.

The short-beaked echidna is widely distributed on the Australian continent, whereas the platypus and long-beaked echidna have relatively restricted habitats.

A short-beaked echidna in Tasmania in search of food.

DIPROTODONTIA
KOALAS, WOMBATS, AND KANGAROOS

Koalas (Phascolarctidae), wombats (Vombatidae), and kangaroos (Macropodidae) are families from the order Diprotodontia. Diprotodonts belong to the mammalian infraclass of marsupials (Metatheria), which occur exclusively on the American and Australian contents and differ from other mammals in that, at the time of their birth, they are scarcely more developed than embryos. They therefore have to grow for a few more weeks or months in the mother's pouch—where, in most species, the teats are located. Only when they have reached an appropriate stage of development do they leave the pouch.

KOALAS

The koala (*Phascolarctos cinereus*) is a connoisseur that feeds almost exclusively on the peppermint-tasting leaves and shoots of very specific eucalyptus species. Koalas will eat only about 20 of the 350 eucalyptus species, and their favorite food consists of just five species. This unbalanced diet is proving to be life-threatening to the koala because large parts of Australia, the home of this marsupial, are constantly being plagued by devastating forest and bush fires, which cause severe damage to flora and fauna. The few koalas that survive these disastrous fires often starve to death because they can no longer find food.

Protective measures are vital to their survival

Not so very long ago, there were millions of these leaf-eaters living in the open woodlands of Australia. Then, at the end of the nineteenth century, the populations were decimated by a series of epidemics. Finally, early in the last century, the koala's beautiful, soft, silver-gray fur was discovered by the fashion industry, with millions of furs being exported during parts of the 1920s. Not until the 1930s did the Australian government enact protective measures—not least in response to international pressure—and work began on reintroducing koalas to their original ranges. Nevertheless, the Australian Koala Foundation puts the numbers of animals living in the wild today at fewer than 100,000 individuals in the whole country and, because of the specific needs of koalas in terms of habitat and food, fears that they will be eradicated in the not-too-distant future unless more far-reaching measures are taken to protect them.

WOMBATS

Until the first quarter of the last century, little was known about the life of the nocturnally active wombats, which occur in southern

Above: After birth, koala young remain for 5 to 6 months in the mother's pouch before they begin to venture on excursions into their immediate surroundings.

Below: Koalas are excellent climbers, leaving "their" eucalyptus tree only reluctantly.

Australia, on the islands of the Bass Strait, and on Tasmania. It is now known that, depending on their habitat, the animals can vary greatly in size and in fur color.

Declining populations

Two genera, the coarse-haired or common wombat (*Vombatus ursinus*) and the hairy-nosed wombats (*Lasiorhinus* spp.), are distinguished. Numbers of both have declined sharply everywhere as a direct result of hunting and also due to habitat destruction and competition with sheep and cattle for food. The situation of the northern hairy-nosed wombat (*Lasiorhinus krefftii*) is particularly critical: the IUCN lists the species as critically endangered, because there are only about 100 specimens still surviving, in a national park in Queensland, Australia.

KANGAROOS

There are over 75 kangaroo species, the smallest of which is only about as big as a rat. The largest, when standing erect, has a head-and-body

Right: The severely threatened hairy-nosed wombat is now found only in a few regions in the south and in the northeast of Australia.

Below: Several subspecies of the common wombat inhabit a number of areas in southeastern Australia and Tasmania. It is vulnerable outside protected areas.

The bridled nail-tailed wallaby is critically endangered due to the destruction of habitats and heavy hunting pressure.

With some luck, it is possible to observe the shy pretty-faced wallaby (*Wallabia canguru*) in the early morning or late evening hours.

Goodfellow's tree kangaroo (*Dendrolagus goodfellowi*) is considered to be endangered due to the continuing clearance of the rainforests.

length of up to 6 feet (2 meters), not including the long, powerful tail, which the animal uses for retaining balance when running and like an extra leg when hopping slowly. The front legs are generally short and carry five clawed toes, whereas the hind legs and feet are elongated and, in some species, are very powerful.

Many species are fast runners with great stamina: large kangaroos, for example, can reach top speeds of just under 45 mph (70 km/h).

Different lifestyles

Kangaroos live in open grassland, in rocky mountainous regions, on river banks, in swamps, and in trees or in open scrubland. They are herbivores, and in a small number of cases, also ruminants. Some species are solitary, with partners spending time together only during the mating period, whereas others live in fairly small groups, which as a rule consist of a male, several females, and their young.

Many threatened species

It is not so much hunting as the introduction of alien species, i.e. the introduction by humans of enemies such as foxes, and, above all, the conversion of habitats into grazing land for farm animals that constitute the chief problems for kangaroos. Four species have become extinct in modern times, and numerous further species are classified by the IUCN as vulnerable, endangered, or critically endangered, including five species of tree kangaroo (*Dendrolagus*), some species of rock wallaby (*Petrogale*), and, in particular, the bridled nail-tailed wallaby (*Onychogalea fraenata*), which had been deemed extinct until a tiny colony was discovered a few years ago.

AFROSORICIDA
TENRECS

Tenrecs (Tenrecidae), together with golden moles (Chrysochloridae), belong to the tenrecomorphs (Afrosoricida)—an order of very primitive insectivores comprising about 45 species.

Varying habitats

The family of tenrecs lives almost exclusively on Madagascar, Mauritius, the Seychelles, and other surrounding small islands. Because no larger predators are found in any of these places, this family of mammals was able to find a refuge there and evolve into various species that, over time, colonized different habitats. Most tenrecs are ground dwellers, but some species live largely underground and adopt the role that elsewhere is filled by moles, whereas others fill the role of shrews or otters in the ecology of the islands. All tenrecs feed predominantly on invertebrates, insects, and—depending on their size—also on small vertebrates. Some species enter a kind of hibernation during the Madagascan winter, from May to October.

Some tenrec species are threatened due to the destruction of their habitats.

Habitat loss decimates populations

Due to large-scale environmental destruction on Madagascar and the surrounding islands, the tenrecs are increasingly being robbed of their habitat, which was in any case extremely small. Whereas some species are synanthropic and are still relatively common, others are not doing so well. The IUCN classifies six species as vulnerable or endangered, including the aquatic tenrec (*Limnogale mergulus*), measuring approximately 5 inches (13 cm) in length, which lives on river banks and has developed an otter-like form. There is also the risk that other species in this subfamily, which have so far scarcely been researched at all, will be eradicated before suitable protective measures can be taken to save them.

CHIROPTERA
FRUIT BATS AND TRUE BATS

Numbering over 1,000 species distributed worldwide, the bats (Chiroptera) are the second-largest order of mammals after rodents (Rodentia)—and they are the only mammals with wings and the ability to fly. Although fruit bats (Megachiroptera) and true bats (Microchiroptera) are alike at first glance, they each form a separate suborder.

OLD WORLD FRUIT BATS

The family of Old World fruit bats (Pteropodidae) comprises about 40 genera, with over 170 species known to date. These all live in humid forests of tropical and subtropical areas of Asia, Africa, Australia, and Oceania. Most roost in trees, but some occupy caves or human-built structures.

The largest known species, with a head-and-body length of 16 inches (40 cm) and a wingspan of a good 5 feet (1.5 meters), is the Indian flying fox (*Pteropus giganteus*), and the smallest species is the lesser long-tongued fruit bat (*Macroglossus minimus*), which occurs only on Java and the surrounding islands and grows to no more than 2½ inches (6 cm) long with a wingspan of 10 inches (25 cm). As a rule, the arms and hands, which have been transformed into wings, are hairless, and the body is covered with soft, short fur. All fruit bats have claws on the first digit.

In contrast to the true bats, which primarily orient themselves acoustically by means of echolocation, the color-blind Old World fruit bats use their eyes, which are adapted to darkness, and their excellent sense of smell to find their way around.

Important function for vegetation

Old World fruit bats are herbivores; some are out-and-out nectar suckers, whereas others are petal-eaters or fruit-lovers that do not consume their meal where they find it, but instead fly with the fruit in their mouths to their roost trees. In doing so, they perform a very important function in the dense rainforests: they are responsible for transporting seeds and for pollinating flowers.

The wings of Old World fruit bats consist of a double layer of skin that is stretched between the four greatly elongated fingers of the hand.

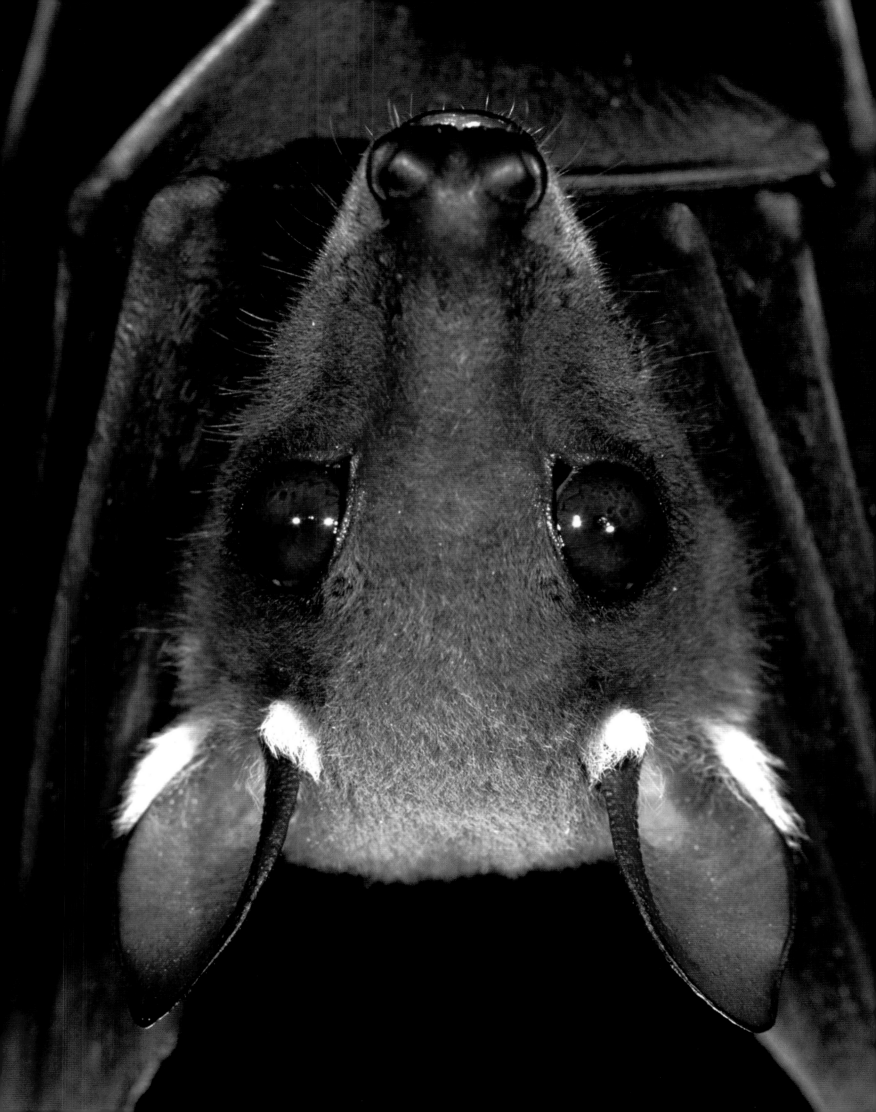

Populations of Old World fruit bats are in decline across their entire geographical range, with many species listed by the IUCN as being vulnerable, endangered, or critically endangered.

The main reason is the loss of habitat caused by clearance of the rainforests. In addition, Old World fruit bats, which live in colonies of up to 500,000, can become a real plague for farmers when they leave their roosts in the hours around dusk and descend on fruit and vegetable plantations; as a result, they are persecuted, shot, or poisoned on a large scale.

Because Old World fruit bats normally produce just one young per year, it is scarcely conceivable that stocks will recover.

Populations of true bats have also declined sharply as a result of the destruction of overwintering and resting places and the large-scale use of insecticides. In particular, many species from the families of evening bats (Vespertilionidae) and the horseshoe bats (Rhinolophidae) are threatened and are recorded on the Red List in various categories.

TRUE BATS

The second suborder of bats, of which there is a wealth of species with a wide variety of forms, is that of the true bats. Unlike the Old World fruit bats, they lack the claw on the second finger and have a tail. In addition, their ears are separated at the base, which—combined with an elongated tragus (ear flap)—helps improve their already highly developed hearing ability.

True bats are relatively small. The largest species is the Australian ghost bat (*Macroderma gigas*), which measures 6 inches (15 cm) from the top of the head to the tip of the tail. The pipistrelles (*Pipistrellus*) from Europe, however, are truly tiny, measuring at most 1½ inches (4 cm) in length. Apart from the patagium (flying membrane) and the pinnae (outer ears), the whole body is usually covered in hair.

Background: By day, the sleeping flying foxes hang—as here in Sri Lanka—in their roost trees. They wake as dusk falls.

Facing page: In contrast to true bats, fruit bats are guided primarily by their senses of sight and smell and don't echolocate.

The legend of the blood sucker

Many true bat species are predominantly insectivorous, although a few species feed on fruit or have become nectar and pollen specialists. Yet other species hunt small vertebrates, and there are even fish specialists.

The legend of the blood-sucking vampire was probably based on the vampire bats (Desmodontinae) of tropical and subtropical areas of the Americas, whose saliva contains anti-coagulant agents and which feed exclusively on the blood of other animals. The common vampire bat (*Desmodus rotundus*), for example, makes an incision in the skin of larger mammals and laps up the blood.

Echolocation

These mainly nocturnal mammals largely rely on echolocation when searching for food. They emit sounds in the ultrasonic range and recapture the echo with their large ears (some also with their strangely shaped noses and mouths). They also can identify the size, shape, and texture of anything they encounter and react in fractions of seconds to avoid an obstacle or hunt down a prey animal.

A nursery colony of the Alpine long-eared bat (*Plecotus macrobullaris*), a recently discovered species, in a Swiss church.

The soprano pipistrelle (*Pipistrellus pygmaeus*), from central Europe, was only discovered in 2000 and is strictly protected.

PRIMATES
LEMURS

According to the latest taxonomic classification, the lemur family (Lemuridae) comprises the prosimians from the suborder of wet-nosed primates (Strepsirrhini), which are found on Madagascar. These are characterized by their moist, dog-like noses and are heavily dependent on their sense of smell. Lemurs are very primitive, mouse-to-dog-sized primates with bushy tails, are closely related to the insectivores (Eulipotyphla), and are predominantly nocturnal.

Named after spirits
Lemurs were given their name by European researchers on account of their eerie nocturnal songs and their eyes, which glow an unearthly red and yellow in low light. The name refers to the wandering souls of the restless dead from Roman mythology. Even the indigenous inhabitants of Madagascar find some lemurs frightening: depending on the region, some species are considered to be good or evil spirits.

Special tools for grooming
Numerous lemur species live in groups in which mutual grooming—common in many primate species—serves to reinforce social bonds. Lemurs possess two special features for this purpose, namely, long claws on the second toe of the foot and a so-called tooth comb, a connected row of incisors and canines in the lower jaw that jut forward at an angle of 45° and are thus perfectly suited to combing the fur.

Even the common species are threatened
The best-known representative of the lemurs must be the ring-tailed lemur (*Lemur catta*), which, because of the purring sounds it produces, is often called the Madagascar cat. It lives in groups, usually of one to two dozen animals, in the dry forests in southwestern Madagascar and is dark to pearl gray in color, with black and white markings on its face, ears, and tail (which may be up to 21 inches/

55 cm long). Although one of the more common lemur species, it, too, is listed as vulnerable on the Red List.

Brown lemurs plant trees
The five species of the genus of brown lemurs (*Eulemur*), which are found predominantly in northern and eastern Madagascar, are to a great extent responsible for distributing the seeds of about 20 tree species in the Madagascan forests by eating their fruit and depositing the seeds with their feces at a different location. As the number of animals decreases, so does the dispersal of the seeds. The fact that four of the five species are classified as vulnerable has a massive impact on tree stocks.

Crowned lemurs (*Eulemur coronatus*) inhabit fixed territories in small groups. With a total population of 10,000 animals, they are considered to be vulnerable.

Slim chances of survival
For a long time, popular belief among Madagascar's indigenous people protected the animals from hunting and persecution. Nowadays, however, traditional beliefs are no longer able to preserve them. As a result of extensive biotope destruction—the World Wildlife Fund (WWF) estimates that 90 percent of the original forest cover on Madagascar has already been destroyed— and heavy hunting pressure, almost all lemurs are indirectly or directly threatened. As long as their habitats continue to be recklessly destroyed despite legal protection, their chances of survival are very slim because the island location greatly limits their opportunities of escape. Even switching location on the island is practically impossible: most lemurs are so specialized that adapting to a new habitat where conditions are different would scarcely be possible.

Due to the continuing destruction of habitats, all Madagascar's lemur species are under threat—even the once very common ring-tailed lemur.

The threatened mongoose lemur (*Eulemur mongoz*) lives in Madagascar's dry forests and on the Comoros islands.

Like all lemurs, the threatened black lemurs (*Eulemur macaco*) are social animals. They live together in groups that may number up to 20 individuals.

PRIMATES
OLD WORLD MONKEYS

Numbering approximately 80 species, the Old World monkeys (Cercopithecidae) are the most species-rich group of catarrhine monkeys and apes, which also include the hominoids (Hominoidea), and are found exclusively in the Old World. All species of Old World monkeys, which are divided into the subfamilies of cheek-pouched monkeys (Cercopithecinae) and leaf-eating monkeys (Colobinae), are today found only in Africa and across broad parts of Asia. One species does occur on Gibraltar, but only because it was introduced there.

Differing diets

Old World monkeys are diurnal and extremely gregarious, usually living in fairly large groupings and exhibiting marked social behavior. As a rule, the groups are headed by an older male (the highest ranking one) who is responsible for the safety of the group and searches for feeding sites. Their diets vary: leaf-eating monkeys are predominantly vegetarians, whereas cheek-pouched monkeys are omnivores, feeding on fruit, seeds, twigs and leaves, insects, and small vertebrates. Their name stems from their cheek pouches, in which they can store food.

HANUMAN LANGUR

One of the most graceful representatives of the langurs is the Hanuman langur (*Semnopithecus entellus*), 15 subspecies of which are distributed across India—from the slopes of the Himalaya to tropical Cape Comorin. The young are born jet black, but over the first three years of their lives, the color of their fur changes to the silver-white of the adult animals, their faces remaining dark.

One of the most striking of the Old World monkeys is the male mandrill. Some populations of the species are endangered.

Although bonnet macaques are highly adaptable, and as synanthropes, also live in cities, they have been eradicated from large parts of their original ranges.

The males of the proboscis monkey from the primeval forests of Borneo are easily recognized by their conspicuous noses.

Below: Old World monkeys and apes belong to the parvorder of catarrhines which are found almost exclusively in Africa south of the Sahara and in Southeast Asia. In the Americas, their counterparts are the New World monkeys, whose range extends from Central America into central South America.

Above: As a result of intense logging activity in the forests where they live and the war in Vietnam, douc langurs are now critically endangered.

Distribution of Old World monkeys
Distribution of New World monkeys

The Celebes crested macaque (*Macaca nigra*)—shown here is a mother with child—is on the IUCN's Red List.

The legend goes that the wise monkey minister Hanuman once helped Prince Rama to free his wife Sita, who was being held captive by the giant Ravanna. As a punishment, Ravanna wanted to burn Hanuman on the pyre, but the clever monkey fled, although with slightly burned hands, feet, and face—and these have been black ever since. All the subspecies are on the Red List, in different threat categories.

PROBOSCIS MONKEY

Another member of the langurs is the strange proboscis monkey (*Nasalis larvatus*) from forested areas along the coasts and river banks of Borneo. It is a remarkably good swimmer and, in the event of danger, jumps into water to swim away.

The males grow up to 30 inches (75 cm) in length and can weigh as much as 55 lb (25 kg), whereas the females are considerably smaller and lighter. The animals live together in troops and feed exclusively on plants; not much more is yet known about them. Their populations are deemed to be endangered.

DOUCS

The doucs (*Pygathrix*), which owe their nickname of "costumed ape" to their characteristic coat patterns, also belong to the langur group. All three known species inhabit the rainforests of central China and Indochina and are herbivores. A group is likely to consist of one or two adult males and several females with young, but little else is known about the lives of douc langurs. There is reason to fear that it will not be possible to rescue their wild populations, which have been significantly reduced, principally by intensive hunting for their fur and the clearance of rainforests.

Like most primates, the Old World monkeys are also suffering from the spread of humans into their habitats, which forces the monkeys into ever-smaller areas. In addition, many of these monkeys are highly specialized, i.e. they are dependent upon particular food or on very specific conditions in their habitats—which would make moving to different areas difficult.

The magnificent coats of many species in the family of Old World monkeys are one reason why the animals are hunted intensively; another is their meat. The trade in monkey meat has increased sharply since the 1990s and is having serious impacts on populations, especially as bushmeat is no longer being sold just in Africa but is also sometimes being sold illegally in Europe—notwithstanding the fact that monkey meat carries a considerable health risk and very probably transferred the HIV virus and Ebola to humans.

*In many parts of Africa, primates—shown here is a moustached monkey (*Cercopithecus cephus*)—are seen as desirable sources of bushmeat.*

DIANA MONKEYS

Numerous species from the genus of guenons are on the Red List. Among them is the Diana monkey (*Cercopithecus diana*), which inhabits the coastal forests of West Africa and the Congo basin. The populations of this strikingly colored guenon species, which is up to 28 inches (70 cm) long, are deemed to be endangered due to large-scale biotope destruction and hunting.

BONNET MACAQUES AND LION-TAILED MACAQUES

The only baboon-like cheek-pouched monkeys living in Asia are the 21 macaque (*Macaca*)

The wonderful roloway monkey (*Cercopithecus diana roloway*) lives in a very small area in the eastern Ivory Coast and in Ghana. It is considered critically endangered.

species, which, over the course of time, have been introduced into several areas of the world, including Gibraltar. Representatives of this group that are particularly flexible and adept at surviving are the bonnet macaques (*Macaca radiata*) from India, which do not shy away from humans. In groups of up to 50 animals, they roam through their territories in the south of India, stripping fruit crops, plantations, and fields bare. They are not considered to be under immediate threat—in contrast to the toque macaques on Sri Lanka (*Macaca sinica*), which are classified as vulnerable.

Another member of the macaques is the lion-tailed macaque or wanderoo (*Macaca silenus*). It lives in the deep forests of the Western Ghats mountains of southern India and is classified as endangered because of reckless land-grabbing by the exploding human population.

BABOONS

Except for the macaques, all other members of the Old World monkey tribe Papionini live in Africa, mostly south of the Sahara and in southern Arabia. Baboon troops, which comprise between 5 and 200 individuals, are—depending on their size—led by one or more males, which are extremely protective. Even lions and leopards prefer to avoid the troop leaders, whose canines can be inches long, rather than to become involved in a fight.

Striking mandrills

In addition to the imposing yellow and hamadryas baboons from the *Papio* genus of baboons, there are other beautiful and striking species, such as the mandrill (*Mandrillus sphinx*), the male of which has a brightly colored

The drill (*Mandrillus leucophaeus*), which closely resembles the mandrill, is one of Africa's rarest primates; its total population in the wild is estimated at 3,000 individuals.

face and significant ischial callosities (areas of thickened, hairless skin on the buttocks), which play an important role in the social behavior of groups. The mandrill inhabits the tropical forests of Cameroon and is classified as vulnerable, with individual populations listed as endangered.

Geladas

On the other side of Africa, in the Ethiopian highlands, lives the gelada baboon (*Theropithecus gelada*), which has a hairless, crimson triangular patch on its chest. Gelada baboons are hunted principally for their meat and are also increasingly losing habitat to humans. On the Red List they are recorded as being "merely" near threatened—not least due to insufficient data having been recorded.

The threat gestures of gelada baboons are truly terrifying.

PRIMATES
GREAT APES

Hominidae (great apes and humans) is a family within the parvorder Catarrhini, which includes the Old World monkeys, with which the hominids have similarities in terms of dental pattern and the shape of the nose, but from which they differ significantly in other features. For example, hominids have no tail, but have instead a coccyx, a broad pelvis, a barrel-shaped thorax, movable shoulders, well-developed back and arm muscles, movable wrist joints, and an opposing thumb. This body structure makes the hominids—including also humans (Homo)—the only primates able to sit upright, and to stand and move around in an upright position. Hominids also differ from the other Old World monkeys and apes by virtue of their far more complex social behavior.

The hominids are a relatively young family within the order of primates, the earliest representatives of which appeared about 98 million years ago; it was only about 4 million years ago that the last two primate genera—humans and chimpanzees (Pan)—began to diverge, and modern humans finally appeared in East Africa, probably evolving from the Australopithecus, between approximately 1.8 and 2.4 million years ago. This most recent member of the hominids is the only one that is not threatened.

Orangutans spend most of their time in trees. They brachiate on their long arms from branch to branch, particularly when they are in a hurry.

Every day before dusk, these diurnal animals use leaves to build themselves a new sleeping nest in the trees.

ORANGUTANS

The name *orangutan* stems from the Malay language and, literally translated, means "man of the forest." Fossil finds show that the orangutan (*Pongo*) previously also occurred on Java, in Vietnam, and in southern China, but its range is nowadays restricted to the widely separated islands of Sumatra and Borneo, where it inhabits the tropical rainforests—preferring to live close to water or in swampy areas—and is found at almost all elevations. On the basis of pronounced differences in their physique and behavior, the two populations are divided into two species: the Sumatran orangutan (*Pongo abelii*) and the somewhat heavier and darker Bornean orangutan (*Pongo pygmaeus*).

Facing page: In contrast to other hominids, orangutans generally lead solitary lives.

Below: The phylogenetic tree shows the branched relationships of the primates. The division of the hominids and the evolution of the genera occurred at a relatively late stage.

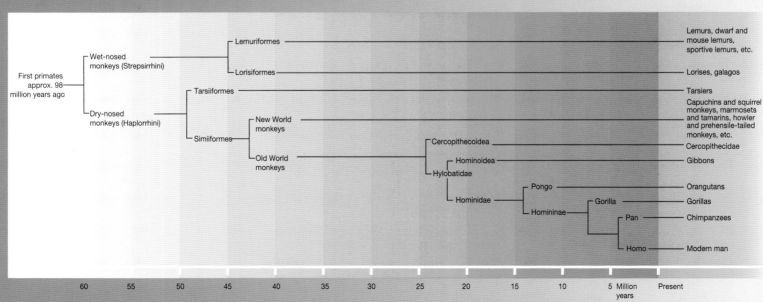

Individual appearance

Orangutans exhibit pronounced sexual dimorphism. Male animals reach a head-and-body length of 4–5 feet (1.25–1.5 meters) and a weight of up to 200 lb (90 kg), making them almost twice as heavy as the females. In addition to the large throat pouch, particularly conspicuous features include the striking bulges, called sagittal and nuchal crests, on the top of the skull in males, and the cheek pads that grow throughout the lifespan and lend each animal a quite individual appearance. Both sexes have beards.

Specialized tree dwellers

Orangutans, which are predominantly vegetarian, are specially adapted for life in the trees. Their arms are long and powerful and reach a span of over 6 feet (2 meters), and the elongated, hook-shaped hands with short thumbs are perfect tools for gripping. The short, highly agile legs, with their hand-like feet, are useful for climbing vertically in trees.

Loose bonds

In contrast to other hominids, orangutans are fairly solitary animals. They maintain only loose contacts with fellow members of their species; close and enduring bonds exist only between mother and child. Unlike the females,

Survival uncertain

Both orangutan species are threatened: the IUCN lists the Sumatran species as critically endangered and the species on Borneo as endangered. The reasons for this lie in the rapid destruction of habitat through the clearing of forests to extract timber. New agricultural areas in the form of giant plantations are currently needed because the countries of Malaysia and Indonesia, to which the natural island habitats of the orangutan belong, are the main producers of palm oil, for which there is great demand; it is an important component of many soaps, washing powders, and personal care products, and has controversially found a new use as a feedstock for biofuel.

In addition, orangutans are still being hunted, partly as sources of meat, but partly also as pests, because they sometimes cause major devastation on the plantations when searching for food.

The young are popular pets in some parts of Asia, so it is assumed that even today—despite the listing of both orangutan species under CITES—every week two babies are being smuggled out of the country and the mothers killed.

To save the orangutans, protected areas and national parks have been established on Borneo and Sumatra, and rehabilitation centers prepare captured young for life in the wild.

An orangutan mother and child in the Tanjung-Putting National Park on Borneo.

the males rarely have fixed territories. They wander freely and frequently react in a hostile manner to fellow males, which occasionally leads to fighting. Females get along more peacefully with one another: sometimes, two or more mothers with their young will remain together, occasionally even in company with a male, for several days on end.

Despite their loose ties, there is a hierarchy in which animals with territory rank higher than animals with no territory.

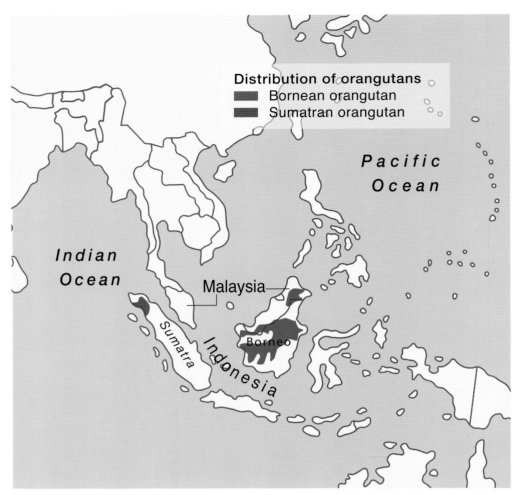

Distribution of orangutans
Bornean orangutan
Sumatran orangutan

Pacific Ocean

Indian Ocean

Malaysia

Sumatra

Indonesia

Borneo

Below: Male orangutans, unlike the females, have pronounced cheek pads.

Above: Because the range of orangutans has now become severely restricted, interbreeding between families is no longer readily possible, and there is a risk of inbreeding.

GORILLAS

Two gorilla species, each with two subspecies, live in the primeval forests of western and central Africa: the western gorilla (*Gorilla gorilla*) and the eastern gorilla (*Gorilla beringei*). The populations of the two species are located about 600 miles (1,000 km) apart and do not mix.

Forest dwellers in different regions

All gorillas are forest dwellers, but they live in different types of forest, depending on the subspecies. For example, some live in lowland rainforests, others in montane rainforests or secondary forests. The mountain gorilla (*Gorilla beringei beringei*), which occurs in the area of the Virunga volcanoes and in the Bwindi rainforest in Uganda, may venture as high as about 13,000 feet (4,000 meters) and consequently has a thick, insulating coat of hair that protects it against both the daily downpours of rain and the cold.

The largest primates

Gorillas are the largest and heaviest animals among the approximately 200 species of primates, the eastern gorilla being generally a little larger and heavier than the western gorilla. There is a considerable size and weight difference between the sexes: although the females grow to about 5 feet (1.5 meters) in height and 165 lb (75 kg) in weight, a male measures about 6 feet (1.8 meters), weighs up to 440 lb (200 kg), and has an arm span of

Right: The female western lowland gorilla suckles its baby. The mother–child bond is very close in gorillas.

Below: The gentle care shown by young gorilla mothers for their young is learned within the family group.

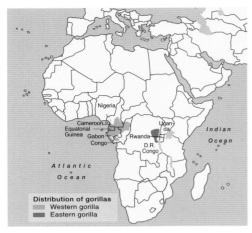

Gorillas live in two totally separate populations in Africa: the lowland gorillas in the west and the mountain gorillas in the high mountains in the east, between Lake Edward and Lake Tanganyika.

The old gorilla males are called silverbacks because of the silver-gray coloration of their backs. This photo shows a magnificent specimen in the Volcanoes National Park in Rwanda.

Many and varied reasons for the decline in numbers

Although accurate population estimates for gorillas are difficult to establish due to their vast range, it is accepted that all the gorilla species are at risk. The IUCN classifies the eastern lowland gorilla (*Gorilla beringei graueri*), whose numbers are estimated at 8,000–17,000, as endangered and the three other subspecies as critically endangered: there are only about 250 Cross River gorillas (*Gorilla gorilla diehli*) and approximately 650 mountain gorillas (*Gorilla beringei beringei*). The last 90,000 surviving western lowland gorillas (*Gorilla gorilla gorilla*) are rapidly falling victim to an Ebola epidemic.

In addition to the Ebola fever, the most serious causes of threat are the large-scale destruction of the forests for the extraction of valuable tropical timbers and the exploitation of mineral resources. Further risks are posed by civil wars in the gorillas' habitat and by poaching: the meat of apes that have been shot is highly sought after and is sold at local markets.

Gorillas continue to be killed illegally by poachers. Shown here is a female displayed for sale in Cameroon.

almost 10 feet (3 meters). For comparison, the arm span of an average-sized human is about 3 feet (1 meter) less.

Eating all day long

Gorillas are strict vegetarians. They feed on more than 100 different plant species, including wild celery, various shoots, and a wide variety of herbs. Because their food is comparatively low in nutrients, the animals have to ingest enormous quantities to meet their daily requirements. Consequently, gorillas spend from 8 to 10 hours a day in search of edible vegetation. They move in family groups and maintain constant visual and voice contact with one another. The head of a family group is always a silverback, a mature male with a silver-colored back, who is accompanied by five or six mature females, some with young.

Nights in the safety of the trees

During the daytime, gorillas remain predominantly on the forest floor; before nightfall, the females climb into trees with their young, build a nest from leaves and branches, and do not descend from the safety of their sleeping places until the next morning. The males are too heavy for such climbing and brachiating exercises. They spend the night on the ground—relatively free from danger because they have no natural enemies to fear.

A family of mountain gorillas. The pronounced size difference between the silverback and his "wives" is clear.

Above: Contrary to wild adventure stories, gorillas are generally docile. However, they do use their enormous physical strength when fighting over their position in the hierarchy or if they feel threatened.

Left: Heavy rainfall is common in the gorillas' habitat, which is why the animals have thick, water-repellant fur.

Gorillas' image as monsters

For a long time, gorillas, especially the males, were considered to be murderous beasts. The fact is, however, that there is scarcely any other animal of comparable size that is as placid as a gorilla. The American zoologist George Schaller (b. 1933), who researched the animals from 1959 onward, and later the behavioral scientist Dian Fossey (b. 1932), who was murdered in 1985 (her book *Gorillas in the Mist* became a worldwide success and was filmed, with Sigourney Weaver playing the leading role), were among the first to rectify the image of the gorilla as a monster. At the same time, they laid the foundation of our current knowledge about these great apes.

CHIMPANZEES

The two closest relatives to humans are found in the chimpanzee genus (*Pan*): the common chimpanzees (*Pan troglodytes*), of which there are four subspecies, and the bonobos (*Pan paniscus*). The bonobos' other common name, pygmy chimpanzee, is misleading. Although the pygmy chimpanzee has a more delicate build, it is not substantially smaller than the common chimpanzee, from which it differs also in having longer, more slender limbs and a more placid nature.

BONOBO

It was not until 1929 that the bonobo was identified as a separate species, from a skull in a Belgian museum. The first detailed descriptions were published four years later. Male bonobos attain a head-and-body length of up to 33 inches (85 cm) and a weight of about 130 lb (60 kg). Sexual dimorphism is pronounced: the males are significantly larger and heavier than the females.

Agile in the trees

On the ground, bonobos—like most African hominids—move around by knuckle-walking, i.e. on all fours, merely supporting themselves on the back of the intermediate phalanges of the forelimbs. In the treetops, where they spend most of their time, they use all their limbs equally, for brachiating, swinging, and climbing; even there, however, they do sometimes walk on two legs.

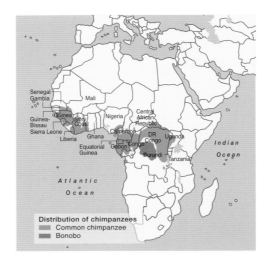

Distribution of chimpanzees
- Common chimpanzee
- Bonobo

Above: Although common chimpanzees are extremely widely distributed, bonobos live only in the tropical rainforests of the Democratic Republic of Congo.

Right: Even when feeding together, bonobos behave very placidly.

Below: Bonobo females give birth to a single young every five or six years after a gestation period of about 250 days. The young bonobo stays with its mother for four years.

Size of bonobo population difficult to estimate

The IUCN classifies the bonobo as endangered, but it is almost impossible, owing to the inaccessible nature of the habitat, to put a figure on the total population; estimates thus range between 29,500 and 50,000 animals, although it is possible that the actual figures could be higher. What is certain is that numbers have declined massively in recent years, a result of the severe deforestation of the rainforests, growing settlement pressure, and hunting.

Above: Because chimpanzee children remain with their mother for a very long time, the females give birth only once every five to six years.

Facing page: Like all primates, including apes and humans, chimpanzees have highly individual and expressive facial features.

Numbers falling

Despite the relatively high degree of flexibility shown by common chimpanzees with regard to their habitat requirements, they, too, are threatened by the destruction and fragmentation of their range. Their populations are becoming ever smaller and also being scattered into small groups that no longer have any contact with one another—this is particularly true for the West African populations.

Their situation is exacerbated by diseases such as Ebola and the civil wars in the animals' habitat. In addition, chimpanzees are highly coveted as game by indigenous people: not only is their meat very popular, but their skin, hands, feet, and heads are sold as trophies.

The latest estimate indicated a population between 173,000 and 300,000, but, as in the case of the bonobos, the number of animals is difficult to estimate. The IUCN designates the species as endangered.

Mimicry and gestures are just as important as the varied verbal utterances as a means of communication.

Without the protection of the mother, with all her life experience, the young animals, which are very curious, would not survive the first months of life.

COMMON CHIMPANZEE

As already mentioned, the common chimpanzee is not that much bigger than its supposedly "smaller brother," the pygmy chimpanzee. A male chimpanzee has a head-and-body length of 26–37 inches (65–95 cm) and a weight of up to 150 lb (70 kg) in the males; females are at least 45 lb (20 kg) lighter.

In comparison to other primates, the common chimpanzee is very flexible in terms of its habitat requirements: it inhabits both rainforests and almost treeless savannas and can also be found in mountainous country at elevations of up to 10,000 feet (3,000 meters).

Close bonds

In contrast to all other hominids except the bonobo, in the female chimpanzee, a clear swelling of the anogenital region occurs during the fertility period, signaling to the male her readiness to mate. After a pregnancy of 220–250 days, the female normally gives birth to a single young weighing $2\frac{1}{4}$–$4\frac{1}{2}$ lb (1–2 kg). It spends the first weeks of its life clinging firmly to the belly fur of its mother, and later it rides on her back and slowly begins to explore the world. Chimpanzees have a relatively long nursing period, not being weaned until they are about four years old, and they are not capable of reproducing until at least three years after that.

In the case of hand-reared animals in captivity, it has been established that a young deprived of social contact, shows of affection, and body warmth and contact, will waste away and is unlikely to survive even if it is provided with an optimum diet. If it does survive, then it is only with severe psychological damage. The close maternal bond and the feeling of security within the group are essential to the survival of a chimpanzee child.

Use of tools

Common chimpanzees are known to be the only primates other than the orangutans to use tools independently in the wild: they use rocks as hammers; sticks as projectiles, as arm extensions, as hooks, or even as spears; and chewed leaves as sponges with which they draw water from an unreachable location and then suck the "sponge" dry. Tool use is not an innate behavior: it is one of the learned behaviors passed on from animal to animal. Accordingly, the ability to use tools differs from population to population.

PRIMATES
GIBBONS

Gibbons or lesser apes (Hylobatidae), which live in tropical and montane rainforests in Southeast Asia, are humans' closest relatives after the great apes. This primate family comprises 12–15 species grouped in the 4 genera of crested gibbons (Nomascus), white-browed or hoolock gibbons (Hoolock), siamangs (Symphalangus), and lar or dwarf gibbons (Hylobates).

Long arms and loud songs

Most gibbon species are pure herbivores. With a diet consisting essentially of fruit, leaves, and buds, they have to ingest very large quantities of food; foraging for edible items occupies them for an average of 9 to 10 hours a day. As a result of remaining almost exclusively in trees and treetops, in the course of their evolutionary development, the tailless gibbons have developed exceedingly long arms relative to their body length. Furthermore, their hands are shaped so as to enable them to grip twigs and branches securely.

Gibbons are renowned for their songs, which fill the forests, particularly in the mornings and evenings. The songs serve as acoustic markers of their territories, which can be up to 120 acres (50 hectares) in size; they are also important for pair bonding. Both males and females "sing"—often in a duet.

Lifelong pair bonding

Gibbons live monogamously, usually maintaining lifelong partnerships. Families are correspondingly small, comprising just one set of parents and one to three young of various ages; young adults have to leave the family and search for their own territories and a partner.

Gibbons—here, a white-handed gibbon (*Hylobates lar*)—live exclusively in Southeast Asia and are the smallest and lightest apes. All species are endangered as a result of the destruction of their habitats.

No fixed mating period

Due to the favorable climatic conditions, gibbons reproduce throughout the year. After a gestation period of about seven months, a tiny baby gibbon is born, usually at night, weighing 14–18 ounces (400–500 g), and is intensively cared for by the mother in the first weeks of its life. Later, the father also takes over part of the care. The young can cling to their mother's fur from birth but are not weaned before the age of eighteen months, and it takes a further five to eight years before the offspring are sexually mature and are themselves able to reproduce.

Above: The endangered black or crested gibbon (*Hylobates concolor*) lives in small family groups composed of a male, a female, and their young.

Below: The siamangs (*Symphalangus syndactylus*) delimit their territories from one another acoustically through melodious songs in which the whole family takes part.

Many threatened species

The IUCN includes all the gibbon species on the Red List, listing most of them as vulnerable, endangered, or critically endangered.

The situation is very grave for the silvery (or Javan) gibbon (*Hylobates moloch*), which is endemic to a very small area of Java and whose population is estimated at 1,000 to 2,000 individuals.

However, other species are also on the brink of complete eradication, including the eastern black crested gibbon (*Nomascus nasutus*), of which only two tiny populations, totaling fewer than 100 animals, are still known to exist.

The principal threat to all gibbons is the rapid rate at which tropical forests are being felled, which led to the decline by as much as 90 percent in numbers of all species within a period of only about 50 years. Gibbons are also hunted heavily. Many ethnic groups in their habitat areas eat ape meat and use bones and other body parts for medicinal and ritual purposes. They are also frequently kept as pets, and when they are caught, in most cases, at least one older animal is shot.

MARMOSETS AND TAMARINS, AND OTHER NEW WORLD MONKEYS

Marmosets and tamarins (Callitrichidae), capuchins and squirrel monkeys (Cebidae), night monkeys (Aotidae), howler and prehensile-tailed monkeys (Atelidae), and titi monkeys, sakis, and uakaris (Pitheciidae), are the five known families from the parvorder of New World or flat-nosed monkeys (Platyrrhini), which differ from the Old World monkeys in that they usually have side-facing nostrils.

All flat-nosed monkeys dwell mainly in trees, have—with one exception—long, powerful prehensile tails, eat a vegetarian diet, and—except for the night monkeys—are diurnal. That is about all that they have in common: the species differ considerably in fur color, size, and weight.

MARMOSETS AND TAMARINS

All the species of marmosets and tamarins live in small groups in the rainforests of South and Central America, and their social behavior is determined by hierarchical rituals. They feed on sap, fruit, nectar, insects, small vertebrates, and eggs. Marmosets and tamarins have claws on all digits except for the big toe, which has a flattened nail.

Impressive markings

Many species have extraordinarily eye-catching fur or facial markings, which can sometimes look quite peculiar. For example, the cotton-top tamarin (*Saguinus oedipus*) wears a snow-white wig; the emperor tamarin (*Saguinus imperator*) has a long, curving white moustache, lending it a very dignified appearance; and many species of lion tamarin (*Leontopithecus*) have strikingly impressive, luxuriant manes.

Many threatened species

Being a highly synanthropic species, the best known of the marmosets and tamarins, the white-tufted-ear marmoset (*Callithrix jacchus*), whose ears are surrounded by an edging of stiff white hairs growing in tufts, has been able to colonize new habitats beyond the boundaries of its original range. It is thus one of the few species that are not endangered at all—in contrast to many other marmoset and tamarin species, including the Brazilian bare-faced

tamarin (*Saguinus bicolor*) and the cotton-top tamarin.

LION TAMARINS

The four species of lion tamarin live in a tiny piece of virgin coastal forest in southeastern Brazil. Such isolated island populations in a very restricted range always carry a potential risk: hunting, poaching, biotope changes, and diseases can cause a population to collapse in a very short period—and that is precisely what befell the lion tamarins in the 1970s.

Due to their very small geographical ranges, little is known about the way in which many tamarins—shown here is a Geoffroy's marmoset (*Callithrix geoffroyi*)—live.

Goeldi's marmoset (*Callimico goeldii*) is a diurnal rainforest dweller. The population in Colombia is deemed vulnerable.

Right: The golden-headed lion tamarin is found only in a small coastal region of the Brazilian federal state of Bahia.

Facing page: The emperor tamarin got its name from its alleged similarity to the German Emperor Wilhelm II.

The strange uakaris, with their striking red faces and shaggy coats, have only a stumpy tail.

The temporary rescue of the golden lion tamarin

By about 1970, only 150–200 specimens of the golden lion tamarin (*Leontopithecus rosalia*) were still in existence, and scarcely any experts believed that this tiny monkey would survive. Intensive protection efforts have made the seemingly impossible, possible: in the course of the decades that followed, zoos managed to breed just under 1,000 lion tamarins, and several hundred of these have been released back into the wild. Today, the population of animals living in the wild stands at between 1,000 and 1,500 individuals. Their range has been severely fragmented by the destruction of forests through slash-and-burn clearance, logging, and the establishment of new human settlements. At the start of the twentieth century, the size of the range amounted to just under 386,000 square miles (1 million km²), but today, just 7,700 square miles (20,000 km²) remain. Therefore, the golden lion tamarins continue to be seen as endangered.

The other three species in the same genus are faring no better: the golden-headed lion tamarin (*Leontopithecus chrysomelas*) is endangered, and the golden-rumped lion tamarin (*Leontopithecus chrysopygus*) and the black-faced lion tamarin (*Leontopithecus caissara*) are critically endangered.

HOWLER MONKEYS

The largest New World monkey species are found in the family of howler and prehensile-tailed monkeys (Atelidae). In all the members of this family, the tail has been transformed into an "extra limb," which the animals use to help them move seemingly effortlessly, and with exceptional agility, through the treetops.

The howler monkeys (*Alouatta*), from the tropical rainforests of Central and South America, are relatively large representatives of the family. They have a head-and-body length of 20–28 inches (50–70 cm), a tail measuring about the same length, and they weigh approximately 22 lb (10 kg). Every now and again they live up to their name by launching into a concert of howling that can be heard up to 3 miles (5 km) away and serves primarily as a means of communication. Some species and

With great ease and elegance, spider monkeys swing through the treetops of the primeval forests. All species are threatened.

subspecies of howler monkeys are listed as endangered on the Red List, among them the Mexican black howler monkey (*Alouatta pigra*) and the red-handed howler monkey (*Alouatta belzebul*).

SPIDER MONKEYS

The spider monkeys (*Ateles*), which live in the tropical rainforests of South and Central America, are true acrobats. They attain a head-and-body length of 22–24 inches (55–60 cm), and the tail is almost twice as long, reaching 37 inches (95 cm). They remain almost exclusively in the top canopy, swinging with ease from branch to branch and crossing even quite large clearings. Three of the seven species are listed by the IUCN as vulnerable.

WOOLLY MONKEYS

Found only in the central and upper Amazon regions, woolly monkeys (*Lagothrix*) are 20–24 inches (50–60 cm) in length and have a prehensile tail measuring approximately 28 inches (70 cm) long. Their fur color can vary, even within the same species, from deep black through gray to light ochre. Troops of woolly monkeys are headed by several males and can number up to 80 animals, which usually behave very placidly and treat each other very affectionately. One of the four species is considered vulnerable and two others critically endangered.

UAKARIS

The uakaris or short-tailed monkeys (*Cacajao*), from the family of titi monkeys, sakis, and uakaris (Pitheciidae), are the only New World monkeys with a short tail. It grows to only 6 inches (15 cm) on an animal with a head-and-body length of 20 inches (50 cm) and is the reason why uakaris cannot jump well—they lack the tool for maintaining their balance.

There are two species, which together have a total of six subspecies: the less-threatened black uakari (*Cacajao melanocephalus*), and the red uakari (*Cacajao calvus*), the four subspecies of which are listed as vulnerable on the Red List as a result of the destruction of their habitat.

The white-bellied spider monkey (*Ateles belzebuth*), which has a white or brown triangular marking on its forehead, is listed as vulnerable on the Red List.

PILOSA
ANTEATERS

The family of anteaters (Myrmecophagidae) belongs to the order of edentates (Pilosa), whose geographical distribution is restricted to Central and South America: there, during the isolation that lasted for millions of years in the Tertiary period, the animals evolved into specialized ant and termite eaters.

A strange shape

The giant anteater (*Myrmecophaga tridactyla*), which is the sole representative of its family, leads an entirely terrestrial life, whereas its smaller relatives are predominantly arboreal. This slender-looking animal grows up to 7 feet (2.1 meters) in length, up to 36 inches (90 cm) of which may be taken up by the tail, and weighs up to 80 lb (35 kg). On the toes of its forefeet, it has powerful claws with which it can rip open ant and termite mounds and, in dangerous situations, deal out powerful blows against its enemies.

The anteater's strong neck becomes increasingly narrow from the trunk forward and merges seamlessly into the head, with its long tubular snout and toothless jaws. The opening of the mouth is very small, just big enough for the thin, approximately 3-feet-long (1-meter-long) tongue, which is covered with sticky mucus and can be extended and retracted at lightning speed—up to 160 times a minute.

The completely toothless anteater feeds exclusively on ants and termites.

Uncertain status of data

The advancing cultivation of land in South America, as well as heavy hunting and—to a lesser extent—increasing road traffic in the anteater's territories, to which growing numbers of animals are falling victim, have reduced giant anteater numbers very sharply in recent decades.

In 1986 it was classified by the IUCN as vulnerable, but since 2006 has been deemed to be merely "near threatened," due to the difficulty of assessing the total population. CITES, however, continues to list it as a vulnerable species as it is still facing a high risk of eradication in the wild.

PILOSA
SLOTHS

Like the anteaters, the two genera from the suborder of sloths (Folivora) belong to the order of edentates. A differentiation is made between two-toed sloths (Megalonychidae), which are found in Central America and in the northern part of South America, and three-toed sloths (Bradypodidae), which live in the tropical rainforests reaching from southern Central America as far as Peru and the Amazon basin in southern Brazil.

True to their name

Sloths are so named because of their lifestyle: they spend up to 18 hours a day sleeping, and, for the remainder of the time, they hang with their backs facing the ground, moving hand over hand in slow motion from branch to branch, eating immense quantities of leaves as they go.

Once a week, they leave the trees so they can defecate on the ground. Because their frame is unable to bear their weight, they can neither

At least one species is threatened

Because all sloth species are rainforest dwellers, they, too, are being adversely affected by the loss of their habitat through slash-and-burn clearance and deforestation. Being hunted for their tasty meat is a further factor threatening them. It is difficult to make precise statements about sloth numbers, and no data are yet available. This lack is probably the key reason why most species are not yet listed as immediately threatened. To date, only the maned sloth (*Bradypus torquatus*), from the family of three-toed sloths, is deemed to be endangered because it has the smallest habitat of all the sloths. It occurs only in a narrow coastal strip in the rainforests of southeastern Brazil that is also densely populated and is therefore being cleared at a particularly fast rate. Organizations like the WWF, USAID, or Conservation International (CI) are working with the locals to protect the habitat of the maned sloth and many other endangered species.

stand nor walk, but have to pull themselves forward by their front legs.

Armed against rain

The fur of sloths has two layers: short, very dense underfur and, over that, long, straw-like hairs with pronounced longitudinal grooves. These—in conjunction with the fact that the hair grows from the belly to the back—cause rainwater to run off more effectively. The color of the fur is actually gray-brown, but it frequently appears greenish on account of the algae living in it.

Three-toed sloths, such as the brown-throated three-toed sloth (*Bradypus variegatus*), are well adapted to their hanging way of life.

ARTIODACTYLA
TRUE PIGS

*The babirusa (*Babyrousa babyrussa*) and the bearded pig (*Sus barbatus*) are two members of the family of true pigs (*Suidae*). This family from the order of even-toed ungulates (*Artiodactyla*) also includes the wild boar (*Sus scrofa*), from which the domestic pig developed.*

BABIRUSA

The deer-hog or babirusa is threatened principally because of its limited habitat on the Indonesian island of Sulawesi, where it inhabits dense swamp forests, mangrove swamps, and the lower areas of forested mountain slopes. It feeds on fruit, nuts, and palm pith.

Babirusas grow to a maximum of 3³/₄ feet (1.1 meters) in length and 32 inches (80 cm) in height. They weigh about 220 lb (100 kg). They are sometimes given the name *deer-hog* because of their strange upper canines: these grow almost vertically upward, passing through the top of the snout, and then curve backward resembling antlers.

As a result of slash-and-burn clearance and deforestation, the habitats of the babirusa have been so severely blighted in the last few decades that the survival of the species is not assured. The IUCN puts the total population of all subspecies at 4,000 individuals and classifies the species as vulnerable.

BEARDED PIG

The bearded pig, with a head-and-body length of about 5 feet (1.5 meters) and a shoulder height of about 30 inches (75 cm), weighs up to 330 lb (150 kg), thus making it the largest and heaviest pig from Southeast Asia. Depending on the food available, bearded pigs undertake lengthy migrations, on which 100 or more animals often band together.

Little is known about populations, but they are certain to be declining due to biotope destruction in their limited habitats. The Palawan bearded pig is classified as vulnerable on the Red List.

Above: With a weight of up to 330 lb (150 kg), the bearded pig is the largest species of wild pig in Southeast Asia. Where they are not hunted, the animals are active during the day and exhibit no timidity.

Below: The babirusa is a very primitive animal that has been able to survive only in the remote regions of secluded islands. Today, it is found only on Sulawesi and adjacent islands.

ARTIODACTYLA
CAMELS

The camel family (Camelidae) belongs to the even-toed ungulates (Artiodactyla) and is subdivided into Old World camels (Camelus) and New World camels, the latter comprising the genera of llamas (Lama) and vicuñas (Vicugna). All the species can live in areas with very low humidity and can drink salt water if necessary. They have unique feet that have given the suborder the name Tylopoda (padded feet): below the distinctive third and fourth toes are cushion-like soles made of thick but elastic connective tissue on which the body weight is supported when the animal is walking; however, the tips of its toes do not touch the ground, unlike those of other even-toed ungulates.

VICUÑA

The delicate vicuña (*Vicugna vicugna*) lives in the high mountains of the South American Andes at altitudes between 11,500 and 16,500 feet (3,500 and 5,000 meters). To cope with the conditions in this extreme habitat, the heart of a vicuña is about 50 percent larger than that of a comparable lowland animal. They need water each day, and in the dry altiplano, they utilize condensation from nighttime fog to meet this need.

Europeans decimate populations

Although vicuñas were valued by the original inhabitants for their fine wool and as a source

The South American guanaco is one of the two wild forms of the llama. Domesticated llamas and alpacas are descended from it.

of meat, populations did not come under pressure until the arrival of Europeans in South America. In the 1960s, the animals were on the brink of extinction. However, the protection programs that were implemented as a matter of urgency have been highly successful, so that today there are again about 100,000 animals living in the wild. Their continued survival is dependent on conservation measures.

GUANACO

Guanacos (*Lama guanicoe*), like vicuñas, are found in the vast mountainous areas of the High Andes, at altitudes up to 13,000 feet (4,000 meters), and they also occur in Patagonia and on the islands off the southern tip of South America, which they reach by swimming. Neither heat nor cold seem to bother them much. With a head-and-body length between 5 and 6½ feet (1.5 and 2 meters), a shoulder height of 4¼ feet (1.3 meters), and a weight of up to 265 lb (120 kg), the guanaco is considerably larger and heavier than the vicuña.

Eradicated from many areas

The guanaco has also undergone a substantial decline in numbers. It is thought that the guanacos living in the wild today, numbering approximately 500,000, make up just one percent of the population that existed before the arrival of Europeans in South America. The species has been eradicated from some regions of its former range, and many populations are threatened. Of the four subspecies, the IUCN lists two as vulnerable and two as endangered.

Left: Guanacos are optimally adapted to the harsh living conditions of the South American highlands and can get by on a meager diet.

Below: the New World camels, the guanacos and vicuñas, live in the high mountain regions of the South American Andes, whereas the

Old World camels—dromedaries and Bactrian camels—inhabit North Africa, Arabia, and the central Asian deserts.

The delicate vicuña, which has never been domesticated, lives in the Andes at extreme altitudes of up to 16,500 feet (5,000 meters).

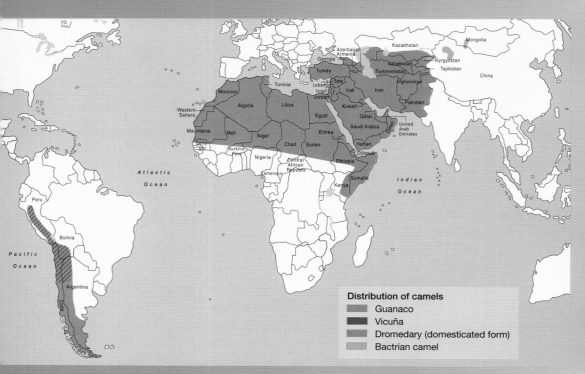

Distribution of camels
- Guanaco
- Vicuña
- Dromedary (domesticated form)
- Bactrian camel

OLD WORLD CAMELS

The genus of Old World camels comprises two species: the dromedary (*Camelus dromedarius*) and the Bactrian or two-humped camel (*Camelus bactrianus* or *Camelus ferus*), which, compared with the New World camels, are relatively large and bulky. In addition, they differ from their smaller relatives in that they have one or two humps.

Adaptation to extreme conditions

The Old World camels are renowned for their modest requirements and their outstanding adaptation to extreme conditions in deserts and semideserts. They can survive in places where no other large mammals can, not least on account of their ability to go for many days without water and food. They are capable of storing up to 40 gallons (150 liters) of water in

Above: The dromedary is considered to be the domesticated form of the Bacterian camel and no wild form is better known. Domesticated camels that have become feral do, however, manage to survive in the wild in many deserts.

their digestive systems and of laying down fat reserves in their humps, which sustains them during particularly hot and dry periods.

Scarcely any animals living in the wild

No wild form of the one-humped dromedary is known, only the form domesticated as a pack animal and riding animal, without which the Sahara would have remained uninhabited for millennia. Approximately 750 Bactrian camels are still to be found living in the wild in central Asia, in particular, in Mongolia. Hunting and habitat loss are the main factors responsible for their constantly declining numbers.

Below: Only about 750 Bactrian camels still exist in the wild, and this species is considered critically endangered.

HIPPOPOTAMUSES

The hippopotamus family (Hippopotamidae) consists of two genera, each comprising a single species: the common hippopotamus (Hippopotamus amphibius), also called the Nile hippopotamus, and the pygmy hippopotamus (Choeropsis liberiensis or Hexaprotodon liberiensis). They belong to the even-toed ungulates, but recent genetic studies have provided evidence that they are more closely related to whales.

COMMON HIPPOPOTAMUS

With a body weight of over 6,600 lb (3,000 kg), the common hippopotamus is one of the heaviest land mammals. Its weight is distributed over a body measuring up to 15 feet (4.5 meters) in length and up to 5½ feet (1.65 meters) in height, and this stout, cylindrical body sits on short pillar-shaped legs. Despite appearances, hippos are not fat. On the contrary, the proportion of muscle is very high, and their meat is considered a delicacy in many regions of Africa. The skin of the hippopotamus is gray

On the way to their feeding grounds, hippos often cover considerable distances at a remarkably high speed.

to pink in color, furnished with mucous glands, and largely hairless, with only the snout region, the edges of the ears, and the tail bearing a few brush-like hairs. Both the nostrils and the ears can be closed and, like the eyes, are positioned such that the animals can breathe, hear, and see when only the top part of the head is projecting out of the water.

Life on and in the water

Nile hippos inhabit river banks, lakes, ponds, and river estuaries on African coasts. They spend most of the daytime in the water in "schools," groups of up to 30 animals that, however, consist only of females and their young; the bulls remain apart. Although the water is their element, hippos are not particularly good swimmers. However, thanks to their specific gravity, they can walk along the bottom under water for up to 10 minutes.

Nocturnal wanderings

Only after the onset of dusk do the animals become really active, and they wander to their pastures, which are often miles away. Each animal consumes up to 110 lb (50 kg) of grass to meet its daily requirements.

As an adaptation to their aquatic lifestyle, hippopotamuses have closable nostrils.

PYGMY HIPPOPOTAMUS

The pygmy hippopotamus lives in West Africa in relatively inaccessible areas and was therefore not discovered by Westerners until the middle of the nineteenth century. Measuring about 5½ feet (1.65 meters) in length and 32 inches (80 cm) in height, and weighing 400–575 lb (180–260 kg), it is not only significantly smaller and lighter than the common hippopotamus, but it is also far more compact and agile. In contrast to the larger common hippopotamus, it is very much a solitary animal.

Above: Adult hippopotamuses have scarcely any enemies. The calves, however, are popular prey, and the mother therefore keeps a sharp eye on her young.

Below: The current range of the hippopotamus is alarmingly small, measured against its range at the beginning of the twentieth century.

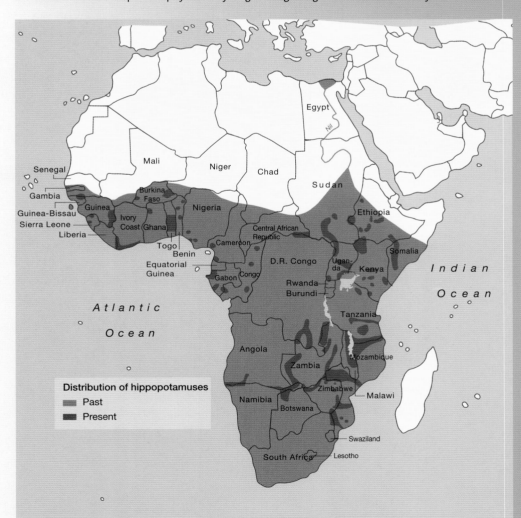

Distribution of hippopotamuses
- Past
- Present

Poor future prospects

The hippopotamus population is estimated by the IUCN to number between 125,000 and 148,000 individuals and is classified as vulnerable. The reasons for the steady population decline are many and varied: as is so often the case, habitat loss is the principal cause, and the civil wars in their range have also had a negative effect. In addition, the hippopotamus is hunted intensively by humans, its only enemy; its tasty flesh, its ivory teeth, and its skin, from which whips are manufactured, are all highly sought after.

The situation is even worse for the pygmy hippopotamus: its population is estimated at between 2,000 and 3,000 individuals, and they are considered endangered. The reasons for the declining numbers are almost the same as in the case of the common hippo, but these smaller animals are hunted not just by humans but also by leopards.

Members of the El-Molo tribe, who live on Lake Turkana (Kenya), cutting up a hippopotamus they have killed.

ARTIODACTYLA
GIRAFFES AND OKAPIS

The family of giraffes and okapis (Giraffidae) comprises two genera, each containing a single species: the giraffe (Giraffa camelopardalis) and the okapi (Okapia johnstoni). Both occur on the African continent and, even though they do not look all that similar, have a number of features in common, such as a blue-black tongue and skin-covered horns.

GIRAFFES

The giraffe is the world's tallest land mammal: the crown of the head of a mature bull can reach a height of almost 20 feet (6 meters), and the animal can weigh up to 4,400 lb (2,000 kg). Females are somewhat smaller and lighter. Even at birth, a giraffe calf already measures an impressive 5½–6 feet (1.7–1.8 meters) in height

and weighs about 150 lb (70 kg). Unlike most other mammals, the mother giraffe does not give birth lying down, but does so standing up, so that its enormous young drops to the ground from a height of about 6 feet (2 meters).

Nine subspecies with differing coat patterns

There are about nine giraffe subspecies that differ from one another in appearance, some considerably, particularly where the pattern of their coat is concerned. The Somali giraffe or reticulated giraffe (*Giraffa camelopardalis reticulata*), which occurs in northern Kenya and western Somalia, is generally deemed to be the most attractive, whereas the rarest is the Rothschild's or Ugandan giraffe (*Giraffa*

The net-like coat pattern of reticulated giraffes differs significantly from the patterns of the other subspecies.

This young Masai giraffe and the hindquarters of its mother display the beautiful, almost star-shaped coat pattern.

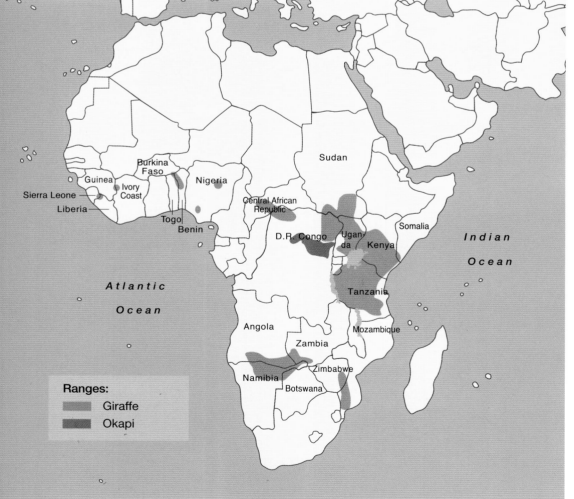

Ranges:
▬ Giraffe
▬ Okapi

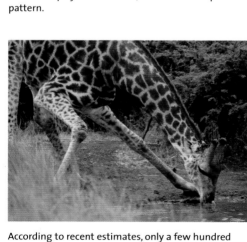

According to recent estimates, only a few hundred specimens of Rothschild's giraffe are still to be found, in isolated areas of Kenya and Uganda.

The various subspecies of giraffe occur in insular populations in Africa south of the Sahara, whereas the okapi lives in a small area in the Democratic Republic of Congo.

On the brink of eradication

The destruction of natural habitats and—to a lesser degree—poaching have brought many populations to the brink of eradication. The North African subspecies and the Angolan giraffe (*Giraffa camelopardalis angolensis*) have already been eradicated, and further species such as the Ugandan giraffe mentioned previously, the Nubian giraffe (*Giraffa camelopardalis camelopardalis*), and the Kordofan giraffe (*Giraffa camelopardalis antiquorum*) are severely threatened and could soon follow them.

Bushmen with the hide of a giraffe that they have killed in the Kalahari.

camelopardalis rothschildi), and the best known is the Masai giraffe (*Giraffa camelopardalis tippelskirchi*).

Adaptation

Giraffes live chiefly in the tree and bush savannas of tropical and subtropical Africa. In the open savanna landscape, giraffes are hard to miss on account of their size, but as soon as they stand in the shade of a few umbrella acacias, they can disappear completely from view.

The long neck of the giraffe, like that of all other mammals, has seven cervical vertebrae and is very probably an evolutionary adaptation to food sources: giraffes feed almost exclusively on the leaves and shoots of various—often very tall—trees. With the aid of their 20-inch-long (50-cm-long), highly flexible tongue, they pluck the leaves from between the very sharpest of thorns; later, in the heat of the day,

With the grace of dancers, male Masai giraffes perform ritualized fights to determine their dominance within a hierarchy. Occasionally, this results in fatalities caused by broken necks.

they ruminate the food they have ingested in a shaded area of open woodland or in the shade of a single acacia.

OKAPI

Measuring 5¼ feet (1.6 meters) at the shoulder and weighing 440–550 lb (200–250 kg), the okapi, also called the short-necked or forest giraffe, is significantly smaller and lighter than the giraffe. It lives a largely solitary life in a fixed territory, feeds predominantly on leaves, and is extremely shy—at the first sign of danger, it disappears into the leafy undergrowth.

Secluded life

The okapi, of whose existence the Western world did not learn until 1901—its discovery was a scientific sensation at the time—has a natural range that is very small. Consequently, it is far more vulnerable to any potential threat than are species with large areas of distribution.

The fact that this animal, scarcely ever encountered in the wild, was discovered so recently is linked to its habitat: it lives in the Congo basin, in the dense virgin forest of the Democratic Republic of Congo, and even today, scientists are not certain how large its range is or how many of these animals exist.

Numbers unknown

The IUCN classifies the okapi as being only "near threatened," an assessment that is probably based on insufficient data. Practically nothing is known about the numbers of this shy animal, and all the figures in circulation should be treated with great caution. What is certain, however, is that the okapi's habitat, which, to make matters worse, also lies in a region rocked by civil wars, is diminishing daily as a result of slash-and-burn clearances and of logging operations by international corporations, which are taking tropical timber out of the country without regard for the environmental consequences.

Above: Although it bears striped markings reminiscent of zebras, the okapi is related to giraffes.

The numbers of okapi in the wild can only be guessed.

The okapi strips leaves from trees with its flexible blue tongue.

ARTIODACTYLA
DEER

All the members of the deer family (Cervidae) and its various subfamilies, all of which belong to the group of horned ruminants (Pecora), share one striking feature: the horns adorning the heads of the male animals. However, that is where the similarities, or at least the purely superficial ones, end.

Highly diverse species

In Europe, Asia, and the Americas, as well as in northwestern Africa, deer live in all habitats, even in the desert and the Arctic tundra. They have also been introduced into other regions, such as Australia and New Zealand.

The various species differ considerably in size, among other things: the smallest species, the southern pudu (*Pudu puda*) from the southwestern tip of South America, is no more than 14 inches (35 cm) tall, whereas the European elk (*Alces alces*), the largest representative of the deer family, can reach up to 7 1/2 feet (2.3 meters) in height at the withers. As a rule, the species in the north are larger than those in the south, and the females are smaller and lighter than the males—there is pronounced sexual dimorphism.

THOROLD'S DEER

Thorold's or white-lipped deer (*Cervus albirostris*), from the high mountains in the border area between Tibet and China, prefer particularly extreme habitats: they live at altitudes between 11,500 and 16,500 feet

Above: The Persian fallow deer is considered to be the world's rarest deer. Most of the animals still alive today are to be found in zoological gardens.

(3,500 and 5,000 meters) and feed on herbs, grasses, lichens, and mosses.

Like most deer, they are sociable and form herds ranging in size from fairly small to fairly large, with only the old males remaining solitary. Thorold's deer is hunted intensively, not just for its meat but also for its antlers, which are used in Chinese medicine. It is listed by the IUCN as vulnerable.

SIKA DEER

Sika deer (*Cervus nippon*) were once numerous in the forests and montane forests of Asia; today, one subspecies, Dybowski's sika deer (*Cervus nippon dybowskii*) has been eradicated in the wild, and various other subspecies appear on the Red List as endangered or critically endangered. Folk medicine is a key

Many subspecies of sika deer are listed as threatened in the wild.

Thorold's deer, found in Asia, are skillful climbers, living in separate male and female herds outside the mating season.

factor behind the intensive hunting of sika deer: the antlers, enriched with sex hormones, are highly sought after as an aphrodisiac.

PERSIAN FALLOW DEER

In the troubled border region between Iran and Iraq lives the Persian fallow deer (*Dama dama mesopotamica*), which was at one time considered to have been eradicated. It was not rediscovered until the 1950s. The IUCN now estimates that its population numbers some 350 animals and classifies it as vulnerable, not least because its range lies within a politically troubled area.

BARASINGHA

The habitats of the barasingha (*Cervus duvaucelii*), which was previously common in India, have been decreasing, so that only a few small populations are still to be found in protected areas, and the species is classified as vulnerable. A subspecies, Schomburgk's deer (*Cervus schomburgki*), is thought to have been eradicated in the 1930s, and the same fate threatens the closely related Eld's deer (*Cervus eldii*): its population is estimated at 2,000–3,000 individuals, and it is questionable whether the species will survive.

PÈRE DAVID'S DEER

Père David's deer, or milu deer (*Elaphurus davidianus*), are listed by the IUCN as critically endangered. Nonetheless, they represent an

Above: There are numerous subspecies of the sika deer in its Asian native habitat, and some of these have been crossbred in Western zoos.

Below left: The barasingha, which, with its widely splayable hooves, is outstandingly well adapted to boggy ground, lives in swampy regions of Assam.

Below right: Only through selective breeding measures has it been possible to save Père David's deer (*Elaphurus davidianus*).

example of a successful rescue of an animal species that had already been eradicated in the wild.

This deer, with its slender elongated head, large eyes, antlers (whose tips extend backward), long tail, and widely splayable hooves, was for a long time unknown to the Western world. It was not until 1865 that the French Jesuit Father Armand David, to whom the deer species owes its name, became the first European to see the animal, in the hunting park of the Chinese emperor in Peking; at this time, the species had probably already been eradicated in the wild.

Breeding in Europe

In subsequent years, a few specimens from the emperor's herd were given as gifts to France, the United Kingdom, and Germany, and, not long afterward, most of the animals remaining in Peking were killed in a disastrous flood. The few surviving deer that had fled into the wild were probably killed and eaten during the Boxer Rebellion in 1900. Once it became known that Père David's deer had become extinct in its native country, all the animals kept in Europe were transferred to the Duke of Bedford in England. On his extensive estates, he established a breeding center with 18 Père David's deer, and just a few years later, the center was able to pass on offspring that had been bred there to zoos in Europe and America, with the result that several breeding herds were established. Today, over 1,000 Père David's deer are in existence worldwide, and efforts are being made to reestablish the species in its natural habitat, the swampy areas of eastern Asia.

When the first European discovered Père David's deer in an imperial park, the species had probably already been eradicated in the wild for centuries.

ARTIODACTYLA
PRONGHORN ANTELOPE

Pronghorn, also called pronghorn antelope (Antilocapra americana), are not related to antelope, despite the similarities between them, but are the sole species in the pronghorn antelope family (Antilocapridae).

Fast endurance runners

Pronghorn are somewhat larger than roe deer, stand up to 3 feet (1 meter) high at the shoulder and weigh approximately 150 lb (70 kg). Females are smaller and lighter than males, and they have horns that are just finger-long, or they have none at all.

These animals are very fast runners, reaching between 43 and 50 mph (70 and 80 km/h) in spurts, and can clear up to 20 feet (6 meters) in a single leap. To find water or food, they occasionally travel distances of up to 90 miles (150 km).

Settlers responsible for collapse in populations

Up to the end of the nineteenth century, pronghorns lived in large numbers in the North American prairie and in the semideserts and deserts of the United States. The native American inhabitants never posed a serious threat to their enormous numbers, any more than did the pronghorn's natural enemies: golden eagles, wolves, and coyotes. However, as North America was being settled by Europeans, the situation changed: not only were the animals decimated by introduced infectious diseases such as anthrax, but the settlers also shot them down in great numbers simply for pleasure.

It was not until 1920, when there were about 20,000 pronghorns still in existence, that serious protection regulations were enacted. Today, over a million animals live in the United States and Canada although there has been some recent decline, possibly due to overgrazing by sheep. The Mexican subspecies, however, never recovered: the Sonoran pronghorn (*Antilocapra americana sonoriensis*) and the peninsular pronghorn (*Antilocapra americana pensinsularis*) are considered endangered and critically endangered, respectively.

A small group of pronghorn antelopes in Yellowstone National Park in Wyoming.

The pronghorn antelope is not related to the antelopes of Africa and Asia.

ARTIODACTYLA
ANTELOPES, CATTLE, GAZELLES, GOATS, SHEEP, AND RELATIVES

The family of bovids (Bovidae) comprises approximately 135 species, ranging from the 6¹/₂-feet-tall (2-meter-tall) buffalo, through sheep and goats, down to small antelopes measuring just 10 inches (25 cm) tall. These diverse animals are found on all the continents except Antarctica, although they were introduced to Australia and Oceania. The greatest diversity of species is found in Africa.

CATTLE

The tribe of cattle (*Bovini*) includes the water buffaloes (*Bubalus*), the oxen and true cattle (*Bos*), and the bisons (*Bison*), which are subdivided into the American bison (*Bison bison*) and the European bison or wisent (*Bison bonasus*).

AMERICAN BISON

The American bison or American buffalo, often simply called buffalo, stands up to 6¹/₂ feet (2 meters) in height and weighs just under 2,200 lb (1,000 kg). There are two subspecies, the plains bison (*Bison bison bison*), which feeds predominantly on grasses and herbs, and the wood bison (*Bison bison athabascae*), which eats leaves, branches, tree bark, and lichens. Like all cattle, both are ruminants.

American buffaloes are protected against cold temperatures, often as low as −22°F (−30°C), by a thick, long-haired coat with a dense undercoat that provides such good thermal insulation that snow will lie on the coat without melting.

Settlers annihilate populations

In the eighteenth and nineteenth centuries, there were 50 million to 60 million buffaloes living on the North American continent, but increasing settlement of their habitats—the prairies east of the Rocky Mountains—led to both their habitats and their populations

Bison used to trek in their millions through the prairies of North America until European settlers caused populations to collapse on a massive scale.

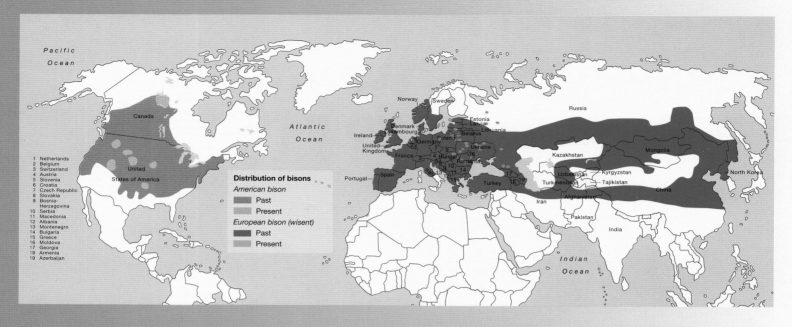

Distribution of bisons

American bison

Past

Present

European bison (wisent)

Past

Present

Above: The ranges of the American bison and of the European bison have shrunk enormously compared with earlier times. The European bison, in particular, has been eradicated from many parts of its original habitat.

Below: It has recently been possible for European bison bred in captivity to be reintroduced into the wild in some areas of their habitat—shown here is a cow with calf in Masuria, Poland.

shrinking. The animals were hunted partly for their meat and partly for their hide, which was in demand for the manufacture of leather. However, millions were also shot down purely for pleasure, so the American buffalo came close to being eradicated.

Only the establishment of a sanctuary in Yellowstone National Park secured the animals' survival. Today, there are once more about 400,000 bison in the United States and Canada, in reserves and on large farms,

which is why the IUCN, although no longer classifying the species as facing immediate threat, nonetheless considers them still to be dependent on conservation measures. The wood bison also appears on the CITES list.

AUROCHS

The aurochs or urus (*Bos primigenius*)—powerful animals measuring about 6½ feet (2 meters) in height and weighing about 2,200 lb (1,000 kg), rivaling the size of the American

bison—were found in Europe up to the early seventeenth century. The last specimen of this wild cattle species was killed in Poland in 1627, eradicating the species.

In the 1930s, two zoo directors, Heinz Heck in Munich and Lutz Heck in Berlin, began an attempt to breed the aurochs back, using approximately 40 primitive breeds of cattle. Animals were produced that, although similar in appearance and, in part, also in behavior to the wild aurochs, are not real aurochs.

WISENT

The wisent, which is closely related to the North American bison, used to roam in herds of between 10 and 30 animals through the forests in large parts of Europe. It became a threatened species early on: intensive hunting, together with the felling of forests and the increase in domestic cattle, resulted in populations beginning to dwindle as long ago as the late Middle Ages, so that by the nineteenth century, populations had reached a critical point.

Rescued at the last minute

Of the original three subspecies, lowland bison (*Bison bonasus bonasus*), Carpathian bison (*Bison bonasus hungarorum*), and Caucasian bison (*Bison bonasus caucasicus*), it proved possible to rescue only the lowland bison—

and that, at the last minute. In 1923, when there were no longer any animals living in the wild, the International Society for the Protection of the European Bison was founded, and it is thanks to this organization that these mighty wild cattle survived. Of the last 56 European bison in several European zoos, the most suitable were assigned to the breeding program, which ran so successfully that, in 1952, it was possible to release the first of the captive-bred animals back into the wild. Their new home was the forests of Bialowieza, which are located in Poland and Belarus, and in which an estimated 800 individuals of this species now live. European bison have also been introduced in the Caucasus and in the Baltic states. In addition, there are groups of breeding animals in several animal parks and zoos. The total population of European bison today stands at about 3,000 individuals, and they are still considered to be endangered.

ASIATIC CATTLE

In Asia there are large numbers of cattle that, in the course of the last 10,000 years, have been domesticated to a greater or lesser extent, but their wild forms are, almost without exception, threatened. The main reasons are the destruction of natural habitats and the overgrazing of biotopes by domestic cattle,

European bison bulls that have been returned to the wild, fighting in deep snow.

The mighty gaur from South and Southeast Asia is the largest cattle species.

goats, and sheep; infection with epizootic diseases; and direct persecution by hunters and poachers. Added to these factors is the frequent crossbreeding of wild cattle with their domesticated counterparts, which threatens the continued existence of the wild animals in their pure-blooded form.

Above: The banteng, a smaller and lighter Asiatic cow, is endangered, although domesticated forms of it are common across large parts of Southeast Asia.

Below: The cold-tolerant wild yak (*Bos grunniens*) lives at altitudes of up to 20,000 feet (6,000 meters) in the Himalaya mountains. Increasingly few pure-blooded specimens of this species exist, which is why it is considered vulnerable.

Threatened wild forms

The gaur (*Bos frontalis*), which, in its domesticated form, is called the gayal, is frequently kept in a semidomesticated state as a farm animal. Its wild form has been so severely depleted in numbers by cattle diseases and the felling of open deciduous forest that it is considered vulnerable. Today, 90 percent of gaurs live in India, where numbers are stable. In other Southeast Asian countries, by contrast, only small populations of a few hundred animals remain, and their survival is not assured.

The situation facing the stockily built, mainly reddish-colored bantengs (*Bos javanicus*) from Southeast Asia, known in their domesticated form as Bali cattle, is even worse. They are considered to be endangered: Thailand alone has lost over 85 percent of its banteng population within the last 20 years due to the destruction of rainforests, and it has vanished completely in Malaysia. On Borneo, it still occurs relatively frequently, but the pure breed is threatened by interbreeding with domestic cattle.

The rarest wild cattle

Among the rarest wild cattle in the world are the lowland anoa and mountain anoa (*Bubalus depressicornis* and *Bubalus quarlesi*), which live on the island of Sulawesi. Both species, which stand at only 28–32 inches (70–80 cm) at the shoulder and weigh 330–440 lb (150–200 kg), are listed as endangered on the Red List. Their

total population probably does not exceed 3,000 individuals, and there is still a downward trend in numbers.

The situation facing the water buffalo (*Bubalus bubalis*) is equally dire. Interbreeding with domesticated cattle makes it difficult to assess the size of the population of the purebred form, and estimates of the number of animals living in the wild range from a minimum of 200 up to a maximum of 4,000. It is also listed as endangered.

TRAGELAPHUS

The genus *Tragelaphus*, the spiral-horned bovines, includes some of the most impressive African antelope species, all occurring exclusively south of the Sahara. Most of them are large and imposing. The eland (*Tragelaphus oryx*), the largest and heaviest of them all, can reach a weight of 2,000 lb (900 kg) and a shoulder height of 5¼–6 feet (1.6–1.8 meters), and, even though it appears somewhat heavy-

Above: Nyala and mountain nyala differ not only in appearance but also in terms of their habitats. The endangered mountain nyala is now found almost exclusively in Bale Mountain National Park in Ethiopia.

Below: The greater kudu is suffering increasingly from habitat destruction and intensive hunting. The same is true of the lesser kudu (*Tragelaphus imberbis*), which has a comparatively restricted geographical range.

In the wild, the bongo (*Tragelaphus eurycerus*) lives in insular populations in the rainforest regions of western and central Africa as well as on the slopes of Mount Kenya and in the Aberdares.

Heavy hunting of all antelope species

No antelope was or is safe from hunting—neither the tiny dik-diks (*Madoqua*), which weigh just 6½–9 lb (3–4 kg), nor the eland, which weigh almost a ton. Hunters chase them with cattle dogs, wire slings, traps, spears, bows and arrows, and, of course, with guns. The local people, often chronically undersupplied with protein, are only too grateful to receive the—usually illegally killed—antelope, which is why the trade in bushmeat is booming throughout sub-Saharan Africa.

Because the destruction of habitats entails an additional potential threat and is taking place on an ever-increasing scale, populations of almost all Tragelaphus species and their subspecies are, to a greater or lesser extent, severely threatened, the situation being particularly bad for the eastern bongo (*Tragelaphus eurycerus isaaci*) and the mountain nyala (*Tragelaphus buxtoni*), which are both listed as endangered on the Red List of the IUCN.

In many regions of Africa, antelopes are still seen as sought-after additions to the menu and—as here in South Africa—are hunted heavily.

footed, it can jump 6 feet (2 meters) from a standing start with ease. Other *Tragelaphus* species also have considerable jumping ability: the bushbuck (*Tragelaphus scriptus*), for example, which measures only 28–36 inches (70–90 cm) at the shoulder, can clear obstacles up to 6 feet (2 meters) high.

Differing lifestyles

The habitats of the animals in this genus are quite varied: some species live relatively concealed lives in forests, whereas others are content with gently hilly areas in which they can find adequate cover. In open savanna, only the eland and greater kudu (*Tragelaphus strepsiceros*) are seen regularly; the sitatunga or marshbuck (*Tragelaphus spekei*) confines itself to wetland areas.

The various species also exhibit a variety of social behaviors. The bushbuck, for example, is a solitary animal, whereas the greater kudu lives in small family groups; nyalas (*Tragelaphus angasii*) gather in herds of 10–20 animals, and eland in herds of more than 50.

Ruminating can save lives

All *Tragelaphus* species are ruminants, which is presumably an adaptation to the high levels of predation pressure: the animals initially swallow the food virtually unchewed. They

Facing page: The black wildebeest occurs only in a few grass and thornbush savannas in southern Africa.

Below: The largest antelopes are the mighty eland, which, despite declining numbers, are still subject to uncontrolled shooting.

then withdraw to a safe location, from which the surroundings can readily be observed, regurgitate the food from their multi-compartment stomachs, and break it down through thorough chewing into a fluid pulp. Big cats, hyenas, and other potential enemies cannot easily approach unobserved to kill the ruminants; they have to wait until the animals are grazing or drinking at waterholes, where they do not have such a good view of their surroundings.

WILDEBEEST AND BONTEBOKS

The bovid subfamily of cow antelopes (Alcelaphinae) contains some very striking and varied antelopes, including two species from the wildebeest genus (*Connochaetes*) as well as the bontebok (*Damaliscus pygargus*) from the genus *Damaliscus*. Like all cow antelopes, they occur only in Africa and are relatively large. They possess, not least on account of their horns, a certain resemblance to cattle,

Grounds for hope

With the arrival of Europeans in Africa, wildebeest herds grew steadily smaller. Although Africa's indigenous inhabitants had hunted the animals from time immemorial, they did so only to meet their need for meat and to make use of the skins and not, like the new settlers, on a grand scale. The loss of habitats also decimated stocks.

The blue wildebeest continues to record heavy losses in some parts of Africa, but because the number of animals in other areas now totals over 1.5 million as a result of highly effective protection programs, populations are currently considered to be not immediately threatened.

The black wildebeest, which is more endangered, was extinct in southern Africa at the start of the twentieth century. However, with the aid of animals bred in zoos, it has been possible to reintroduce it into its original range throughout most of Lesotho, Swaziland, South Africa, Namibia, and Kenya. Numbers have now grown to about 10,000 individuals, and there are grounds for hope that both species can be preserved in the wild.

although they are not closely related to them.

WILDEBEEST

The wildebeest genus comprises two species: the black wildebeest (*Connochaetes gnou*) and the blue wildebeest (*Connochaetes taurinus*).

These medium-sized animals have a shoulder height of 4–4¹/₂ feet (1.2–1.4 meters), weigh about 440 lb (200 kg), and have a short, smooth coat and a shaggy mane. Their large, heavy heads, sitting on squat necks, their ridged napes, and their strangely curved horns give these harmless vegetarians a rather

threatening appearance. They live in different regions: whereas the range of the black wildebeest is restricted to southern Africa, the blue wildebeest is found in the vast grasslands of East and southern Africa as far as Namibia.

The migrations of the blue wildebeest

Blue wildebeest, in particular, are famous for their annual migrations from the Serengeti in Tanzania to the Masai Mara game reserve in Kenya. The migrations are timed to coincide with the rainy season and associated plant growth. At times, thousands of animals gather at the Mara river to cross it, and many of these fall victim to the crocodiles lurking in the water and to the big cats waiting on the other bank. However, far more ominous for the wildebeest is the fact that, at the end of their migration, they reach a densely populated region in which they are heavily persecuted by humans.

BONTEBOKS AND BLESBOKS

Like the wildebeest, the bontebok, of which there were once two subspecies occurring

Above: As a result of breeding in zoos and animal parks, it has been possible to reintroduce blesboks into parts of their original range.

Below: About 1.5 million blue wildebeest take part each year in the migration, which is up to 1,250 miles (2,000 km) long, from Tanzania to Kenya.

exclusively in South Africa, was also almost completely eradicated by European settlers. At one point, only 17 specimens of the true bontebok (*Damaliscus pygargus pygargus*) remained, but thanks to intensive breeding efforts, it has been possible to increase their numbers back up to almost 1,000. Nevertheless, the species is still deemed vulnerable. The situation is somewhat better in terms of numbers of blesbok (*Damaliscus pygargus phillipsi*), of which there are about 250,000 living in the wild. Although it is on the Red List, it is not considered to face immediate threat, but merely to be near threatened.

GEMSBOK AND OTHER HORSE ANTELOPES

The bovid subfamily of horse antelopes (Hippotraginae) contains the three genera *Addax*, *Hippotragus* (true hippotragus antelopes), and *Oryx* (oryxes), together comprising eight species. All the animals range in size from that of a deer to that of a horse, and both sexes carry striking horns. However, in some species, the horns are long and spear-like, in others, twisted spirally lengthwise, and in yet others, curved backward in the shape of a saber. The weapons on their foreheads frequently enable the horse antelopes to defend themselves successfully against attacks by wild dogs or lions.

The majestic addax occurs in the wild only in very small numbers on the southern edge of the Sahara.

ROAN AND SABLE ANTELOPES

The true horse antelopes, which live in sparse scrub and need regular water, include the roan antelope (*Hippotragus equinus*) and the sable antelope (*Hippotragus niger*). In the case of the latter, it is only the males that live up to their name, because only they are black, whereas the females have a chestnut-brown coat. Currently, only the giant sable antelope (*Hippotragus niger variani*) is classified on the Red List as immediately threatened (critically endangered). There was a third species of horse antelope, but this has already become

The scimitar-horned oryx, closely related to the oryx, has also been unable to survive in the wild. Captive-bred animals are now being released in suitable biotopes.

Many species in peril

In the case of horse antelopes, after the loss of habitats, uncontrolled hunting is the prime cause of the threat to many species. Not only are they shot for their meat and for their skin, but they also fall victim in large numbers to trophy collectors because of their magnificent horns which can measure up to 5 feet (1.5 meters). As long as hunting was seen as a luxury for the privileged few, and animals were killed only as sources of meat, the antelopes were never under serious threat. However, once these fast endurance runners could be pursued using cars, motorcycles, and planes, they lost any chance of escaping within their habitat, which offers scarcely any opportunities for cover, and their numbers were drastically reduced within a short time.

extinct: the last southern African blue buck (*Hippotragus leucophaeus*) fell victim to a bullet in about 1800.

ADDAX

The addax (*Addax nasomaculatus*) is better adapted to living in the desert than any other antelope. It tolerates the extreme temperatures by excavating a hollow when the weather is very hot; this cools the animal from below. It is thought that the animals can scent increased air humidity and plant growth from a great distance. Not all that long ago, the sturdy addax would travel through the Sahara in groups of up to 30 animals—sometimes even in huge herds that joined forces in the search for food and waterholes; now, however, their numbers in the wild have dwindled to between 350 and 400 individuals. The IUCN classifies them as critically endangered, and their future is uncertain, despite attempts being made to save the species through a number of projects aiming to release animals back into the wild.

ARABIAN ORYX

Among the oryxes that inhabit the semideserts and deserts of Africa and Arabia, some of which can manage without water for days or weeks, is the Arabian or white oryx (*Oryx leucoryx*). Standing about 36 inches (90 cm) at the shoulder and weighing 150 lb (70 kg), it is the smallest species in its genus.

Its original geographical range extended from the Sinai peninsula across Mesopotamia, covering the entire Arabian peninsula, but as early as the nineteenth century, this white antelope species was to be found only in southern Arabia. In 1972, it was thought that all specimens in the wild had been eradicated. Immediately after this news was announced, a worldwide breeding program to preserve the species was launched; after a few years the young bred from the animals kept in zoos and animal parks were able to be released into the wild in the original ranges.

Despite this success, the IUCN still lists the species as endangered, because the populations in some countries have again shrunk to a fraction of their original sizes, not least because the white oryx is again being hunted illegally in some areas.

SCIMITAR-HORNED ORYX

The scimitar-horned oryx (*Oryx dammah*), weighing approximately 440 lb (200 kg), is up to 4 feet (1.2 meters) tall and differs from all other oryxes in that it has backward-curving horns that can be over 3 feet (1 meter) long. Scimitar-horned oryxes usually live in pairs or in quite small groups. In the past, like other species, they occasionally gathered together

Above: Only through appropriate breeding measures has it been possible to preserve the white oryx from eradication.

Facing page: Despite very stringent protection regulations, the white oryx is again being hunted in the Arab countries. This species has already been eradicated in the wild once before.

to form huge groups of up to 1,000 animals to search for food and water. These times are over, however, because the scimitar-horned oryx has probably been eradicated in the wild as a result of intensive hunting. In Egypt, it had already vanished by about 1850. A few populations survived in the central Sahara until the 1970s, but a search expedition sent out in 1998 found no scimitar-horned oryx there.

The scimitar-horned oryx can still be seen in large numbers in zoos throughout the world because this species, which has probably been eradicated in the wild, is the second most commonly kept animal species in captivity.

GAZELLES AND RELATIVES

Among the most striking members of the bovid family are the gazelles (*Eudorcas*, *Gazella*, and *Nanger*), from the subfamily Antilopinae. Their long slender legs, with small, triangular hooves, give them a rangy appearance; they have spiral horns, which are less prominent or absent altogether in the females. All gazelle species inhabit East and North Africa, the Arabian peninsula, Mesopotamia between the Euphrates and Tigris, and northwest India, with only the goitered gazelle (*Gazella subgutturosa*) extending its range well into central Asia.

Hunting pressure and habitat destruction
Many members of the Antelopinae subfamily are severely endangered to a greater or lesser extent. Some subspecies of the Asiatic and Arabian species, which have traditionally been heavily hunted, have already been eradicated, whereas others appear on the Red List as critically endangered, endangered, or vulnerable. In Africa, too, all populations are affected by habitat destruction by humans and are under heavy hunting pressure, especially since motorized hunting has become common practice.

The Dorcas gazelle (*Gazella dorcas*) has been a sought-after game species for centuries and is now considered vulnerable. Despite its speed, it has little chance of evading its motorized pursuers in the desert, which offers little cover.

The dama gazelle's preferred habitat is the semidesert landscape of North Africa, with its bushes, shrubs, and small stretches of grass.

The medium-sized goitered gazelle of central Asia is one of the world's fastest land mammals.

In Africa, legend relates that the gerenuk is an antelope that never needs water, but quenches its thirst by absorbing the moisture from dew-covered leaves.

DAMA GAZELLE

Several subspecies of the dama gazelle (*Gazella dama* or *Nanger dama*) were formerly distributed throughout the Sahara and undertook seasonal migrations: during the rainy season, the enormous herds moved north, into the heart of the Sahara, and during the dry season, they moved back into the Sudan. Two subspecies are now considered to have been eradicated, and populations of the three remaining subspecies, which are listed by the IUCN as critically endangered, are severely threatened.

GOITERED GAZELLE

The goitered gazelle, many subspecies of which only occur in Asia, owes its name to the unusual thickening of its throat and of the nape of the male animals during the rutting season. Goitered gazelles are very fast and tireless runners and can reach speeds up to 43 mph (70 km/h). Tough and resilient, they measure between 20 and 26 inches (50 and 65 cm) at the shoulder and weigh up to 90 lb (40 kg).

GERENUK

Stemming from another Antelopinae genus is the gerenuk (*Litocranius walleri*), considered one of the most beautiful gazelles. This graceful animal, which has a shoulder height of about 3 feet (1 meter) and weighs up to 110 lb (50 kg), lives in the driest savannas and scrubland of East Africa and moves around its territory in small groups. When danger threatens, gerenuk do not flee blindly but attempt to slink away quietly.

Gerenuk feed predominantly on acacia leaves, twigs, and flowers, their long necks giving them an advantage here. To be able to reach even further, they often stand up on their hind legs before stripping the branches with their tongues and elongated lips.

The IUCN estimates the total population of the species to be 70,000 and includes it on the Red List as a vulnerable species.

The woolly coat of the saiga antelope consists of a top layer of long hairs and a very thick, soft undercoat. Its winter coat, at up to 3 inches (8 cm) long, is nearly twice the length of its summer coat.

SAIGA

The saiga antelope (*Saiga tatarica*) has only recently been assigned to the Antilopinae subfamily. In the past, it was found across the vast steppes of Eurasia, in the United Kingdom, Germany, Russia, and Alaska; however, changes in the world's climate mean that its habitat now comprises only central Asia and the Russian part of Europe.

Saiga antelopes, which can be differentiated from other Antilopinae by the trunk-like shape of their noses, were on the brink of eradication in the early twentieth century but have since recovered. However, numbers are now once again causing concern: hunting and habitat loss have led to the number of these animals falling from two million in the 1950s to a few tens of thousands now, so the IUCN classifies the species as critically endangered.

GOATS, SHEEP, AND OTHER RELATED SPECIES

The subfamily of caprids (Caprinae) is one of the groups in which scientists have lumped together a wide variety of genera and species, which are all medium-sized, have horns and, apart from a few exceptions, live in Asia and Europe.

GORALS AND SEROWS

The gorals (*Naemorhedus*) and the serows (*Capricornis*) are two Asiatic goat genera. They are closely related and both live in mountainous areas, including in and around the Himalaya, the somewhat larger gorals ascending to heights of up to 13,500 feet (4,000 meters), whereas serows climb only up to about 8,000 feet (2,500 meters). Two of the three species in each genus, which are hunted for their coats and their meat, and which are suffering the effects of habitat loss, are included on the Red List as vulnerable.

The Asiatic serows, from the family of bovids and the subfamily of Caprinae, are true mountain dwellers.

Below: Although the Goral (*Naemorhedus caudatus*) prefers dry mountainous regions, it also descends to sea level, such as the one shown here in the Ussuri region, in the far east of Russia.

For a long time, there was dissent among scientists over the taxonomy of the takin. The scientific name of the Mishmi takin (*Budorcas taxicolor taxicolor*) reflects this: *Budorcas* means "ox-gazelle."

The rutting season begins in December for the Himalayan tahr (*Hemitragus jemlahicus*). At this time, the bucks' tail glands give out a scent that the female tahrs find irresistible.

The markhor is a wild goat from the mountainous regions of Asia. It is popular with hunters, principally because of its magnificent horns.

TAKIN

Whether or not the takin, which occurs in Asia, belongs to the Caprinae was for a long time a matter of dispute. This powerful animal has a head-rump length of 6¹/₂ feet (2 meters) and a shoulder height of about 3¹/₂ feet (1.1 meters), and it weighs up to 770 lb (350 kg). With its heavy head and short horns, it is more reminiscent of a cow than a goat. Its range is in the eastern foothills of the Himalaya, extending from Tibet across Sikkim and Bhutan as far as southwest China, where its preferred habitat lies at elevations between 3,000 and 13,000 feet (1,000 and 4,000 meters). Populations of its subspecies are vulnerable or endangered— for the same reasons as serows and gorals.

MARKHORS AND WILD GOATS

Markhors (*Capra falconeri*) are striking members of the genus *Capra* (goats). They live at intermediate to high altitudes in the mountainous regions of Kashmir, Afghanistan, Turkmenistan, Uzbekistan, and Tajikistan. They are heavily hunted, partly for their meat and leather, but principally for their magnificent horns. The IUCN designates two of the three subspecies as endangered, and the other as critically endangered.

The situation is similar for the wild goat (*Capra aegagrus aegagrus*), considered to be the ancestral species of the domestic goat. Although it once lived in many mountainous areas between eastern Turkey and Afghanistan, intensive hunting has reduced stocks to a few remnant populations, and it is now considered vulnerable.

IBEXES

Ibexes are also members of the *Capra* genus, their smallest and southernmost representative being the Nubian ibex (*Capra nubiana*). It lives in rocky mountains in Israel, Eritrea, and the Sudan, and grows to a maximum of 32 inches (80 cm), but has long, magnificent horns despite its small size. It is heavily hunted, particularly in Arabian regions, and is classified on the Red List as endangered. Other ibex species have small, insular distributions, and their populations are therefore particularly at risk, as is the case with the Walia ibex (*Capra walie*), which is considered to be critically endangered.

Saving the Alpine ibex

The Alpine ibex (*Capra ibex*) only narrowly escaped total eradication. These animals, which previously occurred in most areas in the Alps, were already being heavily hunted as far back as the early Middle Ages because of superstitious belief in the healing powers of the horn and bones. In many regions, they were wiped out or brought to the brink of eradication. It is thanks to protection measures implemented by a nineteenth-century king of Piedmont-Sardinia, Victor Emanuel II, that ibexes can now once again be seen in the Alps. Up until the beginning of the twentieth century, animals from Italy were introduced into Switzerland, where they were used for breeding. In 1911, the first ibexes were released into the wild; after some early setbacks, they multiplied splendidly. There are now about 35,000 ibexes across large parts of the Alps, so it has even become necessary for limited numbers to be culled.

AOUDADS

No less striking than markhors and wild goats, with their enormous horns, are aoudads (*Ammotragus lervia*), from the genus *Ammotragus*. They live in the rocky desert areas of North Africa, where they are popular prey for hunters, and are considered vulnerable. At least one subspecies, the Egyptian Barbary sheep (*Ammotragus lervia ornata*), has already been eradicated.

TAHRS

Tahrs (*Hemitragus*) also occupy a place midway between goats and sheep. There are three species, living in geographically separate areas: the Himalayan tahr in the Southern Alps of New Zealand (*Hemitragus jemlahicus*), the Nilgiri tahr of southern India (*Hemitragus hylocrius*), and the Arabian tahr of Oman (*Hemitragus jayakari*). According to the Red List, the first of these species is vulnerable, despite its large range, and populations of the Nilgiri and Arabian tahrs are declining even more sharply; they are listed as endangered.

Even though it is endangered, the Siberian ibex (*Capra sibirica*) is still persecuted by trophy hunters.

The Barbary sheep's magnificent horns almost spelled disaster for this animal.

Wild goats excel at climbing and jumping; they move nimbly in mountainous terrain.

The Alpine ibex almost disappeared forever from the entire Alpine region.

SHEEP

Sheep (*Ovis*) have the largest geographical range not only of all caprids, but also of all bovids living in the wild: it stretches from Europe through the Middle East and central Asia as far as North America and Mexico.

Almost eradicated—the mouflon

One very well-known representative is the wild European mouflon (*Ovis orientalis musimon*), which was originally common between eastern Europe and the Mediterranean, but was later to be found only on the Mediterranean islands of Sardinia and Corsica. The small populations on these islands would also have been eradicated if it had not been for the fact that breeding groups were established all over Europe, so that populations have been able to recover despite occasional minor setbacks, and are today considered reasonably secure.

An animal characteristic of the North American Rocky Mountains is the bighorn sheep, which inhabits these mountainous regions in groups ranging in size from fairly small to large flocks.

Tibetan antelopes live in extremely high mountain regions of Asia: in Tibet, their range starts at an altitude of 11,500 feet (3,500 meters) and extends to elevations above 16,500 feet (5,000 meters).

European settlers endanger the bighorn sheep

The bighorn sheep (*Ovis canadensis*) is found in the Rocky Mountains, a true mountain-dweller that can climb outstandingly well and feeds on grasses, lichens, mosses, and herbs. The rams' large, heavy horns are striking; those of the females are considerably smaller. They live in large herds, but do not have the strict dominance hierarchy of the mouflon.

Before the arrival of European settlers, over two million bighorn sheep lived in the Rocky Mountains, but trophy hunting and diseases introduced by domestic animals drastically decimated stocks. Around 1900, only about 60,000 animals remained, and populations have still not recovered today. Two subspecies, *Ovis canadensis nelsoni* and *Ovis canadensis sierrae*, have been eradicated in many areas, and some others are endangered.

TIBETAN ANTELOPE

Modern research methods have revealed that the golden-brown Tibetan antelope (*Pantholops hodgsonii*), also known as the chiru, is a member of the caprids. Although it was one of the most common Tibetan animals about 50 years ago and had a total population of about a million animals, only small populations now remain on the high plateaus of Tibet and Kashmir and in China: the population is estimated at between 50,000 and 60,000 animals, and it is accordingly included on the Red List as endangered. The main reason for the huge decline in chiru numbers is poaching. In particular, they are hunted for their coats, from which the famous shahtoosh wool is produced, but also for their horns, which are used as remedies in Chinese medicine.

The mouflon, which is considered to be the ancestral form of the domestic sheep, has always been highly sought after by hunters. Some species have now been eradicated or are severely threatened.

PERISSODACTYLA
HORSES

Horses or solidungulates (Equidae) belong to the order of odd-toed ungulates (Perissodactyla). All members of the family—horses, donkeys, and zebras—are easily recognized as such from their external appearance. Some horses are threatened or have already been eradicated; in North America and in western Europe, they became extinct 10,000 years ago for unknown reasons, whereas in eastern Europe, the tarpan survived into the nineteenth century. Since the Iranian and Iraqi population of the Asiatic wild ass (Equus hemionus) *disappeared during the twentieth century, the last remaining wild solipeds are those in southern and eastern Africa and in central Asia.*

A number of shared external characteristics

All solidungulates have certain features in common. They are all powerfully built animals with long limbs that attain a head-rump length of 6 to 9 feet (2 to 3 meters), a height between 3 and 5 feet (1 and 1.6 meters), and a weight between 175 and 1,000 lb (80 and 450 kg). Their coats are usually short and smooth, with only their mane and tail consisting of long hair. Their most striking feature, however, are their legs and hooves: only the third digit, the last phalanx of which is covered with a layer of horn, is fully developed, and this is the only one on which horses walk, which is why they are also called ungulates. This anatomical peculiarity represents an adaptation to their preferred habitats, savannas and steppes, and deserts and semideserts, because it enables them to flee swiftly from enemies such as wolves, lions, and other predators.

Differing lifestyles

Although solidungulates can be observed in their ranges at any time of day, it is predominantly in the twilight hours and at night that they search for food—mainly grasses and herbage, sometimes also leaves and buds.

Their social behavior varies among the different species: in the cases of the mountain zebra (*Equus zebra*), the quagga (*Equus quagga*), and Przewalski's horse (*Equus ferus przewalskii*) a stallion guards a herd that is, however, led by a mare; sometimes groups join together to form large herds with a strict hierarchy. In the cases of Grevy's zebra (*Equus grevyi*) and the African wild ass (*Equus africanus* or *Equus asinus*), stallions sometimes have vast territories of up to 40 square miles (100 km²), and close relationships between adult animals are not as common as in the case of the more markedly gregarious animals.

With a height of up to 5 feet (1.5 meters) at the withers, the beautifully striped Grevy's zebra is the largest of the zebra species.

ZEBRAS

The three species of zebra, with their striking black-and-white-striped coats, today live in an area extending from the southern Sudan as far as South Africa. The plains zebra is the most widely distributed, and its populations are not immediately threatened, although the majority of the animals live in a few national parks and reserves in Kenya and Tanzania.

Vulnerable despite recovery of populations

The situation is worse for the two other zebra species. Some of the subspecies of the mountain zebra, which lives in South Africa and Namibia, have already been eradicated and others are threatened. Although populations have been able to recover somewhat, thanks to specially established national parks, Hartmann's mountain zebra (*Equus zebra hartmannae*) and the Cape mountain zebra (*Equus zebra zebra*) have been classified by the IUCN as endangered, both now being found solely in reserves and protected areas. Also included on the Red List as endangered is Grevy's zebra, which has been completely eradicated in many African countries and, in others, has recorded population declines of up to 70 percent. All zebra species are suffering from loss of habitat and, in addition, have been hunted since time immemorial for their skins.

ASIATIC WILD ASS

The Asiatic wild ass, which is sometimes called the half-ass and, unlike the African ass, has never been domesticated, is distributed across Asia between Iran, India, and Mongolia. All the subspecies—which in some taxonomies are designated as species—are included on the Red List.

Severely threatened subspecies

The Indian wild ass (*Equus hemionus khur*), numbers of which are estimated by IUCN to lie between 800 and 900 animals, is endangered. It has been eradicated in Iran and Pakistan since the 1960s, mainly due to habitat loss, with only one small population in northwestern India surviving. Two further subspecies, the onager (*Equus hemionus onager*) from northern Iran

In the case of Grevy's zebra, up to 15 mares and young animals will form a social group escorted by a stallion, which has a fixed territory.

Hartmann's mountain zebra lives on the high plateaus of Namibia. Its population has shrunk by about 85 percent in the last hundred years.

Cape mountain zebras live almost exclusively in protected areas in South Africa. Only about 700 specimens remain.

The Indian wild ass lives in small herds in just a single state in India, Gujarat, and is still hunted today.

The kiang (*Equus kiang*) is a close relative of the Asiatic wild ass and is sometimes listed as a subspecies of it.

and the kulan (*Equus hemionus kulan*) from Turkmenistan and Kazakhstan, are deemed critically endangered. Numbers have fallen rapidly; they are not only suffering from habitat loss, but also from heavy hunting and poaching, because they are extremely easy to shoot down at the few available waterholes.

AFRICAN WILD ASS

The African wild ass is considered to be the ancestral form of today's domestic donkey. Like many domesticated donkeys, this smallest member of the horse family has bold black horizontal stripes on its legs. At least one subspecies, the Atlas wild ass (*Equus africanus atlanticus*), is now extinct, and another, the

Nubian wild ass (*Equus africanus africanus*), is probably extinct also. Small remnant populations of the third subspecies, the Somalia wild ass (*Equus africanus somaliensis*), are today widely scattered across Ethiopia, Eritrea, Somalia, and the Sudan; with an estimated population of about 570 animals, it is one of the most severely threatened large mammals of all and is listed by the IUCN as critically endangered. However, in 1969 and 1972, some wild animals in Somalia and Ethiopia were captured and placed in various breeding groups in zoological gardens. Offspring are now being produced on a regular basis, and there is some hope that the species will be preserved.

PRZEWALSKI'S HORSE

When, in 1878, the Russian Nikolai Mikhailovich Przewalski returned to the tsar's court from one of his expeditions to central Asia with the hide and skull of a horse that up until that time was almost unknown in the West, Przewalski's horse was already rare in its original range; less than 100 years later, in 1969, the animal was last observed in the wild. However, around the turn of the century, 55 specimens that had been caught in the wild had been imported to

Above: The Somalia wild ass, one of the subspecies of the African wild ass, is considered to be the sole ancestral form of all domestic donkeys.

Below left: Like most wild asses in Africa and Asia, the kulan inhabits dry steppes and semideserts in central Asia.

Below: From the point of view of its genetic makeup, the onager is more closely related to horses than to donkeys.

Europe and distributed among various zoos, all of which set about attempting to breed the species—with success. After the end of the Second World War, there were only 40 animals remaining, but today, the numbers have risen to about 2,000. Reintroduction programs are now up and running: captive-bred offspring from zoos have been reintroduced in their original habitat, including China and Mongolia, as well as in semi-reserves in Hungary, where about 70 animals are currently living in semi-wild conditions. These sturdy, hardy horses with their upright manes can endure temperatures down to −22°F (−30°C) and are the only surviving species of wild horse.

TARPAN

Unlike Przewalski's horse, the tarpan (*Equus ferus gmelini*) and the forest horse (*Equus ferus silvaticus*) were eradicated during the course of the eighteenth and nineteenth centuries from southern Russia and central and eastern Europe. Polish farmers often crossed the tarpan with their domestic horses, creating the konik.

These have been used by various zoological gardens, animal parks, and private individuals since the 1930s, to try to recreate the tarpan through "back-breeding" and to release it in its original ranges as well as in other regions, but ultimately these bred animals are just domestic horses with a tarpan-like appearance. Once a species has been eradicated, it is not possible to reproduce it, and it remains lost to the world forever.

Above: The survival of Przewalski's horse is due to the efforts of various breeders. Nowadays, some animals are being reintroduced into the wild.

Below: In contrast to Przewalski's horse, the tarpan has been eradicated. All the specimens alive today have been back-bred.

PERISSODACTYLA
TAPIRS

Tapirs (Tapiridae), from the order of odd-toed ungulates, are very old animals from an evolutionary point of view. Fossils have been used to demonstrate their existence in North America as early as the Eocene, i.e. about 50 million years ago. They arrived in South America, where three of the four extant species now live, between one and two million years ago, in the Pleistocene era; there is also evidence of the only Asian species, the Asian tapir (Tapirus indicus) from this time onward. The ancestral forms of the tapir also existed in what is now Europe, but they became extinct there a long time ago.

Solitary vegetarians

All tapirs are very shy, nocturnal inhabitants of dense forests and thickets. At the slightest hint of danger, they flee or submerge themselves in nearby water. Tapirs measure between about 2½ and 4 feet (0.8 and 1.2 meters) in height. Their striking feature is their flexible proboscis, which these vegetarians use to grasp leaves that are higher up.

They are solitary creatures, meeting up only for mating; however, mothers and their young, which are born after a gestation period of just under 14 months, remain together for a year.

Tapirs are "hiders"

The calf is ready to flee danger just one hour after its birth. Unlike the adult animals, the calves are brown with distinct white longitudinal stripes, which disappear in the course of the first year of life. This coloration is presumably for camouflage because, although the calves are born completely covered with hair and with their eyes open, they are what is known as "hiders," meaning they spend the first two to four weeks of their lives hidden under bushes while their mothers are out and about.

The Brazilian tapir always lives close to water in the tropical rainforests of the lowland regions of South America. It is fond of bathing and is an excellent swimmer.

Facing page: The Brazilian tapir is threatened not only by the destruction of its habitat: its flesh is considered to be a delicacy, and it is therefore a popular prey among hunters.

Below: Geologically speaking, tapirs are an ancient family that was once very species-rich and widely distributed. Now there are only four species remaining, in areas isolated from one another.

Although at first glance there appear to be few similarities, the tapirs (shown here is an Asian tapir) make up, together with rhinos and horses, the order of odd-toed ungulates.

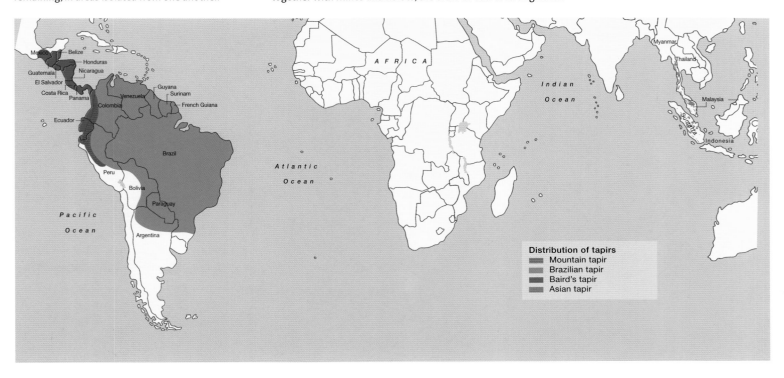

Distribution of tapirs
- Mountain tapir
- Brazilian tapir
- Baird's tapir
- Asian tapir

All tapirs are vulnerable

As with many other species, the main threats to the survival of the tapir are the transformation of its habitats into cultivated land, deforestation, and slash-and-burn land clearance; in some regions, it is also hunted for its meat and its skin. In the medium term, it is likely that tapirs will survive only in well-protected forest reserves, but the establishment of such reserves is still some way off. Therefore, populations of all tapirs are threatened. The Brazilian tapir (*Tapirus terrestris*), which covers large areas of tropical South America as far as northern Argentina, but is absent from the Andes, is classified as vulnerable. In the alpine zones in the west of the continent the mountain tapir (*Tapirus pinchaque*) lives in the Colombian, Ecuadorian, and Peruvian Andes, where it dwells at altitudes between 6,500 and 10,000 feet (2,000 and 3,000 meters), in the summer, even up to 13,000 feet (4,000 meters). It is considered to be endangered, as is Baird's tapir (*Tapirus bairdii*), the population of which is estimated to have fallen to below 5,000 because of the destruction of over two-thirds of the primary forests, and which is probably the most threatened species in its family.

It is essentially unknown how many specimens of the Asian tapir (*Tapirus indicus*), the only two-toned tapir, still exist. What is certain is that enormous damage has been inflicted on this species by the destruction of the rainforests in Southeast Asia, so the IUCN classifies it as vulnerable.

PERISSODACTYLA
RHINOCEROSES

Rhinoceroses (Rhinocerotidae) are a family of odd-toed ungulates that can weigh over a ton whose members are some of the most ancient mammals alive in modern times. Their evolution can be traced directly back about 40 million years.

Habitats and social behavior

The five extant rhinoceros species live in extremely varied habitats in Africa and Asia: the white rhinoceros (*Ceratotherium simum*) prefers grass savannas; the black rhinoceros (*Diceros bicornis*), scrub with open grassy areas; the Indian rhinoceros (*Rhinoceros unicornis*), flooded river plains; and the Sumatran rhinoceros (*Dicerorhinus sumatrensis*) and Javan rhinoceros (*Rhinoceros sondaicus*), dense tropical forests.

With the exception of the white rhinoceros, the predominantly crepuscular and nocturnal rhinoceroses are not particularly gregarious; they avoid one another. Although black rhinoceroses do meet up in their grazing areas and use communal dung heaps, they spend the bulk of their time alone. The same is true of the Indian rhinoceros.

Reproduction and life expectancy

Cows do not become sexually mature until the age of at least 4 years, bulls at 7 years. After a gestation period of 14 to 16 months, a single hornless calf is born, which is suckled by its mother for about a year. The spacing between births is from 2 to 4 years, so rhinoceroses reproduce relatively slowly, which exacerbates their threat status. In the wild, the animals live to a maximum age of 40, but the chance of a rhinoceros reaching this age in the wild is relatively slim, because pressure from humans—through biotope destruction and poaching—is enormous. In addition, calves in Africa often fall prey to lions, and diseases also take their toll.

AFRICAN RHINOCEROSES

Although the white rhinoceros is currently not considered to be immediately threatened, the second African species, the black rhinoceros, is critically endangered. The black rhinoceros is significantly smaller and lighter than the white rhinoceros and far less gregarious. In its habitat, thornbush savanna, it finds cover and sufficient food in the form of twigs and leaves, which it pulls into its mouth using its pointed upper lip. Even finger-long thorns do not bother it.

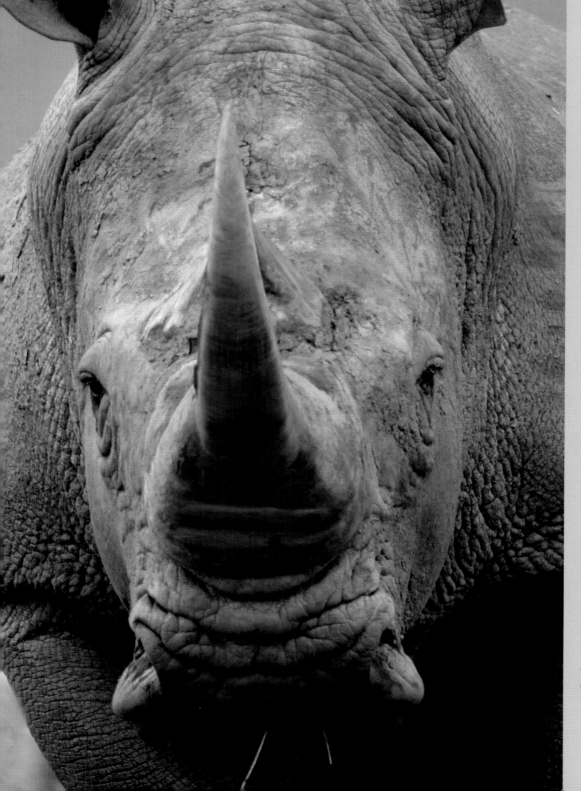

The white rhinoceros is actually gray. The name comes from the Afrikaans word *wyd*, which means *wide*, referring to the characteristic broad mouth.

A member of the "big five"

The rhinoceros together with the elephant, the buffalo, the lion, and the leopard make up the "big five," the prey most coveted by European and American big-game hunters in Africa. Although the rhinoceros, one of the heaviest living land mammals, can reach considerable speeds of about 30 mph (50 km/h), and frequently attacks without warning when it is disturbed, it is far less dangerous when shot and injured than the other four. This is probably not least because it has poor eyesight and cannot make out an enemy clearly; in many authenticated cases, it has merely knocked down its attacker and then bolted. Wounded buffalo and elephants, on the other hand, will attack hunters repeatedly, and will continue to do so until they breathe their last.

ASIAN RHINOCEROSES

The three Asian species of rhinoceros live in the Southeast Asian tropics. They were still common 100 to 150 years ago, but today, they survive only

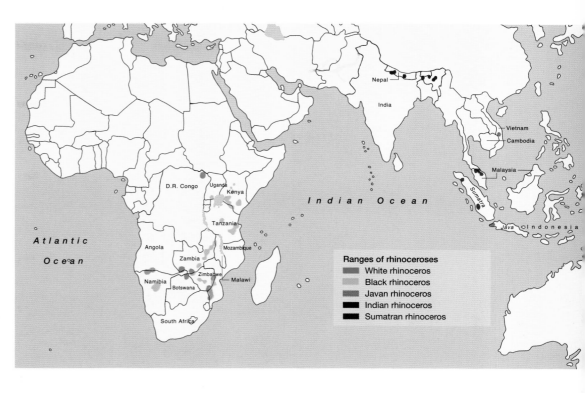

Ranges of rhinoceroses
- White rhinoceros
- Black rhinoceros
- Javan rhinoceros
- Indian rhinoceros
- Sumatran rhinoceros

Above: The fact that the ranges of the five rhinoceros species are either isolated from one another or are very small, or both, increases the danger of eradication.

Below: Unlike its larger cousin, the white rhinoceros, the black rhinoceros prefers eating leaves. With its pointed and flexible upper lip, it tears foliage from bushes and trees.

Alarmingly low numbers

in limited areas. The Indian rhinoceros, with the folds of its thick hide giving the impression of armor plating, now occurs only in the grasslands of Nepal and northeastern India and is classified by the IUCN as endangered. The other two Asian species, by contrast, live in dense jungle: the Sumatran rhinoceros on Borneo and Sumatra and possibly also in Myanmar and Malaysia, and the Javan rhinoceros on Java and in southern Vietnam, where signs of it were recently discovered for the first time.

The Sumatran and Javan rhinos are listed on the Red List as critically endangered. The total population of the Sumatran rhinoceros, the smallest of all rhinoceroses and the only Asian rhino with two horns, is probably fewer than 500 individuals, most of which (250, up to a maximum of 300 animals) are found in three national parks in Sumatra. The Javan rhinoceros is one of the rarest large animals in the world: it is estimated that only between 50 and 80

Black rhinoceroses, unlike the white rhinoceros, which often grazes in herds, are predominantly solitary.

specimens have survived the destruction of their habitat and hunting slaughter, and 8 to 10 of these are in southern Vietnam. The species is given a very low chance of survival.

Rhinoceros horn worth its weight in gold

The threat facing the five extant rhinoceros species has various causes. The key factors, in addition to habitat loss, are civil war in Africa and, in particular, hunting and poaching. For years, the animals were killed mercilessly and purely for shooting enjoyment: there are reports of Indian maharajahs having killed up to 1,000 Indian rhinoceroses within a period of 10 years, and British "sportsmen" and other big-game hunters from a wide range of countries were not far behind.

Traditional Chinese medicine has also played a part in wiping out stocks. Although rhinoceros horn is simply keratin, the same protein fingernails are made of, powdered it is supposed to cure a variety of ailments such as fever, arthritis, headache, food poisoning, etc., and even "devil possession," and to be an aphrodisiac. It is therefore worth its weight in gold, and its value continues to rise because of the falling numbers of animals and the strict ban on trading in their horn. The horn is also in demand in Asia for carving, including the making of dagger handles, which are seen as a symbol of manhood in some countries.

Poaching poses the greatest threat to rhinoceroses all over the world.

Above right: The daily mud bath not only contributes to the animal's wellbeing but is also necessary to rid the skin of irritating parasites.

Center right: The skin of the Indian rhinoceros forms folds at the joints that are reminiscent of armor plating.

Below right: The Sumatran rhinoceros, which leads a secluded life close to waterholes in tropical mountain forests, is the smallest extant rhinoceros species.

SIRENIA
DUGONGS AND
MANATEES

The members of both families of sea cows (Sirenia), the manatees and the dugongs (Trichechidae and Dugongidae), are among the few mammals that live in water. Although some 50 million years ago, they were originally land dwellers, over the course of time, they switched to an aquatic lifestyle, and they now no longer spend any time on dry land.

Gentle giants

Sea cows are distributed across a wide variety of geographical regions, although in all cases in the warm waters of the Tropics or Subtropics: the Amazonian manatee (*Trichechus inunguis*) lives only in fresh water, the dugong (*Dugong*

Left: A female West Indian manatee suckles its young.

Below: The various species of sea cow live in geographically separate populations in different coastal waters and rivers.

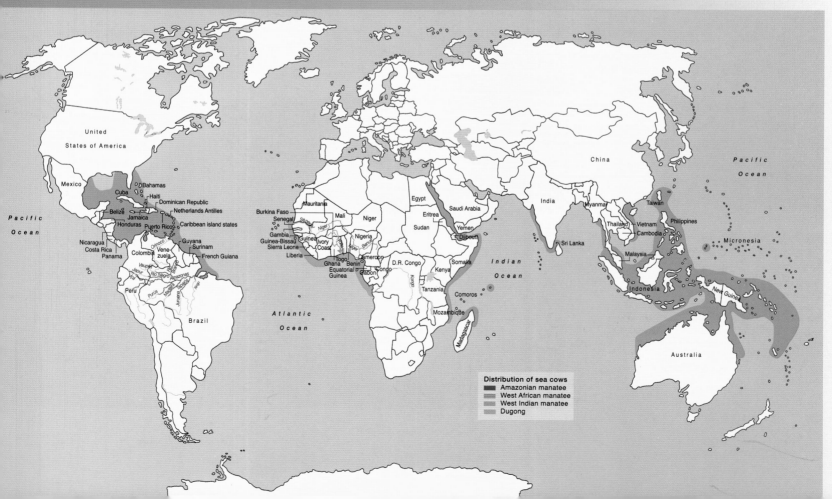

Distribution of sea cows
Amazonian manatee
West African manatee
West Indian manatee
Dugong

Collapse of populations

Sea cows have always been hunted for their delicious meat by inhabitants of the coastal regions in which they live, but it was not until these areas were colonized that the populations became seriously endangered. Now many animals also end up in fishing drift nets, and increasing numbers are severely injured by the propellers of motor boats. However, the exploitation and pollution of the waters off South America and Africa are the main reasons why populations of all four species have shrunk dramatically, even collapsing completely in places. They require the strictest possible protection measures, although these will be extremely hard to implement, especially with regard to the contamination of water with fertilizers and pesticides. All four extant species of sea cow are classified by IUCN as vulnerable; a fifth, Steller's sea cow (*Hydrodamalis gigas*), was eradicated less than three decades after its discovery in 1741.

Dugongs, which are less bulky than manatees, live in the waters of the Indopacific region.

dugon) lives only in salt water, and the West Indian manatee (*Trichechus manatus*) and the West African manatee (*Trichechus senegalensis*) live in both fresh and salt water.

They all feed almost exclusively on hard grasses and other plants in shallow waters, which they graze using their large, downward-pointing mouths surrounded by tactile hairs. Sea cows are considered to be lethargic and very

All sea cows are very large, cumbersome, and extremely placid animals. They are supposed to have inspired the legend of the mermaids and are therefore also referred to as sirens.

gentle, generally live in small groups, and communicate by means of twittering or squeaking sounds.

Sea cows—shown here is an Amazonian manatee with young—are very distantly related to elephants.

PROBOSCIDEA
ELEPHANTS

The elephant family (Elephantidae), from the order of Proboscidea, includes the three largest land mammals of modern times. The smallest of these is the African forest elephant (Loxodonta cyclotis), which lives in the enormous virgin forests of the Congo, and the second largest is the Indian or Asian elephant (Elephas maximus). The largest representative is the African elephant (Loxodonta africana): bulls can reach a shoulder height of more than 13 feet (4 meters) and an equivalent head-rump length—excluding the trunk. The heaviest animals killed weighed almost 13,225 lb (6,000 kg). Cows are between 20 and 30 percent lighter.

AFRICAN ELEPHANTS

African elephants spend most of the day and the night engaged in the search for food—18 hours on average. They require vast quantities of greenery of all kinds: a day's ration weighs at least quarter of a ton and includes grass and herbage, roots and bark, even bushes and the thorny branches of acacias; elephants are particularly fond of wild fruits, succulent marsh plants, and reeds.

Elephants live together in groups ranging from small family units to large herds. These are always led by an experienced cow elephant.

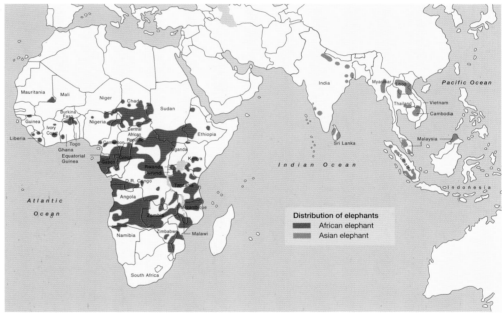

African populations are recovering

In some areas of Africa, elephants had been decimated to an alarming extent, in some cases, even exterminated. A fundamental reason for this is the loss of habitat for these giant animals, which are forced to retreat into small areas where they cause lasting damage to the vegetation. It often takes many years for such overgrazed tracts of land to recover, which leads to elephants dying because they cannot find enough food, particularly where they have no more space to retreat to.

Furthermore, elephants were and still are in extreme danger from poachers, who hunt them for their tusks, which can be up to 11 feet (3.3 meters) long. Although officially there has been no trading in ivory since a ban was introduced in 1989, and the species is scheduled under CITES, African elephant populations continue to be threatened and conservation groups say that poaching is at its highest level since 1989. However, populations are recovering slowly, which is why the IUCN no longer classifies them as endangered, but only as vulnerable. CITES has downgraded the protection status of the African elephant, but only in a few areas. In sub-Saharan Africa, between 25,000 and 50,000 elephants are killed illegally each year and their tusks smuggled to China, where there is great demand for the "white gold": it is used in carvings, but above all, as a treatment for impotence.

Above: Water is essential for elephants to survive; they drink between 25 and 40 gallons (100 and 150 liters) daily. The trunk sucks up 2½ gallons (10 liters) at a time.

Right: Today, several subspecies of elephant live in two geographically distinct areas of Africa and Southeast Asia. Populations of both species are declining rapidly or are threatened.

Below: For elephants, as for all pachyderms, the hygiene of a daily bath in water, mud, or dust is critical to their survival.

Family-oriented lifestyle

These gray giants are very caring and family-oriented animals. Biologists discovered only a few years ago that they carry out animated conversations that are inaudible to the human ear because they are at such low frequencies.

Female elephants live in family groups that are always led by an old, experienced cow; after her death, her eldest daughter usually takes over the herd. However, if the leader is shot suddenly, clans frequently fall apart, which sooner or later leads to the death of any young, single animals. The bulls form bachelor herds of between 4 and 10 animals, in which there is a definite hierarchy. The weaker animals keep out of the way of the stronger ones, so serious fights are extremely rare and usually only occur when strange bulls enter an area that is already occupied by other elephants.

Just one bull responsible for all offspring

Studies in Amboseli National Park have shown that all the animals in a herd and in a clan (several families) are related to one another.

Distribution of elephants
African elephant
Asian elephant

By means of DNA analysis, it was also possible to establish the paternity of the calves. The results surprised even experienced elephant experts: all the calves had the same father, meaning that one dominant bull sired the entire younger generation within a region, even though there were other adult bulls there capable of fathering young.

Elephant cows give birth, following a gestation period of about 22 months, to a single calf, approximately every five or six years. The calves, which at birth weigh just over 220 lb (100 kg) and are so small that they fit under the mother's belly, are watched over with sharp eyes and defended with life and limb. Not

The cow elephant's mammary glands lie immediately behind the forelegs.

only the mothers, but also the other members of the herd, care for the helpless young and protect them by keeping them in their midst. Nonetheless, the calves are exposed to many dangers, including disease, drought, and lack of food, as well as predators, such as lions.

Elephants get six sets of teeth

In the wild, elephants, which are mature at 15 to 16 years of age, seldom live to be older than 50, but in zoological gardens, they can live up

Facing page: Old bulls are solitary animals and only search out the herd when one of the cows is in estrus.

to 15 years longer. They get six sets of teeth in a lifetime. Once the last set is worn, it means a slow death because the elephant is no longer able to crunch up its food—hard grasses, bark, and branches. It usually spends the last years of its life in areas where it can find more tender vegetation, but eventually loses a lot of weight over a period of three to four years before it finally dies.

As late as the twentieth century, even elephant experts believed that the animals sought out particular sites at which to die because explorers and hunters were constantly finding sites containing dozens of skeletons. However, we now know that, where possible, old elephants spend the last months of their lives near swamps and flood plains, where they can find soft and succulent grasses they can still chew with their damaged teeth. They then eventually die at these locations.

ASIAN ELEPHANT

Although very similar in terms of lifestyle and social behavior, the Indian or Asian elephant can be distinguished from its African relative by its appearance: its ears are substantially smaller; it has an extra, fourth, toe on its hind feet; its head has two rounded bulges; and its highest point is its back, whereas in the case of the African elephant, it is the head. Recent studies have shown that the Asian elephant, as the only surviving representative of the genus *Elephas*, is more closely related to the mammoth than to the African elephant.

Elephants as working animals

As long as 4,000 years ago, Asian elephants were being caught, tamed, and used as working animals, particularly in forests and jungle areas. However, demand is falling: in Thailand, for example, a hundred years ago there were still an estimated 100,000 elephants kept in captivity, but today there are only between 3,000 and 4,000. Myanmar, with about 5,000, has the largest numbers of elephants used for work purposes.

Young bulls playfully test their strength against one another, simultaneously honing their social behavior.

African elephants can be distinguished from their Asian relatives by, among other things, their substantially larger ears.

Asian elephants seek out a waterhole at least once a day.

RIGHT WHALES, DOLPHINS, AND OTHER WHALE FAMILIES

Some of the families from the order of whales (Cetacea) contain the largest creatures that have ever populated Earth and its oceans. It has been proven that their ancestors were insect-eating land mammals that, after the disappearance of the dinosaurs, first colonized the beaches and shallow water zones. Primitive whales spent all their time in the water; fossil remains found in 50-million-year-old strata show they measured about 65 feet (20 meters) in length and had a long snout and foreshortened rear limbs. Although these primitive whales became extinct about 25 million years ago, they are among the direct ancestors of modern whales.

One of the things for which many whales are famous is their complex songs, which are audible over long distances. These differ from species to species, and often from group to group, and may lie in the high-frequency or in the low-frequency range.

Baleen whales and toothed whales

The whale order consists of the suborders of toothed whales and baleen whales (Odontoceti and Mysticeti), comprising a variety of families, genera, and species. The gigantic baleen whales, the smallest of which is the 20-feet-long (6-meter-long) pygmy right whale (*Caperea marginata*), feed mainly on krill, tiny

crustaceans that drift in the water. For this, they make use of their baleen, horny plates hanging from the gums with hair-like fringes on the inside. A baleen whale searching for food fills its mouth with water and then pushes it out again with its tongue, leaving the krill hanging in the baleen as if in a net.

Toothed whales, on the other hand, have teeth. They are hunters, feeding on small and large fish, squid, and even other marine mammals, such as seals.

BLUE WHALE

The blue whale (*Balaenoptera musculus*) is thought to be the largest animal that has ever lived. It out-measures any of the dinosaurs: it can attain a length of over 100 feet (30 meters) and a weight of 180 tons, its heart is as large as a small car, and its mouth is up to 20 feet (6 meters) wide. Blue whales were abundant in nearly all oceans until the beginning of the twentieth century.

Heavy hunting in the first half of the century led to severe population collapses, which were only halted by a hunting ban introduced in the 1960s. Since then, at least portions of the blue whale populations have recovered, but the species is still listed on the Red List as endangered.

The sperm whale, shown here near the Azores off Portugal, is the largest and most impressive toothed whale. The bulls are up to 60 feet (18 meters) long.

The huge blue whale can dive for up to 20 minutes at a time; normally, however, it comes to the surface every two minutes.

Facing page: Whale experts can identify the various species by their size and the shape of the tail fins. Shown here is a humpback whale.

Below: Acrobatic leaps during which they heave their whole body out of the water are characteristic of humpback whales.

BOWHEAD WHALE

A stocky dark-colored whale without a dorsal fin, the bowhead whale (*Balaena mysticetus*), also known as the Greenland right whale, or Arctic whale, can live for up to 200 years and reach a length of up to 60 feet (18 meters). Its baleen are up to 15 feet (4.5 meters) long and would tower over a one-storey house. Because it lives in the Arctic regions of the Atlantic and the Pacific, it has a 24-inch-thick (60-cm-thick) layer of blubber to protect it from the icy cold.

The layer of blubber, and the long baleen, made the bowhead whale a particularly attractive target for whalers, and massive declines in the nineteenth and twentieth centuries led, in 1931, to whales becoming the first animals to be placed under the protection of the League of Nations. Individual regional populations are still endangered or critically endangered, although, as with all whales, the number of animals is difficult to estimate.

Left: The black-and-white killer whale, from the family of pilot whales, is an excellent hunter.

Below: The three species of freshwater river dolphins live in areas totally isolated from one another, in the great river systems in the northern part of South America, in northern India, Pakistan, and eastern China.

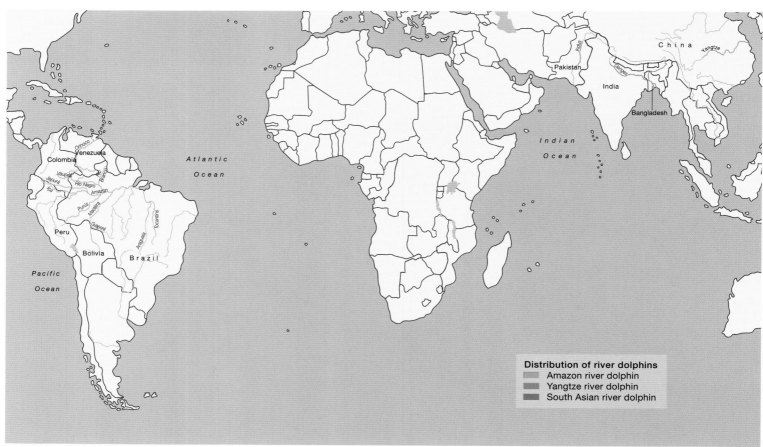

Distribution of river dolphins
Amazon river dolphin
Yangtze river dolphin
South Asian river dolphin

The "blow"—air exhaled through the blowhole after diving—can help to distinguish between whale species. Shown here are killer whales.

The Yangtze river dolphin is thought to be extinct. It has not been sighted since 2002.

HUMPBACK WHALE

Humpback whales (*Megaptera novaeangliae*), from the suborder of baleen whales, reach a maximum of 50 feet (15 meters) in length. They have extremely large pectoral fins, which they often slap against the surface of the water while lying on their sides, presumably to communicate. They are also famous for their songs and for their high breaches. Like other whales, the humpback undertakes seasonal migrations over huge distances; in its winter quarters, it eats its fill, but in the summer, during the mating season in warmer waters, it hardly takes in any food.

It is estimated that 97 percent of humpback whales were eradicated during the twentieth century. However, the hunting ban issued in 1963, which is still in force today, is now having effect: populations are recovering, albeit very slowly. The IUCN has now downgraded the humpback whale from endangered to vulnerable.

SPERM WHALE

The sperm whale (*Physeter catodon* or *Physeter macrocephalus*), which is classified on the Red List as vulnerable, is the largest toothed whale: a bull can be up to 60 feet (18 meters) long and weigh about 45 tons, whereas the female, with a length of just 40 feet (12 meters), is considerably smaller. The sperm whale regularly dives to depths of over 1,000 feet (300 meters), but is thought to reach depths of about 10,000 feet (3,000 meters), making it the record-holder for deep-sea diving among whales. When these animals are hunting giant squid in the deep ocean, they sometimes become entangled in cables and drown because they are lung breathers and need to surface at regular intervals.

KILLER WHALE

One of the best-known toothed whales is the elegant black-and-white orca (*Orcinus orca*), also known as the killer whale. It belongs to the dolphin family (Delphinidae), and at up to 26 feet (8 meters) in length, and weighing 9 tons, is one of the largest dolphin species. Like other dolphins, killer whales live in pods, groups that are led by an old female, and in which they usually remain lifelong. Killer whales occur in all the world's oceans, but they are most frequently encountered in Arctic and Antarctic waters. They were never a particular target of whalers, and are not immediately threatened at present, but like all marine mammals, they are suffering from the effects of water pollution and global warming.

RIVER DOLPHINS

The term *river dolphins* was for a long time used to cover, in one group, four species occurring in fresh water rather than in the open ocean. However, it is now known that they evolved separately from one another. They are the boto or Amazon river dolphin (*Inia geoffrensis*), the baiji or Yangtze river dolphin (*Lipotes vexillifer*), the blind or South Asian river dolphin (*Platanista gangetica*), and the franciscana or La Plata river dolphin (*Pontoporia blainvillei*), which spends most of its time in salt water. They are all threatened, but the position of the baiji, which lives predominantly in the Yangtze river, is particularly critical. Although it was placed under protection at the beginning of the 1980s, sightings have steadily decreased; the last animal living in the wild was photographed in 2002, and since then, no more have been seen. It is assumed that the species is now extinct.

RODENTIA
SQUIRRELS AND HUTIAS

The most species-rich order of mammals, the rodents (Rodentia), includes the families of squirrels (Sciuridae) and hutias (Capromyidae). They live in totally different regions of Earth, but—like all other members of this order—have one thing in common: enlarged front teeth.

HUTIAS

Hutias belong to the suborder Caviomorpha. Until the time of their discovery by the Spanish conquistadors, there were probably about 15 species of these rats, measuring 8 to 20 inches (20 to 50 cm) in length and weighing up to 22 lb (10 kg), on the Greater Antilles and some neighboring Caribbean islands. They were already a popular source of protein among the natives and were heavily persecuted, which is the reason why we know of the existence of some species only from bone remnants found in ancient fire sites. Most of the primitive rodents had been able to survive in remote refugia, but

Left: The sounds made by prairie dogs, several subspecies of which inhabit the prairie regions of North America, resemble the barking of small dogs.

Below: Like the prairie dogs, the marmots also belong to the order of rodents. They live principally in burrows in mountainous and steppe regions.

when Europeans came to the islands with dogs, cats, rats, mice, and later, even with mongooses, further species died out.

All hutias are threatened

Of the original 15 species of hutia, only 7 are nowadays seen from time to time. Some of them are now so rare that even occasional reports of sightings are considered to be strokes of luck. The entire hutia family is threatened, with five species classified on the Red List as endangered. Only few studies about their life in the wild are available, and hardly anything is known about their social and reproductive behavior, so there is the risk that further species will become extinct before steps can be taken to save them.

ALPINE MARMOT

Marmots (*Marmota*) form a genus of their own within the squirrel family, comprising 13 species in Europe, Asia, and North America. The threat status of the various species differs: the woodchuck (*Marmota monax*) is now so common in Canada and the United States that it is considered a pest; the status of other species is far worse.

One relatively well-known representative of this genus is the Alpine marmot (*Marmota marmota*), which lives above the tree line at heights up to 10,000 feet (3,000 meters) in the Alps, the Carpathians, and the High Tatras, and

feeds on herbs and grasses. It has a head-rump length of 16 to 20 inches (40 to 50 cm), and its tail measures 4–8 inches (10–20 cm). It weighs 6½ lb (3 kg), but its weight fluctuates seasonally and can double prior to hibernation.

Disastrous folk beliefs

Alpine marmots have never been particularly widespread, but in the past they were seen frequently. Hunting and, in folk medicine, a belief in the healing powers of rendered-down marmot fat—so-called marmot oil—for people with rheumatism and other joint disorders, led to their being persecuted heavily and eradicated in some areas.

PRAIRIE DOGS

Another member of the squirrel family is the North American prairie dog (*Cynomys*): the vast prairies of North America were originally— quite literally—riddled with five species of prairie dog. These animals, measuring about 12 inches (30 cm) in length, live in extensive underground systems of tunnels and caves in large social groups, which have developed a sophisticated warning system.

Poisoning campaign against prairie dogs

Prairie dogs were almost eradicated in the early twentieth century: because they were eating

their way through entire fields and destroying harvests, the U.S. government launched a poisoning campaign, to which about 99 percent of the animals fell victim. Most species have now recovered again, the most threatened among them being the Mexican prairie dog (*Cynomys mexicanus*), which is on the Red List as endangered.

Above: Prairie dogs are diurnal animals, spending the nights in their underground burrows.

Below: The hutias from the Caribbean region are a very primitive family. Nowadays they are highly endangered, and it is questionable whether they will be able to survive.

RODENTIA
BEAVERS

Unlike most other rodents, beavers (Castoridae) are generally well loved by humans—they are the national animal of Canada. They are semi-aquatic rodents and their tree-felling and dam-building activities make them less popular with foresters, however, which, in the case of the Eurasian beaver (Castor fiber), was one of several reasons for its virtual eradication.

Outstanding adaptation

Eurasian beavers can attain a weight of 65 lb (30 kg) and a length of up to 3 feet (1 meter). They are preordained for a life in and around water by their spindle-shaped bodies and short, sturdy legs; their hind feet are webbed. The flat, club-shaped, scaly tail is used in the water to power and steer the animal.

Beavers are renowned for their dams made of mud and stones, as well as for their lodges, built from branches gnawed from trees that they have felled themselves and, in some cases, transported over long distances.

Below: A beaver's thick pelt protects it from the cold and wet.

In contrast to rats and mice, the beaver is a rodent that is truly popular with most people.

Beavers do not hibernate. They live on stockpiled reserves of food, which they can find beneath layers of ice.

Recovery of populations

The Eurasian beaver used to be widespread in river meadows and on the banks of rivers and lakes in North America, Europe, and Asia. However, they were heavily hunted not only because of the damage they caused to commercial forests, but also for their thick pelts, tasty meat, and beaver fat, which was popularly used in folk medicine for its alleged healing powers.

The beaver was eradicated from large parts of its original range quite early on—it disappeared from the United Kingdom as early as the twelfth century, and from Italy in the sixteenth century. By the end of the nineteenth century, there were scarcely any beavers left in large parts of Europe, but intensive reintroduction programs have since had some success: beaver lodges and dams can now once again be admired in several countries. Today, the Eurasian beaver is protected under the Convention on the Conservation of European Wildlife and Natural Habitats.

RODENTIA
HAMSTERS

The family of cricetids (Cricetidae) includes the subfamily of hamsters (Cricetinae), whose range stretches in the Northern Hemisphere from Europe eastward as far as China; only one hamster genus occurs in the Southern Hemisphere, in South Africa. These mouse-to-rat-sized animals, with their cylindrical bodies, are outstandingly well adapted to their way of life and to moving around in the underground tunnels they dig.

GOLDEN HAMSTER

The golden hamster (*Mesocricetus auratus*), popular these days as a pet, was thought to be extinct when, in 1930, an expedition in Syria found a female with 12 young, brought it to Israel, and bred the animals there. Practically all the golden hamsters which are now kept as pets or as laboratory animals are descended from this litter.

The animal has also survived thus far in the wild. Because the natural habitat of this 6- to 7-inch-long (15- to 18-cm-long) desert dweller is restricted to the Aleppo plateau, it is listed on the Red List as endangered.

COMMON HAMSTER

The common hamster (*Cricetus cricetus*), which occurs only in central Europe, can reach up to 12 inches (30 cm) in length. It is considered to be aggressive, which is also the reason why, unlike other hamster species, it cannot be tamed.

Until the 1970s, common hamsters were still common, but since then, populations have declined very sharply across the whole of central Europe because of increasing cultivation and the consolidation of agricultural land holdings. It is now classified, at least in some regions, as vulnerable, and, in others, even as critically endangered. In many places, there are now breeding and release programs to ensure the survival of the common hamster.

A characteristic feature of the hamster is the cheek pouches running along the lower jaw, which are used for transporting food.

RODENTIA
CHINCHILLAS

The family of chinchillas (Chinchillidae) includes, in addition to mountain viscachas (Lagidium spp.) and plains viscachas (Lagostomus maximus), true chinchillas (Chinchilla spp.), which are now widely familiar as pets, as well as being reared for their fur.

Frugal rodents

True chinchillas are crepuscular and nocturnal rodents that live in rock crevices or in burrows that they have dug themselves, in the High Andes in western South America. There are two species: the long-tailed chinchilla (*Chinchilla lanigera*), with a head-rump length of about 12 inches (30 cm) and a tail measuring 4 to 6 inches (10 to 15 cm) in length, and the short-

Fatal fur

Chinchillas were common in large areas of the Andes until the eighteenth century, when people began to cherish their long-haired pelts—they have about 60 hairs sprouting from each hair follicle which makes it extremely soft. This gave rise to a period of ruthless hunting that almost led to the eradication of chinchillas in the wild; and it is now probable that they

only occur in the Andes in northern Chile. Hunting chinchillas is now banned; to meet the demand for their silver-gray pelts, which are still extremely popular, the animals are bred in special farms, where the majority of these rodents now live. In the wild, there are scarcely any sizeable populations left, so the IUCN lists the long-tailed chinchilla as vulnerable and the short-tailed chinchilla as critically endangered.

tailed chinchilla (*Chinchilla brevicaudata*). Both species are frugal in terms of their dietary requirements.

Chinchillas are highly gregarious animals that live in large colonies in mountainous regions at elevations between 10,000 and 16,500 feet (3,000 and 5,000 meters).

CARNIVORA
BADGERS, OTTERS, WEASELS, AND RELATIVES

The badgers, otters, weasels, and their relatives (Mustelidae) belong to the suborder of caniform carnivores and are a species-rich family containing a wide variety of representatives, including the otters (Lutrinae spp.), the 13 or so species of which are distributed almost all over the world, being absent only in Oceania and on Madagascar.

Otters live mainly in fresh water

Otters lead a largely aquatic life. They mainly live in fresh water, but two species occur exclusively in salt water, the sea otter (*Enhydra lutris*) from North America, and the marine otter (*Lontra felina*) from South America.

Otters can stay underwater for eight to nine minutes and are outstanding swimmers and divers because they have evolved webbing between their toes and a slim, cylindrical body that is well adapted to moving in the water.

The largest representative

The giant otter (*Pteronura brasiliensis*), which lives in the Amazon, is one of the heaviest,

weighing 45 lb (20 kg), and, with a head-tail length of 6½ feet (2 meters), it is the largest mustelid. Unlike many other species, it is not a solitary creature, but lives and hunts in groups of up to 12 animals. The young, which usually number between one and four, are supervised

Above: Otters swim like seals, in that they steer by positioning their legs and use their long, powerful tails to propel themselves.

Below: Otters do not have a particularly thick insulating layer of fat; instead, the animals are protected from the cold by up to a million hairs.

and looked after communally; because the young animals have many enemies—from ocelots and jaguars to caimans, raptors, and large fish—this improves their chances of survival. However, their way of life cannot protect the otters from humans: the giant otter has been eradicated in many areas of its original range, and remaining populations are at risk as a result of biotope destruction, hunting, and poaching. It has been classified as endangered by the IUCN since the end of the 1990s.

The largest otter species is the amphibious giant otter, which lives on rivers in South America, and, because of the clearing of the rainforest, is deemed to be endangered.

On the verge of eradication

For their wellbeing and survival, otters need clean water, which should be as unspoiled as possible, and have natural, healthy fish stocks. For this reason, the destruction of biotopes in North America and in Europe has led to a very sharp decline in their numbers.

Another reason for the worldwide population collapse has been and continues to be relentless hunting: all otters have extremely well insulating and exceptionally fine fur, which is made into coats, hats, and cloaks. The threat has been exacerbated by the otters' relative fearlessness and tendency to approach human beings. They are extremely easy to hunt, being active through the day and highly inquisitive. Otters are also persecuted as fish predators and food competitors. The increasing pollution of waters with the environmental toxin PCB, heavy metals, artificial fertilizers, and pesticides has also contributed to the decimation of most otter species.

In the case of the Eurasian otter (*Lutra lutra*), water pollution even led to infertility in the species. Its rescue has been one of the all-too-infrequent success stories in wildlife conservation. As a result of the restoration of rivers to a natural state, the establishment of purification plants, and the banning of PCBs, the animals have finally been able to reproduce again. Numbers have increased gradually over the last 15 years, and today, populations are small but stable. In most countries in its range, the otter is still protected, and hunting is not permitted.

CARNIVORA
RED PANDA

Conservation status unclear

The red panda originally had no enemies, but it is now under extreme pressure from incursion by humans into even the most remote mountain forests. China and Nepal have rapidly growing human populations and their need for timber, fuel, and grazing land causes widespread losses of forested land that supports bamboo undergrowth. Moreover, although it is protected under CITES, it is still poached for its fur and for selling to zoos and animal parks.

As far as is known, most populations have declined sharply in the last 20 years. In 1996, the IUCN therefore reclassified the red panda from vulnerable to endangered. However, there is still a general uncertainty about the actual threat it is under because even experts are unable to provide reliable information on the total population. What is clear is that as long as the bamboo belt continues to be destroyed, then the species is in great danger, simply because of its specialized requirements in terms of habitat and food.

The red or lesser panda (Ailurus fulgens) is the only species in the family of lesser pandas (Ailuridae). It inhabits the bamboo belt in the eastern Himalaya between Nepal and the Chinese province of Sichuan and lives at altitudes between 6,500 and 15,000 feet (2,000 and 4,500 meters).

Specialized bamboo feeder

This animal, which is about 24 inches (60 cm) long and has a tail of about the same length, is a first-rate climber, far happier in the highest treetops and at the top of bamboo groves than on the ground. It spends its days sleeping in trees. At dusk, it sets out to look for food, which, to a substantial extent, consists of bamboo shoots but also of berries, fruit, mushrooms, roots, acorns, lichen, and grasses. It is known to supplement its diet with young birds, fishes, eggs, small rodents, and insects on occasion.

Above: The lesser or red panda is sometimes called the red cat-bear, and it does show many cat-like behavioral characteristics, especially with regard to grooming.

Left: Red pandas generally lead solitary lives, only coming together to mate.

The red panda is considered a threatened species.

CARNIVORA
BEARS

The family of bears (Ursidae), which belongs to the suborder of caniform carnivores, includes the largest land predators on Earth. They are mainly distributed in the Northern Hemisphere; there are no bears in Africa or Australia. Most species are omnivores that can adapt their diet to a wide variety of circumstances, depending on the season. Bears are also generalists when it comes to habitats: depending on the species, they are found in Arctic regions, in mountains and grassy plains, and in tropical rainforests.

SPECTACLED BEAR

The spectacled bear (*Tremarctos ornatus*) is the only species in the subfamily of Tremarctinae or short-faced bears, and it is also the only bear in South America. During the ice age, the ancestors of this relatively small bear, with a head-rump length of about 4¼ feet (1.3 meters), were widely distributed across North and South America, but today, this species, also known as the Andean bear after its range, lives alone or in small families at elevations of 5,000 to 8,000 feet (1,500 to 2,500 meters) in humid forests in Colombia, Venezuela, Peru, Ecuador, and Bolivia.

The spectacled bear is a good climber; it not only builds sleeping nests in trees, but also often searches in trees for food. Although it is predominantly herbivorous, in rare cases, it attacks sheep, cattle, or llamas; for this reason, as well as for its fur and its meat, it is still hunted today.

The IUCN classifies it as vulnerable—hunting and advancing cultivation of its habitats have rendered it a threatened species.

Above: The only large bear on the South American continent is the spectacled bear. It got its name from the white markings on its black face.

Right: As the smallest and lightest members of the bear family, spectacled bears are excellent climbers that live in the subtropical and tropical high alpine rainforests of the Andes.

Heavily persecuted at all times

People have always treated bears with great respect as is reflected by the role of the bear in many folk tales—and with good reason: although these animals normally avoid humans, when they do meet, even if it is accidentally, bears present a serious danger. Even now, people are still dying from attacks by bears that see themselves, their young, or their prey or food stores as being in danger.

Bear attacks on people have always been a justification for the wholesale hunting of these animals, but they have also been relentlessly persecuted for other reasons: they have been seen as competitors robbing humans of their food—grazing animals, fish, and honey—and they have been killed for their flesh and fur as well as their claws and teeth, which are made into ornaments. The Asiatic species, in particular, have suffered from the fact that traditional Chinese medicine attributes healing powers to certain body parts of the bear, notably their gallbladders and bile. Furthermore, at times there has also been a flourishing trade in live animals, which were sold as dancing bears, for bear fights, or to zoos.

The hunting problem is compounded by the settlement and destruction of their range by humans.

BROWN BEAR

The most widely distributed bears are the members of the genus *Ursus* in the subfamily Ursinae. The best-known species is the brown bear (*Ursus arctos*), several subspecies of which range from Europe and Asia to North America. These bears increase markedly in size and weight in Eurasia from west to east and in North America from south to north. Thus, the Alpine bears and their relatives from the Abruzzo and the Carpathians are not very large or heavy, with a head-rump length of about 5½ feet (1.7 meters) and a weight of 150 lb (70 kg), whereas bears in Scandinavia and Russia, with an overall length of about 7½ feet (2.2 meters) and a weight of 550 to 660 lb (250 to 300 kg), are considerably more powerful. However, the subspecies in North America are even larger.

Just as varied as their sizes are brown bears' habitats, food, and even fur color. For example, the Himalayan brown bear (*Ursus arctos isabellinus*) from the Himalaya is sand-colored, the Syrian brown bear (*Ursus arctos syriacus*) from the Middle East is light brown, and the Kodiak bear (*Ursus arctos middendorffi*) from Alaska is very dark, almost black.

In the Yukon Territory, on the border between Canada and Alaska, grizzlies can be seen catching salmon in late summer.

Many endangered subspecies of brown bear

Although the species as a whole is not considered to be immediately threatened, brown bears are listed on the Red List as potentially threatened, and stocks of numerous subspecies are threatened. Many populations were eradicated long ago: the last brown bear in the United Kingdom was killed in the tenth century; the last one in Germany, in the nineteenth century; and not much later, the last one in Switzerland. Only relict populations remain today in western and central Europe. The same is true of the brown bear subspecies of North America, including the grizzly (*Ursus arctos horribilis*), numbers of which have been decimated, leaving just small populations in the northwest. The Syrian brown bear, too, has been almost eradicated, and the total population of the Himalayan brown bear, which is endangered due to poaching, is estimated at 600 to 800 animals.

Above: Young brown bears are very playful and can climb up trees—something adult bears are unable to do because of their weight.

Below: A brown bear in the Bavarian Forest National Park, which, although it is resting, is keeping a sharp eye on its surroundings.

AMERICAN AND ASIATIC BLACK BEARS

The genus *Ursus* includes two species of black bear: the American black bear (*Ursus americanus*) and the Asiatic black bear (*Ursus thibetanus*). The American species is relatively small, with a shoulder height of about 3 feet (90 cm), and is found in many areas of the United States, Canada, and Alaska. It is not currently considered to be immediately threatened; on the contrary, it is one of the most common bear species. However, because the American black bear is heavily hunted, for the same reasons as other bears, and is losing parts of its habitat, some of its populations are deemed to be threatened and are under strict protection regionally.

In contrast, its somewhat larger Asiatic relative, which inhabits large swathes of

Left: The smallest bear of all, the Malayan sun bear, is tolerated close to human settlements. Little is known about its numbers, but it is protected.

Below: The sloth bear is heavily hunted for its bile, to which healing powers are ascribed.

In some parts of its original range, the North American black bear has already been eradicated or is severely threatened.

the continent that gives it its name, from Afghanistan through Nepal and Tibet as far as China and South Asia, is listed by the IUCN as vulnerable, and some subspecies are on the brink of eradication. Because traditional Chinese medicine attributes healing powers to its bile, many animals are caught and kept in abysmal conditions so that bear bile can be extracted.

SLOTH BEAR

The sloth bear (*Melursus ursinus*) lives in India and Sri Lanka, and also in Bangladesh, Bhutan, and Nepal, where it is less common. They are the most nocturnal of bears, although sows with cubs will move in daylight. With a head-rump length between 4½ and 6 feet (1.4 and

1.8 meters) and a shoulder height up to 3 feet (90 cm), it is not particularly terrifying, but the local inhabitants have a lot of respect for it. It is considered highly aggressive, probably because it has poor hearing and eyesight, often only seeing a person approaching at the last minute, and then attacking out of fright. Habitat loss and heavy hunting, in particular, for medicinal purposes, have caused the numbers of this once-common animal to dwindle. The global population is estimated at 7,000 to 10,000, and the species is considered vulnerable.

MALAYAN SUN BEAR

Another Asiatic species of the *Ursus* genus is the nocturnal sun bear (*Helarctos malayanus* or *Ursus malayanus*), from the tropical rainforests

of Southeast Asia. Standing with a maximum shoulder height of 28 inches (70 cm), it is even smaller than the sloth bear. It is a solitary animal, but little else is known of its behavior in the wild, and its threat status is also difficult to assess. The IUCN included it on the Red List, but, due to deficient data on population numbers, made no assessment of the level of the threat to it until 2008 when it was assessed as "vulnerable." It is protected under CITES and in all probability, the Indian population is already extinct, and the Chinese population is on the brink. It is safe to assume that these will not be the only ones, as long as forests continue to be cleared on such a large scale and animals continue to be poached, for, among other reasons, medicinal purposes.

POLAR BEAR

The polar bear (*Ursus maritimus*) is the second-largest land predator after the Kodiak bear and, like the latter, belongs to the genus *Ursus*. Its habitat comprises the Arctic regions around the North Pole.

It is approximately 8 feet (2.5 meters) long, stands 5¼ feet (1.6 meters) high at the shoulder, and weighs from 1,000 to 1,200 lb (450 to 500 kg), although the animals are generally heavier in the winter, during the seal hunting season, than in the summer. The colorless coat not only provides optimal camouflage, but also, in combination with a thick layer of fat, has an insulating effect.

Seal hunting

These solitary, diurnal animals keep predominantly to the coastal fringes or the pack ice, where they also go hunting for seals. Although polar bears are very good swimmers, they rarely hunt underwater, but prefer to lie in wait for their prey at their breathing holes in the ice and grab them as soon as they surface for air. They have an outstanding sense of smell and can scent their prey in the water or even under the ice.

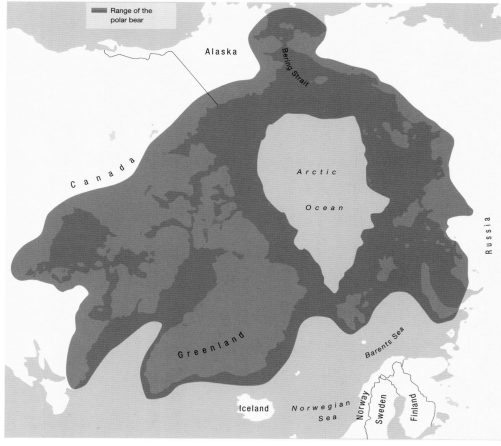

Below: Polar bear cubs, whose greatest enemies are adult males, are suckled by their mothers for 1½ to 2½ years. During this time, she teaches them to hunt.

Above: The polar bear's range is circumpolar, i.e. over the pack ice and the permanent ice around the North Pole and neighboring regions in Europe, Asia, and North America.

Polar bears suffering from global warming and environmental pollution

Polar bears have always been hunted by indigenous peoples for fur and food, but this never posed a threat. The situation changed when, among other things, numerous trophy hunters began hunting, or at least locating, the animals from airplanes in the mid-twentieth century. Numbers fell dramatically, prompting various countries to impose hunting restrictions and later, an extensive hunting ban. These measures have been effective: the estimated total population has increased from between 5,000 and 10,000 to between 20,000 and 25,000 animals today.

Nevertheless, the IUCN considers the polar bear to be vulnerable and is working on the assumption that numbers will soon begin to decline again, citing as factors the increasing extraction of oil and gas in the Arctic regions as well as global warming, which is causing the ice to melt and therefore reducing the polar bear's range.

Polar bears are not only outstanding swimmers, but also can roam long distances without tiring.

The polar bear's paws each have five claws, and the soles of its feet are covered with thick hair so that they do not slip on smooth ice too easily.

Young polar bears at play are building their body strength and learning to fight to survive.

Polar bears are suffering from global warming, which is causing the ice either to melt or to become so thin that it can no longer take the weight of these heavy animals.

Polar bears are solitary creatures. Where there is a plentiful supply of food, short-term feeding communities may form, but these have no social significance.

Famed for being endangered

The giant panda, the total population of which is estimated at about 2,000 animals, is listed on the Red List as endangered, and it is one of the most threatened large animals. As such, it was chosen by the World Wildlife Fund (WWF) as its emblem, and is now internationally known and recognized, as well as being a symbol for the protection of threatened animal species. As a result, the giant panda has acquired worldwide fame for being endangered.

Until the end of the last ice age, the giant panda still lived in large areas of eastern China and Myanmar, but when the climate began to change, so did the vegetation, and this, together with the increasing spread of humans into the panda's habitat, led to the decline of the species over time.

Eventually, only three separate populations survived, and these were drastically threatened by poaching for their fur and for the wildlife trade. The Chinese government recognized the danger and, as early as 1939, placed the giant panda under strict protection. However, numbers have continued to decline, one of the reasons being that poachers continue to hunt the animals despite heavy fines and additional protection through CITES.

Because increasing human population density means that the habitats are shrinking, the vegetation cannot recover quickly enough to provide adequate food for the giant pandas. Additionally, the fragmentation of its habitat means that animals from different areas seldom meet, leading to wide-scale genetic impoverishment, which, in turn, leads to high rates of mortality.

The successful breeding of offspring in zoological gardens is rare, even in Chinese protected areas with breeding stations, despite the use of artificial insemination. In any case, it is currently questionable whether it is possible to release pandas raised by people into their natural habitat; the first attempt in 2006 failed despite a three-year period spent preparing the panda for life in the wild and it was found dead a few months later after fighting with wild-born males.

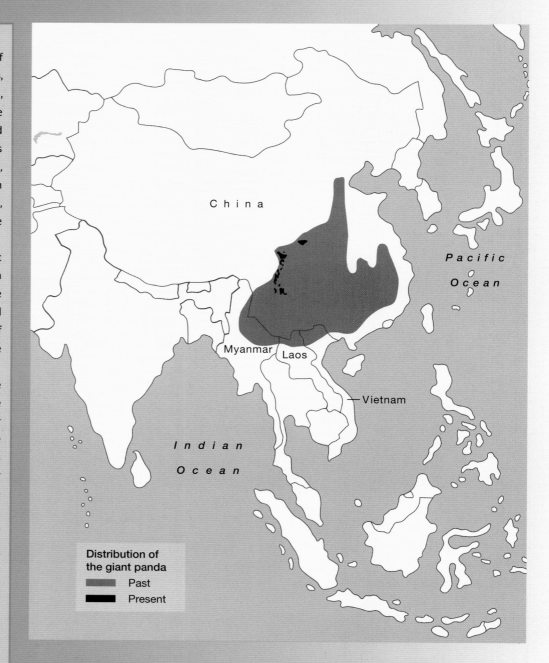

Distribution of the giant panda
■ Past
■ Present

GIANT PANDA

The giant panda (*Ailuropoda melanoleuca*), like all other bears, is a caniform carnivore, but is now classified as the only extant species in a different subfamily called Ailuropodinae. The giant panda was unknown in the West for a long time, and the arrival of the first live panda in Europe (London) in the mid-1930s caused an absolute sensation.

Very exacting habitat and food requirements

Pandas, which are crepuscular and nocturnal, are today found only in a mountainous region of eastern China that covers approximately 2,275 square miles (5,900 km²). They are ground dwellers but can climb and swim well. Their diet consists predominantly of bamboo—they

The habitat of the giant panda has shrunk dramatically in comparison to its former range. The primary causes are thought to be human influences and climate change.

prefer the shoots—but they also eat other plants and, occasionally, small animals. The daily nutritional needs of these animals, which are up to 5 feet (1.5 meters) in length and weigh on average 175 lb (80 kg), are, like those of all herbivores, high, rising to as much as 45 lb (20 kg) of vegetation.

Reproduction

Pandas are solitary, relatively intolerant animals that come together only to mate. After a five- to six-month gestation period, they give birth, usually to a single cub, but sometimes to two or even three. However, the mother will only raise

Giant pandas, which are sometimes known as bamboo bears, are extreme food specialists, feeding predominantly on the shoots of certain bamboo species.

One of the largest protected areas for the giant panda, which acts simultaneously as a research and breeding station, is the Wolong Valley in China.

For reasons that are still unknown, a relatively large number of the youngsters die, so the reproductive rate of the giant panda is very low.

one youngster; in the case of a multiple birth, she will choose one of them.

Young pandas are tiny and undeveloped, weighing only 3 to 4½ ounces (90 to 130 grams), and have only sparse hair growth. The typical black-and-white fur markings do not appear until after they are one month old. After 40 to 60 days, they open their eyes, and at five to six months—when they weigh 11 lb (5 kg)—the cubs take their first solid food. Adult pandas are capable of reproducing when they are about five years old.

Giant pandas are solitary, sometimes very aggressive, creatures, tolerating the company of other members of the same species only during the mating season.

CARNIVORA
DOGS

There are almost 170 species of the dog family (Canidae), from the order of carnivores, distributed worldwide. They have certain external characteristics in common; for example, they can all run fast and untiringly, they have a slender, muscular body and generally long legs with small paws. Their powerful claws (with one exception, they have five on the forepaws and four on the hind paws) cannot be retracted. The skull is, in most cases, elongated with a pointed snout, the ears are triangular and pointed, and the tail is bushy.

WOLVES

Wolves (*Canis lupus*) used to live in almost the whole of Eurasia, from the Arctic to the Mediterranean, and also in Arabia, the Middle East, India, and Japan, as well as in North America from the Arctic Circle down to Mexico. They have now been eradicated in many regions of western and central Europe, and in North America—where populations have also been exterminated locally—it has in many places been necessary to protect them or to reintroduce them.

Of the 15 or so subspecies, the taxonomy of which is still disputed, two have been eradicated: the Hokkaido wolf (*Canis lupus hattai*) and the Honshu wolf (*Canis lupus hodophilax*), from the Japanese islands of the same names. Other subspecies are threatened.

Regional variations in size

The animals increase in size and weight from south to north. An adult male from a northern population can reach a head-rump length of 5¼ feet (1.6 meters) and a weight of 175 lb (80 kg), but the small races from the Middle East and Arabia are only 32 inches (80 cm) long and weigh about 45 lb (20 kg).

People's fear of wolves is reflected in many adventure stories and fairy stories in which the animals are represented as fearsome predators, wild beasts, or cruel hunters.

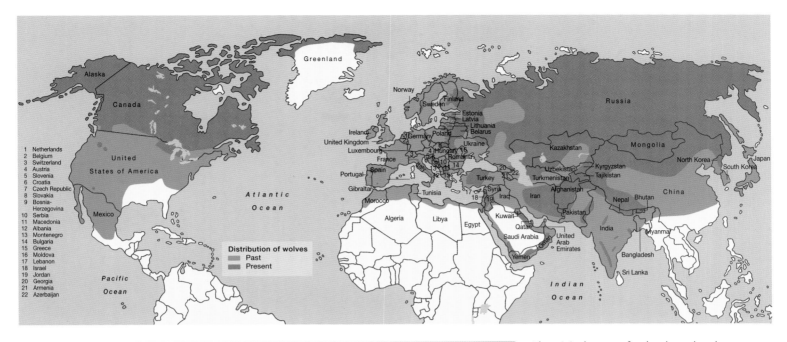

The original ranges of wolves have shrunk enormously over time. Some subspecies have already been eradicated.

Above: Wolves are pack animals with strict hierarchies and rules. They treat one another affectionately and help sick pack members.

Below: The eastern timber wolf, which was once distributed across North America, is only found today in the eastern U.S. and in southeastern Canada.

Eradicated out of fear

Humans are the wolf's only serious enemy and have brought it to the brink of eradication. The wolf has been hunted for its pelt and its skin, but this is not the main reason for its persecution.

Early sedentary peoples hunted it not only as a cattle predator, but also because they felt that their own lives were threatened by wolves. Later, fear of these animals increased, culminating in reports of alleged attacks on people by whole packs of wolves—something that seems unlikely because wolves do not usually attack people. Regardless of the truth of their content, such stories fanned the flames of people's fears, giving birth to many folk tales representing wolves as bloodthirsty man-killers, thus contributing to ruthless hunting aimed at eradicating them.

Although people in southern and eastern Europe tolerated the animals to a certain extent, they were persecuted intensely in large areas of western and central Europe, where they were eradicated in the eighteenth century. Since about 1990, however, wolves from countries to the southeast, and particularly from the countries to the east, have started to come back to central Europe, including to Germany, Austria, and Switzerland.

Above: Hated, persecuted, maligned, and almost eradicated—the African wild dog. It is also very susceptible to diseases that are spread by domestic dogs.

AFRICAN WILD DOG

One African representative of the dog family is the mottled African wild dog or Cape hunting dog (*Lycaon pictus*). It lives in groups of 6 to 10 animals in the savannas south of the Sahara and is very reliant on social contact and the company of members of the same species. A pack is led by an alpha pair, which are the only animals to have the privilege of rearing young. After a gestation period of about 70 days, the female normally gives birth to six to eight pups, which the whole pack helps to bring up,

The scientific name for the African wild dog, *Lycaon pictus*, means "painted wolf," which is no accident.

just as all the animals join in looking after old, wounded, or sick pack members.

Because wild dogs seize domestic animals, they are subject to widespread persecution by farmers and hunters. Populations have also been decimated by diseases of dogs, such as canine distemper and rabies, with the result that there are now only between 3,000 and 5,000 animals remaining, which, due to their insular distribution, are additionally threatened by illness and inbreeding. The species is classified on the Red List as endangered.

DHOLE

The red dog or Asiatic wild dog or dhole (*Cuon alpinus*), not to be confused with the severely endangered red wolf (*Canis rufus*) from North America, lives in a variety of climate zones in Asia, being found both in mountainous steppes and in forests. Because of the destruction of its habitat and diseases passed on by domestic animals, the total population is estimated at only 2,500 animals, and the IUCN lists the species as endangered.

ETHIOPIAN WOLF

The rarest wild dog is the Ethiopian wolf (*Canis simensis*). Its main range is the Bale Mountains National Park in the Ethiopian highlands,

Right: The 11 subspecies of dhole that occur in Asia and on the Southeast Asian islands are considered to be endangered.

where it hunts—principally rats and mice—at elevations between 10,000 and 13,000 feet (3,000 and 4,000 meters). Increasing cultivation of its habitat and, in particular, diseases such as rabies, have caused a rapid decline in the population; the number of these endangered animals remaining in the wild is estimated to be just 700 individuals.

MANED WOLF

The South American maned wolf (*Chrysocyon brachyurus*), whose main range lies in the savannas of southern Brazil and Paraguay, is a quite special wolf. Its lifestyle distinguishes it from all other wolves because it lives not in packs, but in pairs, with males and females in the same territory even hunting alone during the day outside the mating season.

Maned wolves feed predominantly on small animals and insects, also occasionally on fruit; nonetheless, they are persecuted as food competitors for their alleged killing of farm animals such as sheep and cows, although, because of their dentition, they are incapable of killing or eating larger animals. The maned wolf has now disappeared from Argentina and Uruguay and is on the verge of eradication in many areas where there is a dense cattle population.

Below: The long-legged maned wolf now lives mainly in the savannas of southern Brazil. Habitat loss means that it will soon face immediate threat.

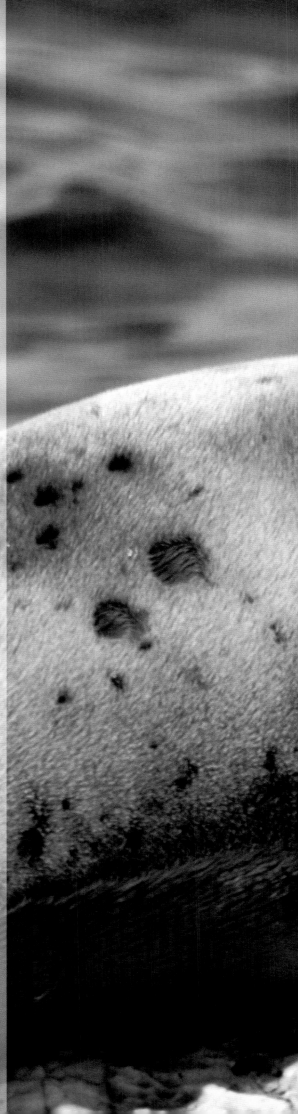

CARNIVORA
SEALS AND WALRUSES

The seal species, of which there are almost three dozen, belong to the superfamily of dog-like carnivores (Canoidea) and are divided into three families: eared seals (Otaridae), true seals (Phocidae), and walruses (Odobenidae). They live—sometimes in huge colonies—in all the world's oceans, but prefer the polar and subpolar regions. From an evolutionary point of view, the pinnipeds (Pinnipedia) are descended from bear-like land predators that made their way back into the water between 25 and 30 million years ago. Fossil finds show that they probably originated in the western North Pacific.

WALRUSES

The family of walruses consists of just one species with two subspecies, the Atlantic walrus and the Pacific walrus (*Odobenus rosmarus rosmarus* and *Odobenus rosmarus divergens*). Its range is restricted to the Arctic and subarctic latitudes of the Northern Hemisphere, where the animals live either in coastal regions or in the pack-ice belt, depending on the season. They are highly gregarious and form colonies that may comprise hundreds of animals.

Below: Walruses use the bristles, which number up to 500, on their upper lips to sense and distinguish their prey in the murky depths.

Heavily hunted for their ivory

As long as only the Inuit were killing walruses for their personal needs, populations remained stable and unendangered. The situation changed when European hunters advanced into their remote habitats and hunted the walruses for their tusks made of ivory. Hundreds of thousands of animals were killed, resulting in the wholesale collapse of populations that had once numbered in the millions of animals.

The Atlantic subspecies, in particular, was on the brink of eradication and has never recovered from these campaigns of destruction. The Pacific walrus, which was almost as heavily depleted, fared much better after the introduction of protection provisions by the United States and Russia: there are now an estimated 200,000 animals once more, whereas the total population of the Atlantic walrus stands at only about 15,000. It is uncertain whether populations will recover in future because the habitat of the walrus is shrinking, and its prey becoming less abundant. It is also probable that they will be affected by the consequences of global warming.

Powerful animals with huge appetites

Walruses are powerful animals: the males can reach up to 11 feet (3.3 meters) in length and weigh 3,300 lb (1,500 kg), the females being smaller and lighter. In keeping with their size, walruses need substantial amounts of food, requiring up to 110 lb (50 kg) daily. Their diet consists largely of mollusks, but they also eat crabs, shrimps, snails, sea cucumbers, squid, and, more rarely, even seals. During their forays for prey they dive to depths of up to 300 feet (100 meters) and can stay underwater for up to half an hour.

BAIKAL SEAL

The Baikal seal (*Pusa sibirica*), from the family of eared seals, is the only seal species that lives exclusively in fresh water, in Lake Baikal in Siberia. In the first half of the twentieth century, it was close to eradication, but it initially recovered from heavy hunting. Sadly, in the last 10 years, the threat to it has intensified once more: populations are declining again because the animals are still being legally hunted, and, in addition, are suffering from diseases transmitted by domestic animals as well as from pollution of the lake with toxins.

HARP SEAL

The press often focuses on the harp seal (*Pagophilus groenlandicus*, previously *Phoca groenlandica*), which has achieved notoriety through its annual massacre by seal hunters,

Left: The Baikal seal has adapted to life in fresh water. It is endemic to Lake Baikal in southern Siberia.

Young harp seals wear the coveted soft fur for only about 20 days.

Fatal fur

The problem for many eared seals is their valuable and exceptionally fine fur, from which coats, jackets, shoes, and wallets are manufactured and, because of which, they have long been persecuted intensively. In many cases, their numbers have been so severely depleted that their populations have dwindled everywhere. Commercial fishers kill these alleged food competitors, and large numbers of eared seals become entangled in long dragnets and driftnets, in which they eventually drown because they can no longer surface to breathe. The pollution of the oceans is also contributing to their decline, and the melting ice masses at the poles are likely to have a negative effect on populations of seal species in the near future.

To avoid damage to the precious pelts with bullet holes, the "seal slaughterers," as they are called, bludgeon these trusting creatures to death with clubs and then skin them.

who slaughter hundreds of thousands of baby seals for their soft white fur. Large proportions of the year's offspring were often killed, which resulted in worryingly sharp declines in populations. Public protests by conservationists and animal rights protesters eventually led, at the end of the 1980s, not only to the collapse of the seal fur market, but also to the Canadian government's extensive ban on seal hunting. Because the seals allegedly present a threat to fish stocks, about 300,000 animals continue to be killed each year (subject to strict regulatory requirements), which inflicts massive damage on populations.

The natural phenomenon of El Niño causes fluctuations in the food supply of the threatened Galapagos sea lion (*Zalophus wollebaeki*), which has a direct effect on populations.

Above: On the Falkland Islands, a blackish cinclodes (*Cinclodes antarcticus*) frees a southern elephant seal (*Mirounga leonina*) from irritating parasites.

ELEPHANT SEAL

The largest and heaviest seals of all are the elephant seals, of which there are two geographically separate populations: the northern elephant seal (*Mirounga angustirostris*) lives in the North Pacific, and the southern elephant seal (*Mirounga leonina*), around the Antarctic. The bulls of the latter species grow up to 16 feet (5 meters) in length and 11,000 lb (5,000 kg) in weight. Both species of elephant seal were on the brink of eradication but are no longer considered to be immediately threatened. However, the population of the southern elephant seal is declining by 5–10 percent annually, for unknown reasons. Moreover, both populations will probably have problems in the long term because of a lack of genetic diversity, which will make adapting to changing climatic conditions more difficult.

EARED SEALS

The family of eared seals comprises about 16 species, of which just under half are considered to be immediately threatened. One of the rarest is the Guadalupe fur seal (*Arctocephalus townsendi*), of which no more than 2,000 specimens have survived, together with the Juan Fernandez fur seal (*Arctocephalus philippii*), numbering about 6,000 individuals, and the Galapagos fur seal (*Arctocephalus galapagoensis*), with between 10,000 and 15,000 specimens—these species are all classified by the IUCN as vulnerable. The survival of the Australian sea lion (*Neophoca cinerea*), numbers of which are estimated at between 3,000 and 4,000 animals, and of the New Zealand sea lion (*Phocarctos hookeri*), is also considered uncertain.

CARNIVORA
HYENAS

The four extant species of hyena appear to resemble the caniforms, but are assigned to the feliform carnivores (Feloidea), where they form the family of hyenas (Hyaenidae). Their distribution is almost exclusively confined to Africa: only the striped hyena (Hyaena hyaena) is also found on the Arabian Peninsula and the countries between eastern Turkey and India.

Not all species are carrion-eaters

Hyenas, which are predominantly nocturnal, had a bad reputation for hundreds of years, being decried as cunning carrion-eaters. These alleged pests were arbitrarily killed, so that, for a time, many populations declined severely. It was groundbreaking research in the 1960s in the Seregenti by the Dutch biologist Hans Kruuk on the spotted hyena (*Crocuta crocuta*), better known as the "laughing hyena" because one of its vocalizations resembles the sound of hysterical human laughter, that first put these animals in a new light: Kruuk established that these hyenas do not feed mainly on carrion, but are excellent hunters, which in packs can kill any animal up to the size of a wildebeest. He was also able to show that hyenas are responsible for the healthy balance of the large populations of ungulates in East and southern Africa, in that they mainly kill old and sick animals.

Two virtually unknown hyena species

Even African wildlife experts are seldom lucky enough to see a brown hyena (*Hyaena brunnea*) or an aardwolf (*Proteles cristatus*).

The brown hyena occurs only in southern Africa between Angola and the Cape. It is a poor hunter and feeds mainly on carcasses of all sizes. In rare cases, it captures a bird or a rodent. Because of the scarcity of food in the

The striped hyena leads a solitary life and exhibits no marked territorial behavior. Its vocal utterances are restricted to a gentle growl.

desert, the brown hyena sometimes adds fruit and vegetables to its diet.

The aardwolf occurs in two geographically separate populations, one in East and one in southern Africa, and is most likely to be seen in northern Namibia, particularly in the Etosha pan. It hides in a burrow during the day and comes out at night to search for food. It has strict dietary requirements, feeding exclusively on termite species living on the surface,

which it licks up in huge quantities. Its weak dentition would enable it neither to rip open the tough hide of an antelope nor to crack its bones.

Above: The aardwolf is usually solitary, but sometimes lives in pairs.

Below: The brown hyena lives in small family groups consisting of parents and their offspring.

Disagreement over the level of threat

Aardwolves and brown hyenas are included on the Red List merely as potentially threatened, not as immediately threatened, although the brown hyena was previously listed as vulnerable. The IUCN's appraisal of these two species was probably reached in the absence of meaningful studies. Conservationists who have been observing the aardwolf for decades are convinced that numbers are declining sharply due to hunting and habitat loss, and that these animals have even been wiped out locally. The situation is similar in the case of the brown hyena, for which there have been no studies of population levels since its reclassification over ten years ago. Experts are also certain that populations of striped hyenas are declining sharply, despite its large geographical range.

Only in the case of the spotted hyena does there seem to be broad agreement: it is considered to be the only species whose populations are currently neither locally nor generally endangered.

CARNIVORA
CATS

The cat family (Felidae) is generally divided into two subfamilies: small cats (Felinae) and big cats (Pantherinae). However, contrary to their names, these are not necessarily distinguishable from one another by their size. Rather, they are assigned to a subfamily according to different criteria; for example, small cats cannot roar, but purr when breathing in and out because their larynx is less developed than that of big cats, which can only produce a purr when breathing out.

SMALL CATS

This subfamily has a worldwide distribution, being absent only from the Oceanic and polar regions, and is considerably more species-rich than that of the large cats, with about 30 species. Small cats are predominantly nocturnal, shy, and solitary creatures. Their food consists largely of meat. They are, moreover, with the exception of the leopard, ambush hunters that can pursue their prey only over short distances.

LYNX

Lynxes (*Lynx*) are powerful animals. The males of the largest species, the Eurasian lynx (*Lynx lynx*), can reach up to 28 inches (70 cm) in height, 4 feet (1.2 meters) in length, and 75 lb (35 kg) in weight. There are two species in Eurasia and two in North America. Because of their magnificent winter coats, but also because, every now and then, they prey on domestic animals up to the size of a calf, lynxes have been persecuted intensely for centuries

and have been eradicated from large parts of their range.

Protection measures proving effective

Thanks to reintroductions and rigorous protection measures, they are now inhabiting parts of their former ranges again. Although the two North American species, the Canada lynx (*Lynx canadensis*) and the bobcat (*Lynx rufus*), are subjected to constant hunting pressure and increasing biotope destruction, they currently seem to be in little danger, unlike the Eurasian lynx, numbers of which have been heavily depleted. The most endangered is the Iberian lynx (*Lynx pardinus*), which is critically endangered and of which only tiny populations remain in Spain and—probably—Portugal.

LEOPARD

The situation also looks bad for representatives of the *Leopardus* genus, which are almost all listed on the Red List as immediately threatened. The best-known small cat in this genus is the ocelot (*Leopardus pardalis*), an inhabitant of dense forests between the southernmost U.S. states and northern Argentina. It was mercilessly hunted for its magnificent spotted coat, and in some places it has been eradicated or is teetering on the brink; in Texas, for example, there are only about 100 animals left. Because the trade in their skins

Facing page: A Eurasian lynx in the Bavarian Forest National Park. Its range used to stretch from Spain to the Urals and on to the coast of the East China Sea. It has now been eradicated in many regions.

is now regulated under CITES, the main threat they face today is habitat loss.

COUGAR

The cougar (*Puma concolor*), also known as the mountain lion, puma, or panther, is the heaviest of the small cats—adult males can reach a weight between 175 and 220 lb (80 and 100 kg). Cougars are able to bring down larger prey, such as tapirs or capybaras, and even domestic cattle. This has led to widespread persecution and the threat of eradication from many areas of their range in South America and western North America. In the United States, they have been chased with dogs and forced up trees, where they can easily be shot down. Cougars remain only in sparsely populated and some protected areas; several subspecies have already been eradicated, and others, like the Florida panther (*Puma concolor coryi*), of which there are a maximum of 100 animals left in the wild, are threatened with the same fate.

Above: A young cougar stays with its mother for about 20 months. After this period, cougars are solitary, coming together only to mate.

Center: Although the cougar creeps up on its prey and then generally reaches it in one mighty leap, it can run very fast over short distances.

Below: The beautifully marked ocelot from Central and South America has for a long time been hunted for its fur and has been eradicated from some regions.

CHEETAH

The slender, long-legged cheetahs (*Acinonyx jubatus*) of the African savanna are the fastest land mammals in the world: they can accelerate from a standstill to just over 60 mph (100 km/h) in four seconds, but can keep up this enormous speed only over a distance of about 200–300 yards (180–275 meters).

They have adapted their hunting behavior to suit their abilities: they creep as close as possible to their prey, making use of the slightest cover, such as clumps of grass, small termite mounds, or stones. If the potential prey looks up, they crouch to the ground and freeze; not until the victim is grazing again do they creep closer, to a distance between 55 and 110 yards (50 and 100 meters). Then, the cats sprint, thereby optimizing their chances of success.

Below: It is thought that about 95 percent of young cheetahs do not survive the first year of life. Lions, leopards, and hyenas, as well as disease, claim countless victims.

Not food specialists

Unlike other cats, cheetahs have neither sharp claws nor powerful teeth, so they are scarcely able to bring down large antelopes or zebras. They have to content themselves with smaller prey—from mice, in hard times, through hares and young warthogs to Grant's gazelles and juvenile wildebeest. From time to time, a guinea fowl, francolin, or other ground-dwelling bird might also fall victim to them. They eat, on average, between 11 and 18 lb (5 and 8 kg) of meat at each meal.

Cheetahs must eat their prey as soon as possible after the kill because they are not strong enough to be able to defend it against other predators, such as leopards.

The cheetah's facial markings are characterized by the black stripes running from the eyes toward the mouth, so-called tear stripes.

Under threat for many reasons

The cheetah, which has now been classified as vulnerable, originally had an enormous range, stretching from southeastern Europe across Turkey, Iraq, and Iran as far as India and across large parts of Africa—except for the deserts and areas of virgin forests. Nowadays, large populations remain only in eastern and southwestern Africa, with total numbers being estimated at between 10,000 and 12,000; Namibia has the greatest population density, with between 2,500 and 5,000 specimens. In Iran, a relict population of the subspecies *Acinonyx jubatus raddei* leads an exceedingly threatened existence; it is thought that there are between 50 and 100 animals there.

The reasons for the decline in populations are manifold and, in part, have their roots far in the past. In the pre-Christian era, people were already making use of the outstanding hunting abilities of the cheetah and training them as hunting companions—some rulers allegedly kept up to 3,000 animals at their courts. The tradition was maintained at least into the Middle Ages, at European courts as well. The main reasons for the sharp decline in the cheetah populations, however, are the illegal, and sometimes legal, hunting of the animals for their skins and as food competitors, as well as progressive destruction and cultivation of their habitats, combined with a growing shortage of prey animals.

BIG CATS

The subfamily of big cats comprises nine species in three genera, including some of the best-known cats, such as the tiger (*Panthera tigris*) and the lion (*Panthera leo*). Big cats occur predominantly in Asia and Africa, although there is also one species distributed across the Americas.

TIGER

The tiger is the largest of the big cats. This mighty subspecies can reach a weight of about 660 lb (300 kg), a shoulder height of 3½ feet (1.1 meters), and a length of almost 12½ feet (3.8 meters), the tail alone measuring about 3 feet (1 meter). Females are considerably smaller and lighter. Tigers live in thick jungles,

in impenetrable bamboo forests, and in inaccessible swamps in Asia; in areas where they are largely undisturbed, for example, in Siberia and in Indian national parks, they are diurnal.

Solitary lifestyle

Like most cats, they are predominantly solitary, with the exception of females and their cubs. Males inhabit territories that can cover up to 1,500 square miles (4,000 km²) in places like Siberia and Manchuria, although they are much smaller on the Southeast Asian islands. The males' territories overlap, and encounters between males in the boundary areas are generally peaceful; people have even observed several males gathering together at a kill.

Hunters that stalk and ambush

There is hardly an animal in the world that an adult tiger cannot overcome. Not even fully grown wild cattle such as gaur, which can weigh between 880 and 1,100 lb (400 and 500 kg), are safe from these big cats, and young elephants can also fall victim to them.

Tigers are ambush hunters: they stalk as close as possible to their victim, wait for a suitable moment when the prey is not alert, and then leap at it and kill it with a bite to the throat or the nape of the neck. Sometimes tigers also follow their prey into water and kill it there. A tiger that has not eaten for a

All tigers are excellent swimmers and frequently spend time in the water. In this, they are different from most other cats.

Poor outlook for the future

The tiger once had a very wide distribution, extending from the Caspian Sea in the west as far as Siberia and Manchuria in the east and to India, Malaysia, and Indonesia in the south. Until the beginning of the twentieth century, there were still about 100,000 tigers from eight different subspecies roaming through their habitat, but now, although it is difficult to count tigers due to their elusive nature, it is thought that there are fewer than 5,000. Three subspecies are deemed extinct: the Caspian tiger (*Panthera tigris virgata*), the Javan tiger (*Panthera tigris sondaica*), and the Bali tiger (*Panthera tigris balica*). The surviving subspecies could follow them—in some cases, perhaps very soon—because populations have been decimated to a large extent.

About a hundred years ago, there were about 40,000 Bengal or Royal Bengal tigers (*Panthera tigris tigris*) living in India, Bangladesh, and Nepal, but nowadays, there are probably fewer than 3,000. It is estimated that there are now 1,500 specimens of the Indochinese tiger (*Panthera tigris corbetti*) remaining on the Southeast Asian mainland. However, it has been entirely or almost entirely eradicated in many countries. The situation is even grimmer for the Amur or Siberian tiger (*Panthera tigris altaica*): populations in the wild are thought to comprise about 200 animals, with a further 200 living in various zoos. The population of the Sumatran tiger (*Panthera tigris sumatrae*) is estimated at just 150 individuals, whereas it is thought that there are only 20 to 50 specimens of the South China tiger (*Panthera tigris amoyensis*) left alive—it will probably not be possible to save this species.

There are a variety of factors behind the critical situation facing the tiger. They are suffering from the spread of humans and the destruction of their habitat. Furthermore, the hunting by humans of many ungulates has reduced the numbers of potential prey animals to such an extent that many tigers have starved to death. Further enormous collapses in populations have been caused by intensive hunting of the tiger as a food competitor and man-eater, as well as for its valuable coat and other body parts, such as its penis and bones, which are much in demand in traditional Chinese medicine as cures for impotence. Even today, the tigers are still poached out of greed for profit, despite its being protected, including under CITES. A third reason now contributing to the fact that many subspecies will probably not be able to recover is the lack of genetic diversity, which makes adapting to changing living conditions difficult.

Despite protection measures (such as the setting up of protected areas), reintroductions into its original habitats, and breeding programs, it currently seems unlikely that it will be possible to save all the remaining subspecies from eradication.

long time can swallow 65 lb (30 kg) or more of meat in one meal; normally the tiger revisits the slaughtered prey at intervals of one to two days to eat some more, which makes it easy for people to kill tigers from a hide.

Man-eaters

In areas that they have to share with humans, tigers attack domestic animals and—in rare cases—also people. Some tigers have become

Right: The tiger subspecies that were previously widely distributed across Southeast Asia now live only in a few refugia in protected areas, such as national parks.

Below: The Siberian tiger, the largest living big cat, requires large quantities of meat. It often takes its prey to a remote spot to be able to eat it in peace.

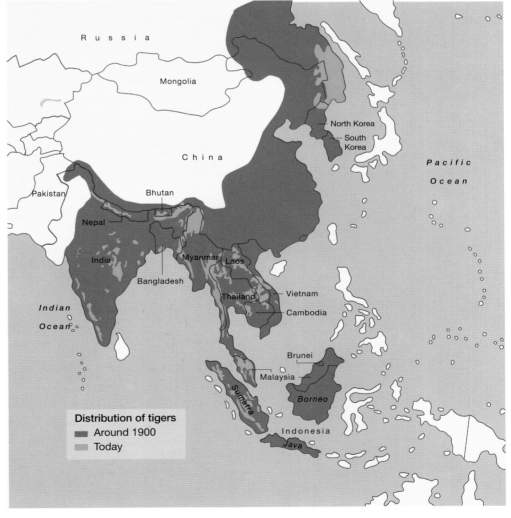

Distribution of tigers
- Around 1900
- Today

man-eaters because they were old or wounded and no longer able to hunt their natural prey, or because there was not enough prey available. In India and Bangladesh in the last century, man-eaters were still a problem that had villages and entire districts holding their breath; in India, in particular, there were some notorious man-eaters that killed over a hundred people before hunters managed to bring them down.

Facing page: Although Bengal tigers have the largest populations of all tigers, their populations have also declined dramatically in recent years.

Below: The Sumatran tiger is considered to be the smallest representative of the species. There are probably now more living in zoological gardens than in the wild.

High mortality rate among young

The favorable climatic conditions in the tropical regions mean that tiger subspecies there, unlike those in Siberia, have no fixed mating season. Following a gestation period between 95 and 114 days, the female gives birth in a hiding place to two or three blind and helpless cubs weighing about 2 lb (1 kg) each. For the first eight weeks, they live purely on milk, and then they slowly begin to eat meat. They are weaned at six months at the latest, but they remain with their mother for at least another year to learn how to hunt.

Shortly before the tiger mother gives birth again, the previous cubs must leave the family and fend for themselves. Because they are still inexperienced and anything but accomplished hunters, the mortality rate among young animals is high; some starve, and others are wounded by powerful prey such as wild boar.

Above: Like all other tigers, the Bengal or Royal Bengal tiger prefers habitats close to water.

Below: An Indochinese tiger cub in the virgin forests of Southeast Asia.

LION

Next to the tiger, the lion (*Panthera leo*) is the best known of all the big cats. No other wild animal is so deeply embedded in human consciousness: it is encountered, for example, in symbolism, sagas, proverbs, and metaphors.

Pronounced sexual dimorphism

With a head-rump length of up to 8 feet (2.5 meters) and weighing about 485 lb (220 kg), the lion is the largest and heaviest cat after the tiger. It is the only big cat, and one of the few cat species at all, to exhibit pronounced sexual dimorphism: the males are not only considerably larger and heavier than the females, but also have a mane. This begins to grow between the ages of 2 and 3 years and is fully developed by about the age of 4 years.

Gregarious lifestyle

The lion is the only one of the more than three dozen cat species that lives gregariously in a pride and hunts together. Lion prides consist either of siblings that, after separating from their mother at the age of about 1½ years,

Right: Despite their huge paws and powerful carnassials, lionesses are loving mothers who handle their tiny cubs remarkably tenderly.

Below: Lions spend a substantial part of the day resting and digesting their food.

Male lions are clearly distinguishable from the females by their manes.

Unlike other big cats, lions are emphatically gregarious animals.

Many extinct subspecies

Numerous subspecies of lion were previously distributed over most of Africa and from southeastern Europe across Iraq and Iran as far as India. Two known representatives of the species disappeared from Africa early on: the Cape lion (*Panthera leo melanochaita*) in 1865 and the Barbary lion (*Panthera leo leo*) in 1922. In the mid-twentieth century, it is estimated that there were still 500,000 lions in Africa south of the Sahara, but populations have declined dramatically. A major cause was heavy hunting by European and American hunters, and by East African Masai warriors, for whom hunting lions was a ritual of manhood to demonstrate their bravery. At the end of the 1980s, the total population was put at about 100,000 animals, concentrated in eastern and southern Africa. Hunting, habitat destruction, and diseases, such as tuberculosis and an immunodeficiency virus, have led to current numbers being estimated at just 25,000 to 30,000 animals, and the species has been entered on the Red List as vulnerable.

In Asia, lions have now been almost completely eradicated through heavy hunting and habitat loss—only in one small area in the Indian state of Gujarat has it been possible, thanks to effective protection measures, to save about 250 specimens of the Asiatic lion (*Panthera leo persica*). It is one of the world's rarest large animals and continues to be classified as critically endangered, because, on account of extensive inbreeding, it has an extremely small gene pool.

African and Asiatic lions (shown here is an Indian lioness) are so closely related that they can crossbreed without any problem.

remain together for a while, or of up to ten females and their (normally 2 or 3) cubs, which are guarded by between one and three adult males. Males generally lead a pride for only a relatively short time; after 3 or 4 years, a younger male will take over the group, often after fierce fighting. If there are still small cubs, they will usually be killed by the new leader of the pride so that the females will become ready to mate, and the new leader will be able to pass on his genes.

LEOPARD

Leopard (*Panthera pardus*) and panther are two names for the same animal, and even the black panther is not a separate species, but a black color phase of the leopard. This black coloration, called melanism—which also occurs in the jaguar—is caused by excessive deposits of black pigmentation. Melanistic animals occur more frequently in dense forests and at high altitudes, and they can be born in the same litter as normally colored cubs.

Wide distribution

The solitary leopard, the best climber of all the big cats, is extremely adaptable and lives in semideserts and savannas as well as in open forests and in the jungle. It once inhabited the whole of Africa, except for the central Sahara, the Middle East, Turkey, and, to the east, the entire subtropical and tropical region as far as southern China: it was even found in southern Siberia. Nowadays, its range is considerably smaller and partially fragmented.

For a long time, leopards were hunted for their magnificent coats, which vary according to the subspecies and the habitat.

Numerous subspecies are threatened with eradication

Populations of leopards have now been severely depleted in almost all parts of its range. The main reasons for this were, for a long time, its persecution as a cattle predator and man-eater, as well as its being hunted for its sought-after coat, which varies in color, depending on the subspecies. Numerous subspecies are listed as critically endangered, including the North Persian leopard (*Panthera pardus saxicolor*), the Amur leopard (*Panthera pardus orientalis*), and the North Chinese leopard (*Panthera pardus japonensis*). The leopard is now protected under CITES, which has largely stemmed the fur trade, although smuggling still occurs, but it is now increasingly threatened by the progressive destruction of its habitats and the spread of the sharply rising human population.

JAGUAR

The jaguar (*Panthera onca*) is the only big cat to occur in the New World and is almost exclusively a forest and scrubland dweller who prefers to live by rivers and swamps. It is encountered most frequently in the Amazon basin, but its range stretches from Mexico and Central America down to Argentina; in the United States it was, in all probability, eradicated in the second half of the twentieth century. Unlike most other cats, the jaguar is not afraid of water. On the contrary, it often pursues tapirs and capybara when they flee into swamps, lakes, or rivers and enjoys swimming.

Similarities with the leopard

Outwardly, the jaguar looks similar to the Old World leopard, but it is significantly heavier and more sturdily built than the latter. Its spot pattern also differs from that of its African and Asiatic relatives: the ring-shaped spots are larger and have spots inside them, which are absent in the leopard.

Above: Jaguars' preferred habitat is the dense vegetation of rainforests—the animal shown here is in the Pantanal in Brazil.

Falling population numbers

The jaguar is less threatened than some big cats: the number of sexually mature animals is currently estimated at about 50,000, but it is assumed that numbers will continue to fall and that the jaguar will soon face immediate threat.

The spread of humans and the clearing of rainforests have led to its complete disappearance from many areas, and its habitat, which has already shrunk by about 50 percent in recent decades, is growing a little smaller every day.

Moreover, it is persecuted by farmers as a cattle thief and poached for its coveted coat, even though it is protected under CITES in most areas. Outlook for the jaguar is poor as, in 2008, the United States approved an unprecedented decision to abandon jaguar recovery as a federal goal.

Below: The cause of the black coloration of jaguars can be traced to excessive pigmentation. Under favorable light conditions, it is possible to see the coat markings shimmering through.

Habitat loss and poaching

The snow leopard is included on the Red List as endangered; despite the establishment of protected areas and despite its protection under CITES, its population is estimated at fewer than 5,000 animals in the wild. The reasons for this are many and various: in addition to habitat loss and the increasing shortage of prey animals, which are shot in large numbers by people, commercial hunting has played a particularly important role. For decades, the snow leopard has been persecuted on a massive scale for its highly desirable and expensive coat; in addition, its bones are used in traditional Chinese medicine, where they are processed into remedies. Despite the ban, animals are still being killed for these purposes because illegal poaching is a financially very lucrative business.

In addition to the 5,000 animals living in the wild, there are up to 500 snow leopards living in zoos all over the world. Captive-bred young are no longer unusual, and paradoxically, there is even a surplus of animals of this endangered species, for which no takers can be found in zoos or animal parks.

Snow leopards are mostly solitary animals, tolerating the companionship of a partner only during the mating season.

SNOW LEOPARD

The snow leopard or ounce (*Uncia uncia*) is a high-mountain dweller whose main range lies at elevations between 6,500 and 18,000 feet (2,000 and 5,500 meters) in the Himalaya. It is unusually sure-footed, even on the most craggy cliffs, and has an enormous leap: when it is fleeing or hunting, it is said to be able to leap up to 30 feet (10 meters). Its food consists, depending on the season and availability, of marmots, wild sheep, and wild goats, but in lean times, it also eats mice, pikas, and birds.

"Snow shoes" and magnificent coat

The snow leopard is famous for its large, fur-covered paws, which act as snow shoes and prevent it from sinking into the snow. It also has a magnificent, thick coat in a variety of shades of gray with black rings or rosettes and spots, which are more visible on the summer coat than on the winter coat.

CLOUDED LEOPARD

The clouded leopard (*Neofelis nebulosa*) from Southeast Asia is the smallest of the big cats, with a shoulder height of 20 inches (50 cm), and is also smaller than many of the small cats. Its coat is distinctively marked with large, irregularly shaped, dark-edged ellipses which are said to be shaped like clouds, hence its name. It lives and hunts predominantly in trees in dense forests as far from humans as possible, and it is magnificently adapted to this way of life: its legs are relatively short and its tail is long and is used for balance. This impressive climber even runs down trees headfirst and hangs upside-down on branches. The clouded leopard is also a very good swimmer.

Declining population

The total population of the clouded leopard amounts to about 10,000 adults, with no population exceeding 1,000 animals, and the species is considered to be eradicated in some regions. Habitat loss and heavy hunting are its main problems. It continues to be hunted by poachers for its magnificent coat, as well as for its bones, which are used in traditional Chinese medicine to cure various ailments. Its extremely long carnassials are also used in ritual ceremonies, and its flesh is sometimes served up to well-to-do Asian tourists in Chinese and Thai restaurants as a delicacy. The clouded leopard is protected, both locally in its geographical range and globally under CITES, but the ban is unfortunately poorly enforced and its overall numbers continue to fall, which is why it is deemed to be vulnerable.

Below: Its wonderful coat markings have been the downfall of the clouded leopard because they have led to the species' being heavily hunted.

Above: A true high-mountain dweller, the snow leopard can withstand extreme temperatures, thanks to its very thick coat.

Galapagos giant tortoise

Rhinoceros iguana

Hammerhead shark

THREATENED ANIMAL SPECIES FROM AROUND THE WORLD

The populations of more than 10,000 animal species worldwide are threatened to some extent. The cross section presented here of the species mentioned in this book shows the level of threat at a glance.

Scientists, committed conservationists, and international conservation organizations regularly attempt to count populations of rare animals so that appropriate protection measures can be put in place. The IUCN's Red List is based on such counts—which, in most cases, are estimates and extrapolations, with correspondingly high error rates. Moreover, for financial reasons, such surveys cannot be conducted annually, but are often carried out only at intervals of 10 years or more. All figures for populations should, therefore, be treated with the utmost caution. The direction of the population trend is a more significant indicator.

Species	Family	Distribution	Reason for threat	Numbers (total population)	Level of threat	Population trend	Related species or subspecies under threat
Yellowfin tuna (*Thunnus albacares*)	Scombridae (albacores, bonitos, mackerels, and tunas)	All seas except the Mediterranean	Hunting (by commercial fishing)	?	!!!	↓	Southern bluefin tuna (*Thunnus maccoyii*) !!!!, Bigeye tuna (*Thunnus obesus*) !!!!, Monterrey Spanish mackerel (*Scomberomorus concolor*) !!!
Great white shark (*Carcharodon carcharias*)	Lamnidae (mackerel sharks, porbeagles, and white sharks)	Tropical and subtropical seas	Hunting (by commercial fishing and sport anglers)	2,000–3,000	!!!/!!!!	?	Longfin mako (*Isurus paucus*) !!! Porbeagle (*Lamna nasus*) !!!!
Great hammerhead (*Sphyrna mokarran*)	Sphyrnidae	Tropical seas, Red Sea, Caribbean	Hunting	?	!!/!!!	↓	Smalleye hammerhead shark (*Sphyrna tudes*) !!/!!!
Poison-dart frogs (Dendrobatidae family)	Dendrobatidae (poison-dart frogs)	Central America, tropical South America	Habitat destruction (deforestation), climate change, diseases	?	!! to !!!!	↓	Skunk frog (*Aromobates nocturnus*) !!!! *Colostethus anthracinus* !!!!
Indian gharial (*Gavialis gangeticus*)	Gavialidae (gharials)	Indian subcontinent	Habitat destruction, hunting (for meat, skin, trophies, use in natural medicine, and eggs)	Under 500	!!!!	↓	
Black caiman (*Melanosuchus niger*)	Alligatoridae (alligators and caimans)	Amazon basin	Habitat destruction, hunting (for meat and skin)	?	!!!	?	Chinese alligator (*Alligator sinensis*) !!!
Red-footed tortoise (*Geochelone carbonaria*)	Testudinidae (tortoises)	Panama to Argentina	Habitat destruction, hunting (for meat and eggs)	?	!!/!!!		Burmese starred tortoise (*Geochelone platynota*) !!!! Travancore tortoise (*Indotestudo forstenii*) !!! Egyptian tortoise (*Testudo kleinmanni*) !!!!
Hermann's tortoise (*Testudo hermanni*)	Testudinidae (tortoises)	European Mediterranean region	Habitat destruction, hunting (for the animal trade)	?	!!/!!!	↓	Spur-thighed tortoise (*Testudo graeca*) !!

Brothers Island tuatara | Indian gharial | Great white shark

Key for population trends

❗ = population falling

➡ = population stable

⬆ = population rising (mainly for species kept in zoos and animal parks)

❓ = due to a lack of population data or estimates, no indication can be given

Key for category of threat (see also p. 12)

! = potentially threatened   **!!!!** = critically endangered

!! = vulnerable   **†** = eradicated in the wild

!!! = endangered   **††** = eradicated

If two categories are shown, separated by a slash—for example, **!!/!!!**—then the category before the slash specifies the threat on a global level and the category after the slash specifies the threat on a local level or to isolated populations.

Species	Family	Distribution	Reason for threat	Numbers (total population)	Level of threat	Population trend	Related species or subspecies under threat
Galapagos giant tortoise (*Geochelone nigra*)	Testudinidae (tortoises	Galapagos archipelago	Hunting (for meat), introduction of alien species (various domestic animals)	10,000–12,000 in total, individual subspecies only 500–600	**!!!/!!!!**	❗	Abingdon Island tortoise (*Geochelone nigra abingdoni*) **††** Sierra negra tortoise (*Geochelone nigra guntheri*) **!!!!** Duncan Island tortoise (*Geochelone nigra duncanensis* (previously *G. n. ephippium*)) **!!!!**
Kemp's ridley (*Lepidochelys kempii*)	Cheloniidae (sea turtles)	Tropical and subtropical seas	Hunting (for meat, shell, and eggs), bycatch	❓	**!!!!**	❗	Hawksbill turtle (*Eretmochelys imbricata*) **!!!!** Loggerhead (*Caretta caretta*) **!!!**
Brothers Island tuatara (*Sphenodon guntheri*)	Sphenodontidae (tuataras)	New Zealand (approx. 30 small islands)	Hunting, competition from domestic animals for food	A few thousand	**!!!**	❓	
Galapagos land iguana (*Conolophus subcristatus*)	Iguanidae (iguanas)	Galapagos archipelago (approx. five islands)	Hunting (for meat and eggs), introduction of alien species (pigs, dogs, and cats)	A few hundred to a thousand	**!!!**	❗	Fiji crested iguana (*Brachylophus vitiensis*) **!!!!** Utila spiny-tailed iguana (*Ctenosaura bakeri*) **!!!!** Guatemalan spiny-tailed iguana (*Ctenosaura palearis*) **!!!!**
Rhinoceros iguana (*Cyclura cornuta*)	Iguanidae (iguanas)	Haiti, Dominican Republic, a few Caribbean islands	Hunting (for meat)	A few hundred, possibly a thousand	**!!!/!!!!**	❗	
Water monitor (*Varanus salvator*)	Varabidae (monitor lizards)	Southeast Asia	Habitat destruction, hunting (for meat, skins, and use in natural medicine)	❓	**!!!**	❗	Komodo dragon (*Varanus komodoensis*) **!!/!!!**

Hazel grouse

Red-breasted goose

Madagascar teal

Species	Family	Distribution	Reason for threat	Numbers (total population)	Level of threat	Population trend	Related species or subspecies under threat
Western capercaillie (*Tetrao urogallus*)	Phasianidae (turkeys, grouse, pheasants, and partridges)	Northern Asia, central and northern Europe (forested regions)	Habitat destruction, hunting	?	‼/‼‼	⬇ to ➡	
Hazel grouse (*Bonasa bonasia*)	Phasianidae (turkeys, grouse, pheasants, and partridges)	Europe and Asia (forested regions and taiga)	Habitat destruction (forests), hunting, disturbance by humans	?	‼/‼‼	? or ⬇	
Hawaiian goose (*Branta sandvicensis*)	Anatidae (ducks, geese, and swans)	Hawaiian archipelago (Hawaii and Maui)	Habitat destruction, hunting, introduction of alien species (dogs and cats)	+/– 1,000	‼‼	⬆	
Red-breasted goose (*Branta ruficollis*)	Anatidae (ducks, geese, and swans)	Arctic areas of Europe and Siberia	Hunting, particularly in overwintering grounds in central Asia, Iraq, and southern Europe	?	‼‼	⬇	
Lesser white-fronted goose (*Anser erythropus*)	Anatidae (ducks, geese, and swans)	Scandinavia to Siberia	Hunting, habitat destruction, environmental pollution (toxins)	?	‼/‼‼, in Scandinavia ‼‼‼	⬇	Swan goose (*Anser cygnoides*) ‼‼
Trumpeter swan (*Cygnus buccinator*)	Anatidae (ducks, geese, and swans)	Central and northern North America	Hunting, habitat destruction (draining of	12,000–15,000	‼‼	⬆	
Madagascar teal (*Anas bernieri*)	Anatidae (ducks, geese, and swans)	Madagascar (western part)	Hunting, habitat destruction	+/– 1,000	‼‼‼	➡, poss. ⬇	White-winged duck (*Cairina scutulata*) ‼‼ Madagascar pochard (*Aythya innotata*) ‼‼‼ Labrador duck (*Camptorhynchus labradorius*) ††
Laysan duck (*Anas laysanensis*)	Anatidae (ducks, geese, and swans)	Hawaiian archipelago (Laysan Island)	Hunting (for guano), introduction of alien species (rabbits)	+/– 500–700 (in 1912, only 12 individuals remained)	‼‼‼	➡, poss. ⬇	Auckland Island teal (*Anas aucklandica*) ‼/‼‼ Brown teal (*Anas chlorotis*) ‼‼ Baikal teal (*Anas formosa*) ‼/‼‼ Campbell Island teal (*Anas nesiotis*) ‼‼‼

Western capercaillie   Andean flamingos

Siberian cranes

Species	Family	Distribution	Reason for threat	Numbers (total population)	Level of threat	Population trend	Related species or subspecies under threat
Great bustard (*Otis tarda*)	Otididae (bustards)	Spain to central Asia (fragmented)	Habitat destruction, hunting	Several small populations of 500–1,000 birds	‼ to ‼‼	↓	Bengal florican (*Houbaropsis bengalensis*) ‼‼, Houbara bustard (*Chlamydotis undulata*) ‼‼ Great Indian bustard (*Ardeotis nigriceps*) ‼
Siberian crane (*Grus leucogeranus*)	Gruidae (cranes)	Northeast Siberia, central Yangtze area, eastern Urals	Habitat destruction, hunting	Probably under 2,000	‼‼	↓	Red-crowned crane (*Grus japonensis*) ‼‼
Black-crowned crane (*Balearica pavonina*)	Gruidae (cranes)	West Africa (savannas and wetlands)	Habitat destruction, hunting	?	‼/‼‼	↓	
Blue crane (*Grus paradisea*)	Gruidae (cranes)	Parts of South Africa and Namibia	Environmental toxins (fertilizers and pesticides), conversion of biotopes to farmland	+/– 20,000	‼/‼‼	↓	
Whooping crane (*Grus americana*)	Gruidae (cranes)	Central Canada, overwintering grounds in Texas	Biotope destruction	400–500	‼‼	↓	
Hooded crane (*Grus monacha*)	Gruidae (cranes)	Siberia, possibly also Mongolia	Habitat destruction, hunting, disturbance by humans	+/– 8,000	‼‼/‼‼	↓	Wattled crane (*Grus carunculatus*) ‼/‼‼ Black-necked crane (*Grus nigricollis*) ‼‼
Andean flamingo (*Phoenicoparrus andinus*)	Phoenicopteridae (flamingos)	Andean regions of Chile, Argentina, Bolivia, and Peru	Habitat destruction (salt lakes), disturbance by humans	A few thousand	‼‼	↓	
Storm's stork (*Ciconia stormi*)	Ciconiidae (storks)	Parts of Southeast Asia	Habitat destruction	500–1,000	‼‼	↓	Painted stork (*Mycteria leucocephala*)
Black stork (*Ciconia nigra*)	Ciconiidae (storks)	Palearctic forested areas, overwintering grounds in South Asia and Africa	Hunting, environmental pollution, accidents (high-voltage lines)	+/– 40,000	‼/‼‼, in Europe rising slightly	?, poss. ↓	Oriental stork (*Ciconia boyciana*) ‼‼ Greater adjutant (*Leptoptilos dubius*) ‼‼
Dalmatian pelican (*Pelecanus crispus*)	Pelecanidae (pelicans)	Southwest Europe, East Africa, South and Southeast Asia	Habitat destruction (wetlands, aquatic environments), hunting (as food competitors)	10,000–20,000	‼/‼‼	↓	

Galapagos penguin   Kea   Hyacinth macaw

Species	Family	Distribution	Reason for threat	Numbers (total population)	Level of threat	Population trend	Related species or subspecies under threat
Galapagos cormorant (*Phalacrocorax harrisi*)	Phalacrocoracidae (cormorants)	Galapagos archipelago (Fernandina and Isabela islands)	Introduction of alien species (dogs, cats, and pigs)	+/− 1,500	‼‼	⚱	Campbell Island shag (*Phalacrocorax campbelli*) ‼/‼‼ Pitt Island shag (*Phalacrocorax featherstoni*) ‼‼ Chatham Island shag (*Phalacrocorax onslowi*) ‼‼‼
Cape gannet (*Morus capensis*)	Sulidae (gannets and boobies)	Coasts of Namibia and South Africa (fragmented)	Lack of prey (overfishing), disturbance by humans	?	‼/‼‼	⚱	
Blue-footed booby (*Sula nebouxii*)	Sulidae (gannets and boobies)	West coast of California down to Ecuador, Galapagos archipelago	Disturbance by humans, hunting (for guano and eggs)	?	‼‼	⚱	Red-footed booby (*Sula sula*) ‼ Tasman booby (*Sula tasmani*) ††
Amsterdam albatross (*Diomedea amsterdamensis*)	Diomedeidae (albatrosses)	Amsterdam Island	Introduction of alien species (goats and cattle)	+/−130	‼‼‼	⚱	Waved albatross (*Phoebastria irrorata*) ‼‼
Galapagos penguin (*Spheniscus mendiculus*)	Spheniscidae (penguins)	Galapagos archipelago (Fernandina and Isabela islands)	Introduction of alien species (domestic animals), lack of food, disturbance by humans	3,000–4,000	‼‼	⚱	African penguin (*Spheniscus demersus*) ‼/‼‼ Humboldt penguin (*Spheniscus humboldti*) ‼‼
Erect-crested penguin (*Eudyptes sclateri*)	Spheniscidae (penguins)	New Zealand (Bounty islands and Antipodes archipelago)	Lack of prey (overfishing), climate change	?	‼‼	⚱	Rockhopper penguin (*Eudyptes chrysocome*) ‼ Royal penguin (*Eudyptes schlegeli*) ‼
Yellow-eyed penguin (*Megadyptes antipodes*)	Spheniscidae (penguins)	Southern New Zealand, Auckland and Campbell islands	Habitat destruction, introduction of alien species (ferrets, stoats, and cats)	4,000–5,000	‼‼	⚱	
Hyacinth macaw (*Anodorhynchus hyacinthinus*)	Psittacidae (parrots, cockatoos, and relatives)	Brazil (Pantanal)	Habitat destruction, hunting (for the animal trade)	A few thousand	‼‼/‼‼‼	⚱	Glaucous macaw (*Anodorhynchus glaucus*) ‼‼‼ Lear's macaw (*Anodorhynchus leari*) ‼‼‼ Blue-throated macaw (*Ara glaucogularis*) ‼‼‼ Red-fronted macaw (*Ara rubrogenys*) ‼‼ Spix's macaw (*Cyanopsitta spixii*) †

Cape gannets

Major Mitchell's cockatoo

Lappet-faced vultures

Species	Family	Distribution	Reason for threat	Numbers (total population)	Level of threat	Population trend	Related species or subspecies under threat
Imperial parrot (*Amazona imperialis*)	Psittacidae (parrots, cockatoos, and relatives)	Lesser Antilles (Dominica)	Habitat destruction, hunting (for the animal trade)	+/−300	!!!!	!	Yellow-headed parrot (*Amazona oratrix*) !!! Puerto Rican parrot (*Amazona vittata*) !!!!
Kakapo (*Strigops habroptila*)	Psittacidae (parrots, cockatoos, and relatives)	New Zealand (Chalky and Codfish islands)	Introduction of alien species (dogs, cats, martens, ferrets, and rats)	100–200 (lowest number: 12 birds)	!!!!	➙, poss. ↑	
Kea (*Nestor notabilis*)	Psittacidae (parrots, cockatoos, and relatives)	New Zealand (South Island)	Introduction of alien species, hunting as pests, habitat destruction	1,000–10,000	!!!	!	
Black-cheeked lovebird (*Agapornis nigrigenis*)	Psittacidae (parrots, cockatoos, and relatives)	Zambia, northern regions of Namibia and Botswana	Habitat destruction, hunting (for the animal trade)	?	!!!	!	
Lilian's lovebird (*Agapornis lilianae*)	Psittacidae (parrots, cockatoos, and relatives)	Tanzania, Malawi, Mozambique, Zimbabwe	Habitat destruction	?	!!!	!	
Major Mitchell's cockatoo (*Cacatua leadbeateri*)	Psittacidae (parrots, cockatoos, and relatives)	Central Australia	Habitat destruction, climate change, hunting as pests	?	!! to !!!	!	
Black cockatoos (*Calyptorhynchus* spp.)	Psittacidae (parrots, cockatoos, and relatives)	Dry areas of Australia	Habitat destruction	?	!!/!!!	!	Philippine cockatoo (*Cacatua haematuropygia*) !!!! Yellow-crested cockatoo (*Cacatua sulphurea*) !!!!
Lammergeier (*Gypaetus barbatus*)	Accipitridae (hawks, eagles, and relatives)	Ethiopia, East Africa, Pyrenees, southwest and central Asia	Habitat destruction, lack of prey, hunting	?	!!!, in Europe (reintroduction) efforts !!	! to ➙	
Lappet-faced vulture (*Torgos tracheliotos*)	Accipitridae (hawks, eagles, and relatives)	Sub-Saharan Africa, savanna areas	Habitat destruction, lack of prey	?	!!/!!!	!	Slender-billed vulture (*Gyps tenuirostris*) !!!! Madagascar fish eagle (*Haliaeetus vociferoides*) !!!! Crowned eagle (*Harpyhaliaetus coronatus*) !!! Egyptian vulture (*Neophron percnopterus*) !!!

Southern cassowary

Philippine eagle

Bali starling

Species	Family	Distribution	Reason for threat	Numbers (total population)	Level of threat	Population trend	Related species or subspecies under threat
Philippine eagle (*Pithecophaga jefferyi*)	Accipitridae (hawks, eagles, and relatives)	Philippines (rainforests)	Habitat destruction, hunting	Max. 500	!		
Pernambuco pygmy-owl (*Glaucidium mooreorum*)	Strigidae (typical owls)	Brazil (Pernambuco: rainforests)	Habitat destruction	?	!		Forest owlet (*Heteroglaux blewitti*) !!!! Mauritius owl (*Mascarenotus sauzieri*) †† Seychelles scops-owl (*Otus insularis*) !!!
Southern ground-hornbill (*Bucorvus cafer*)	Bucorvidae (ground hornbills)	Southern Africa, savanna areas	Habitat destruction, hunting as pests	Fewer than 500 breeding pairs	! to ➡		
Bali starling (*Leucopsar rothschildi*)	Sturnidae (starlings, mynahs, and oxpeckers)	Indonesia (Bali)	Habitat destruction, hunting (for the animal trade)	Fewer than 100 in the wild, +/− 1,000 in zoos	↥		White-eyed starling (*Aplonis brunneicapillus*) !!! Kosrae starling (*Aplonis corvina*) †† White-faced starling (*Sturnus albofrontatus*) !!! Black-winged starling (*Sturnus melanopterus*) !!!
Great gray shrike (*Lanius excubitor*)	Laniidae (shrikes)	Temperate and subarctic regions of the holarctic	Environmental pollution (pesticides), climate change, habitat destruction	?	!		
Southern cassowary (*Casuarius casuarius*)	Casuariidae (cassowaries)	New Guinea, northern Australia	Habitat destruction, introduction of alien species (dogs and pigs), road traffic	2,000–5,000	!		Northern cassowary (*Casuarius unappendiculatus*) !!/!!!
Tokoeka (*Apteryx australis*)	Apterigidae (kiwis)	New Zealand (North and South Islands, Stewart Island)	Habitat destruction, hunting, introduction of alien species (foxes, martens, and rats)	A few thousand	!		Great spotted kiwi (*Apteryx haastii*) !!/!!! Little spotted kiwi (*Apteryx owenii*) !!!

Hairy-nosed wombat   Pretty-faced wallaby   Alpine long-eared bats

Species	Family	Distribution	Reason for threat	Numbers (total population)	Level of threat	Population trend	Related species or subspecies under threat
Long-beaked echidna (*Zaglossus bruijni*)	Tachyglossidae (echidnas)	New Guinea	Habitat destruction, hunting (for meat)	Max. 3,000	‼/‼‼	❗	
Northern hairy-nosed wombat (*Lasiorhinus krefftii*)	Vombatidae (wombats)	Australia (Queensland)	Habitat destruction, hunting, competition from cattle for food	+/–100	‼‼	❗❓	Southern hairy-nosed wombat (*Lasiorhinus latifrons*) ❗❗
Goodfellow's tree kangaroo (*Dendrolagus goodfellowi*)	Macropodidae (kangaroos, wallabies, and relatives)	Eastern New Guinea	Habitat destruction, hunting, introduction of alien species (foxes, dogs,	❓	‼	❗	Doria's tree kangaroo (*Dendrolagus dorianus*) ❗❗/‼ Huon tree kangaroo (*Dendrolagus matscihei*) ‼
Parma wallaby (*Macropus parma*)	Macropodidae (kangaroos, wallabies, and relatives)	Eastern Australia	Habitat destruction, introduction of alien species	❓	❗❗/‼	❓	
Bridled nail-tailed wallaby (*Onychogalea fraenata*)	Macropodidae (kangaroos, wallabies, and relatives)	Eastern Australia	Habitat destruction, introduction of alien species	Probably only a few hundred	‼	❗	Crescent nail-tailed wallaby (*Onychogalea lunata*) ††
Mindanao pygmy fruit bat (*Alionycteris paucidentata*)	Pteropodidae (Old World fruit bats)	Philippines (Mindanao)	Habitat destruction	❓	❗❗	❗	Talaud fruit bat (*Acerodon humilis*) ❗❗/‼ Panay giant fruit bat (*Acerodon lucifer*) ††
Lesser mouse-eared bat (*Myotis blythii*)	Vespertilionidae (evening bats and vesper bats)	Central and southern Europe, parts of Asia and North Africa	Habitat destruction, environmental pollution, road traffic, disturbance by humans	❓	❗❗/‼	❓, probably ❗	Soprano pipistrelle (*Pipistrellus pygmaeus*) ❗❗/‼ Van Gelder's bat (*Bauerus dubiaquercus*) ❗❗/‼ Horn-skinned bat (*Eptesicus floweri*) ‼ Gaskell's false serotine (*Hesperoptenus gaskelli*) ‼
Lesser horseshoe bat (*Rhinolophus hipposideros*)	Rhinolophidae (horseshoe bats and Old World leaf-nosed bats	Central and southern Europe, North Africa, parts of Asia	Habitat destruction, environmental pollution, disturbance by humans	❓	❗❗/‼	❗	

Mountain gorillas   Golden-headed lion tamarin   Chimpanzees

Species	Family	Distribution	Reason for threat	Numbers (total population)	Level of threat	Population trend	Related species or subspecies under threat
Sumatran orangutan (*Pongo abelii*)	Hominidae (great apes and humans)	Sumatra	Habitat destruction, hunting (for meat and the animal trade), diseases	+/– 5,000	‼‼	↓	Bornean orangutan (*Pongo pygmaeus*) ‼
Lowland or western gorilla (*Gorilla gorilla*)	Hominidae (great apes and humans)	Tropical and equatorial Africa	Habitat destruction, hunting (for meat and trophies), civil wars, diseases	Between 700 and several tens of thousands	‼	↓	Mountain gorilla (*Gorilla beringei beringei*) ‼‼ Cross River gorilla (*Gorilla gorilla diehli*) ‼‼
Bonobo (*Pan paniscus*)	Hominidae (great apes and humans)	Democratic Republic of Congo	Habitat destruction, hunting (for meat and for keeping as pets)	Max. 50,000	‼/‼‼	↓	
Chimpanzee (*Pan troglodytes*)	Hominidae (great apes and humans)	Between Senegal and Democratic Republic of Congo (fragmented)	Habitat destruction, hunting (for meat and the animal trade)	Max. 30,000	‼/‼	↓	
Silvery gibbon (*Hylobates moloch*)	Hylobatidae (gibbons and lesser apes)	Indonesia (central and western Java)	Habitat destruction	1,000–2,000	‼‼	?	Kloss's gibbon (*Hylobates klossii*) ‼ Pileated gibbon (*Hylobates pileatus*) ‼ Eastern black crested gibbon (*Nomascus nasutus*) ‼‼
Golden lion tamarin (*Leontopithecus rosalia*)	Callitrichidae (marmosets and tamarins)	Southeastern Brazil (Rio de Janeiro state)	Habitat destruction	Max. 1,500 in the wild, but there are conservation breeding programs	‼‼	↑	Golden-rumped lion tamarin (*Leontopithecus chrysopygus*) ‼‼ Brazilian bare-faced tamarin (*Saguinus bicolor*) ‼‼ Silvery-brown bare-face tamarin (*Saguinus leucopus*) ‼
Maned three-toed sloth (*Bradypus torquatus*)	Bradypodidae (three-toed sloths)	Eastern Brazil	Habitat destruction	?	‼‼	↓	Pygmy three-toed sloth (*Bradypus pygmaeus*) ‼‼
Rothschild's giraffe (*Giraffa camelopardalis rothschildi*)	Giraffidae (giraffes and okapis)	Africa (south of the Sahara)	Habitat destruction, hunting (for meat and hides), civil wars (East Africa)	A few hundred	‼/‼‼	↓	Reticulated giraffe (*Giraffa camelopardalis reticulata*) ‼

European bison   Gaur   Dama gazelle

Species	Family	Distribution	Reason for threat	Numbers (total population)	Level of threat	Population trend	Related species or subspecies under threat
Eld's deer or thamin (*Cervus eldii*)	Cervidae (deer)	Eastern India to southern China, Malaysian peninsula (fragmented)	Habitat destruction, hunting (for meat and antlers)	One hundred to several thousand, depending on subspecies	‼/‼‼, one hundred to several thousand, depending on subspecies ‼‼‼	↕	Bawean deer (*Axis kuhlii*) ‼‼‼ Visayan spotted deer (*Cervus alfredi*) ‼‼‼ Schomburgk's deer (*Cervus schomburgki*) ✝✝ Persian fallow deer (*Dama dama mesopotamica*) ‼‼‼‼
European bison or wisent (*Bison bonasus*)	Bovidae (antelopes, cattle, gazelles, goats, sheep, and relatives)	Eradicated in the wild, but now reintroduced in eastern Europe	Hunting (for meat and hides), habitat destruction, genetic bottleneck	+/– 4,000 (in captivity and semi-wild)	‼‼	↕	
Gaur or Indian bison (*Bos frontalis*)	Bovidae (antelopes, cattle, gazelles, goats, sheep, and relatives)	India, Nepal, Southeast Asia (fragmented)	Hunting (for meat), habitat destruction	10,000–20,000	‼‼/‼‼‼	↕	Wild yak (*Bos grunniens*) ‼‼ Banteng (*Bos javanicus*) ‼‼, Lowland anoa (*Bubalus depressicornis*) ‼‼, Mountain anoa (*Bubalus quarlesi*) ‼‼
Bongo (*Tragelaphus eurycerus*)	Bovidae (antelopes, cattle, gazelles, goats, sheep, and relatives)	Central and West Africa (western subspecies), Kenya and Uganda (eastern subspecies)	Hunting, habitat destruction	?	‼ (western subspecies), ‼‼ to ‼‼‼ (eastern subspecies)	↕	
Arabian or white oryx (*Oryx leucoryx*)	Bovidae (antelopes, cattle, gazelles, goats, sheep, and relatives)	Middle East to Arabian peninsula	Hunting	A few hundred	‼‼	↕, poss.→	Addax (*Addax nasomaculatus*) ‼‼‼ Hirola (*Beatragus hunteri*) ‼‼‼
Dama gazelle (*Gazella dama* or *Nanger dama*)	Bovidae (antelopes, cattle, gazelles, goats, sheep, and relatives)	North Africa (desert areas)	Hunting, habitat destruction	A few thousand	‼‼‼	↕	Goitered gazelle (*Gazella subgutturosa*) ‼/‼‼ Arabian gazelle (*Gazella arabica*) ✝✝ Cuvier's gazelle (*Gazella cuvieri*) ‼‼ Saudi gazelle (*Gazella saudiya*) ✝✝
Markhor (*Capra falconeri*)	Bovidae (antelopes, cattle, gazelles, goats, sheep, and relatives)	Central Asia	Hunting (for meat, skins, and trophies)	?	‼‼	?	Serow (*Capricornis sumatraensis*) ‼‼ Barbary sheep or aoudad (*Ammotragus lervia*) ‼‼
Asian wild ass (*Equus hemionus*)	Equidae (asses, horses, and zebras)	Central Asia (fragmented, e.g. Rann of Kutch)	Hunting, habitat destruction	800–900	‼‼/‼‼‼	↕	
African wild ass (*Equus africanus*)	Equidae (asses, horses, and zebras)	North Africa, Somalia, Eritrea, possibly Ethiopia, and southern Sudan	Hunting, civil wars	? (some subspecies eradicated or on the brink of eradication)	‼‼‼	↕	

Grevy's zebras   Black rhinoceros   African elephants

Species	Family	Distribution	Reason for threat	Numbers (total population)	Level of threat	Population trend	Related species or subspecies under threat
Przewalski's horse (*Equus ferus przewalskii*)	Equidae (asses, horses, and zebras)	Eradicated in the wild; now reintroduced into China, Mongolia, and Hungary	Hunting, habitat destruction, genetic bottleneck	About 2,000 (mainly zoo animals)	!!! (eradicated in the wild)	↕	
Mountain zebra (*Equus zebra*)	Equidae (asses, horses, and zebras)	Mountainous areas of Namibia and South Africa	Hunting, habitat destruction (South Africa)	A few hundred (Cape mountain zebra) to +/– 10,000 (Hartmann's mountain zebra)	!!!	?	
Grevy's zebra (*Equus grevyi*)	Equidae (asses, horses, and zebras)	Northern Kenya; probably extinct in southern Ethiopia and Somalia	Hunting (for skins and meat), civil wars, habitat destruction	A few thousand, possibly only a few hundred	!	↓	Quagga (*Equus quagga*) ††
Black rhinoceros (*Diceros bicornis*)	Rhinocerotidae (rhinoceroses)	East and South Africa (fragmented	Hunting (for horn and trophies)	3,000–5,000	!!!/!!!!	↓	
Sumatran rhinoceros (*Dicerorhinus sumatrensis*)	Rhinocerotidae (rhinoceroses)	Indonesia (Sumatra) and Malaysia	Hunting (for horn and use in natural medicine), habitat destruction	Max. 500, of which 250–300 are on Sumatra	!!!!	?	Javan rhinoceros (*Rhinoceros sondaicus*) !!!! Indian rhinoceros (*Rhinoceros unicornis*) !!!
African elephant (*Loxodonta africana*)	Elephantidae (elephants)	Africa apart from North Africa (fragmented)	Hunting (for ivory and trophies), habitat destruction	250,000–350,000	!!/!!!	↓	
Asian or Indian elephant (*Elephas maximus*)	Elephantidae (elephants)	Southeast Asia (fragmented)	Hunting (for ivory), working animals, habitat destruction	30,000–50,000	!!!	↓	
Gray whale (*Eschrichtius robustus*)	Eschrichtiidae (gray whale)	Western and eastern Pacific	Hunting, environmental pollution	Max. 200 (western Pacific) to a few thousand (eastern Pacific)	!!!	↓	Blue whale (*Balaenoptera musculus*) !!! Fin whale (*Balaenoptera physalus*) !!! North Pacific right whale (*Eubalaena japonica*) !!!
Vaquita (*Phocoena sinus*)	Phocoenidae (porpoises)	Gulf of California	Hunting, water pollution	100–200	!!!!	?	Hector's dolphin (*Cephalorhynchus hectori*) !!!

Spectacled bear

Polar bear

Cheetahs

Species	Family	Distribution	Reason for threat	Numbers (total population)	Level of threat	Population trend	Related species or subspecies under threat
Yangtze river dolphin or baiji (*Lipotes vexillifer*)	Iniidae (river dolphins)	Yangtze River in China	Water pollution, fishing	Max. one dozen, but probably eradicated	!!!!/††	⚡	Amazon river dolphin (*Inia geoffrensis*) !!!
Asiatic black bear (*Ursus thibetanus*)	Ursidae (bears)	East and Southeast Asia to Afghanistan	Hunting, habitat destruction	?	!!/!!!	?	Sun bear (*Helarctos malayanus*) !!! Sloth bear (*Melursus ursinus*) !!!
Spectacled bear (*Tremarctos ornatus*)	Ursidae (bears)	Colombia to north Argentina (Andes)	Hunting, habitat loss	?	!!/!!!	?	
Polar bear (*Ursus maritimus*)	Ursidae (bears)	Arctic (circumpolar)	Hunting (for trophies), lack of prey, climate change	Max. 25,000	!!/!!!	⚡	
Giant panda (*Ailuropoda melanoleuca*)	Ursidae (bears)	Southeast China	Habitat destruction, hunting (for use in natural medicine and for the animal trade)	+/−2,000	!!!	?	
African wild dog (*Lycaon pictus*)	Canidae (coyotes, dogs, foxes, jackals, and wolves)	East and South Africa (savannas)	Hunting, habitat destruction, disease	3,000–5,000	!!!/!!!!	⚡	
Maned wolf (*Chrysocyon brachyurus*)	Canidae (coyotes, dogs, foxes, jackals, and wolves)	Central South America (pampas)	Hunting, habitat destruction, disease	?	!!/!!!	⚡	
Ethiopian wolf (*Canis simensis*)	Canidae (coyotes, dogs, foxes, jackals, and wolves)	Ethiopia (high alpine regions)	Habitat destruction, disease	Max. 700	!!!!	⚡	Falkland Island wolf (*Dusicyon australis*) ††, Asiatic wild dog or dhole (*Cuon alpinus*) !!!, Darwin's fox (*Pseudalopex fulvipes*) !!!!
Cheetah (*Acinonyx jubatus*)	Felidae (cats)	East and South Africa, Iran	Hunting, genetic bottleneck	+/−10,000 in Africa, max. 100 in Iran	!!!, for Iranian population !!!!	⚡	Asiatic golden cat (*Catopuma temminckii*) !!! Iberian lynx (*Lynx pardinus*) !!!! Andean cat (*Oreailurus jacobita*) !!!
Tiger (*Panthera tigris*)	Felidae (cats)	Central, West, East and Southeast Asia (fragmented)	Hunting, habitat destruction	+/−5,000 (all subspecies)	!!!/!!!!	⚡	Snow leopard or ounce (*Uncia uncia*) !!!
Lion (*Panthera leo*)	Felidae (cats)	Africa (south of the Sahara), Near and Middle East, Indian subcontinent	Hunting, poisoning by farmers, habitat destruction	Max. 30,000, of which 250 are in India	!!!!	⚡ (African species) ➔ (Asian species)	African lion (*Panthera leo*) !!! Asiatic lion (*Panthera leo persica*) !!!!

THREATENED ANIMAL SPECIES | 243

GLOSSARY

Biodiversity
Totality of all of Earth's ecosystems and of their plant and animal species, as well as of the genetic diversity of species and populations.

Biosphere
Totality of all of Earth's habitats.

Biotope
Habitat that offers specific conditions for defined plant and animal species, such as wetlands, tidal flats, etc.

Carnivore
Meat eater

Circumpolar
In biogeography, distribution of a species over multiple climatic zones. In general, the term is used to designate the regions around the North Pole and the South Pole.

CITES
Convention on International Trade in Endangered Species of Wild Fauna and Flora, also known as the Washington Species Protection Convention (see entry below).

Culling
In biology, this term refers to the deliberate killing of individuals of a species whose population has become too large, for example, in national parks and protected areas (e.g. elephant, African buffalo, and certain antelope species in South Africa).

Ecological niche
When animals or plants come across competing species in their habitat, they must either fight for their biotope, give way, or search for a niche within the biotope in which there is no competition. This may, for example, take the form of a species specializing in a particular food spurned by other species, or, if its direct competitors are diurnal, of developing a nocturnal lifestyle.

Ecosystem
Biological system consisting of biotic factors (populations of plants and animals) and abiotic factors (physical and chemical elements of a habitat), or, in simple terms, the community of animals, plants, and the environment to which they are adapted.

Evolution
Development of living organisms over long time periods through selection, mutation, isolation, and other factors, principally due to environmental influences and changes. Evolutionary biology is the science of evolutionary processes.

Exoanthropic
Plant or animal species that only live and prosper outside of inhabited areas.

Extant
In biology, plant and animal species that still exist today or only recently became extinct.

Fauna
Totality of all the animal species of an area.

Flora
Totality of all the plant species of an area.

Food chain
A system in which organisms feed on other organisms, which are, in turn, eaten by yet other organisms, and so on. A greatly simplified example of a food chain would be: algae–larvae–fish–birds. If an ecosystem is no longer intact, the animals at the top of a food chain frequently suffer from a shortage of prey.

Gene pool
The set of all the genetic variations within an animal species in a defined area. The larger the gene pool of a population, the greater the capacity it has to adapt to a changed environment (see also evolution).

Genetic bottleneck
Genetic impoverishment that can arise where populations are very small. The result is a higher mortality rate.

Habitat
Equates approximately to the term *biotope*. Where an animal or plant species inhabits several different biotopes, these are grouped together under the term *habitat*.

Herbivore
Plant eater.

Holarctic
The two temperate zones of the Northern Hemisphere: palearctic and nearctic (see entries below).

Homo sapiens
Latin name for modern humans, in contrast to *Homo neanderthalensis*, the Neanderthal, or *Homo habilis*, the extinct "handy man," who lived in East Africa between approximately 1.5 and 2.5 million years ago.

IUCN
International Union for Conservation of Nature previously abbreviated to World Conservation Union, sister organization to WWF (see entry below). The principal function of the IUCN, which was founded in 1948 and has its headquarters in Gland, Switzerland, consists in scientifically recording the threat to animals and plants and in communicating the results to governmental organizations and NGOs (non-governmental organizations).

Kleptospecies
A new category of taxa at the species level, the character of which does not coincide with the biological species concept.

Metamorphosis
In zoology, the transformation from the larval form to the mature animal, e.g. in the case of butterflies or amphibians.

National park
Area designed to protect and preserve an ecosystem or to promote species diversity. Interventions into the ecosystem—such as shooting to control populations—should, if possible, be avoided, but are sometimes necessary.

Nearctic
Biogeographical designation of the North American subregion covering the area from Greenland across North America to the highlands of Mexico.

Omnivore
Animals that eat everything, i.e. feed on both plants and meat.

Palearctic
Biogeographical designation for the temperate zones of the Old World. It covers Europe, North Africa, and Asia, not including the Arabian peninsula and the Indian subcontinent.

PCBs
Abbreviation for polychlorinated biphenyls. Highly toxic chlorine compounds that have been added as plasticizers to plastics, insulating materials, and lacquers, as well as being used in capacitors and hydraulic systems. They were banned in 2001 by the Stockholm Convention.

Population
Members of animal and plant species that, among other things, possess an almost identical gene pool, and reside and interbreed in a defined area.

Red List
A list of threatened animal and plant species published by the IUCN since 1963, subdivided into various categories ranging from a preliminary warning to eradicated species (see threat categories). It is updated every one to two years and, in 2007, comprised almost 17,000 animal and plant species, with the number of entries increasing rapidly.

Selection
Natural, artificial, or sexual selection always results in the genes of one individual fusing with those of another, and new individuals coming into being. Through targeted selection, negative elements can be diminished or eradicated, whereas positive ones are enhanced and accentuated. Derived from the Latin *selectio*.

Sexual dimorphism
Differences between male and female animals, e.g. in size, weight, color, or amount of hair (e.g. lion's mane).

Species diversity
Term used to describe the measure of all the plant and animal species of a certain habitat, e.g. desert, savanna, or rainforest. It is a component of biodiversity.

Threat categories
The International Union for Conservation of Nature and Natural Resources (IUCN) categorizes populations of animals and plants. The terminology used for immediately threatened species is as follows: Extinct (EX), Extinct in the Wild (EW), Critically Endangered (CE), Endangered (EN), and Vulnerable (VU).

Washington Species Protection Convention
Both an organization, founded in 1973, and a convention. The aim is to contribute to species conservation by prohibiting and restricting trade in threatened animals and plants and in products made from these.

WWF
World Wildlife Fund, as it is known in North America, and World Wide Fund for Nature, as it is known in the rest of the world, is a private nature conservation organization spanning the globe that was founded in Switzerland in 1961. Today, local WWF agencies manage about 3,000 nature and environment conservation projects worldwide. The WWF logo, the giant panda, which was designed by Sir Peter Scott, has become known the world over.

BIBLIOGRAPHY

In the production of this book, the authors had access to the following sources, in digital or printed form, although only the principal sources are shown in the list. The authors would like to thank all government offices and NGOs concerned for their support.

Aktionsgemeinschaft Artenschutz

Alpenforum

American Bird Conservancy

Bat Conservation Trust London

Biomedical Primate Research Centre

BirdLife International

BNA (Bundesverband für fachgerechten Natur- und Artenschutz): Association for the Protection of Flora and Fauna)

BUND (Bund für Umwelt und Naturschutz Deutschland): League for the Environment and for Nature Conservation, a branch of Friends of the Earth

Bundesamt für Naturschutz (BfN)

Bundesamt für Veterinärwesen Bern, Switzerland

CITES (Convention on International Trade in Endangered Species of Wild Fauna and Flora)

Conservation International Washington D.C.

Deutsche Gesellschaft für Herpetologie und Terrarienkunde: German Herpetological society

Deutsche Ornithologische Gesellschaft

Deutsche Tierpark Gesellschaft

EEP (Europäisches Erhaltungszucht-Programm): European Captive Breeding Programme

Gesellschaft zum Schutz der Meeressäugetiere

Gesellschaft zur Rettung der Delphine: Association for the Protection of Dolphins

Global Biodiversity Information

Greenpeace International and Germany

GTO (Gesellschaft für Tropenornithologie)

Institut für Zoo- und Wildtierforschung

International Friends of Nature

IPCC Intergovernmental Panel on Climate Change

IUCN (International Union for Conservation of Nature)

Jane Goodall Institute

Klima-Allianz

KORA Schweiz

KWS Kenya Wildlife Services

Marine Conservation Society

Max-Planck-Gesellschaft

NABU Germany

National Audubon Society USA

National Geographic Society, USA and Germany

Nationale Naturschutzbehörden verschiedener Länder

Nature Serve Explorer

Ocean Futures Society

Oro verde Tropenwaldstiftung

Partners in Flight—U.S.

PETA

Pro Natura Switzerland

Quantum Conservation

Ramsar Convention on Wetlands

Regenwaldschutz

Sea Watch Conservation

Senckenberg Museum

Sharkprojekt

Sierra Club USA

Smithsonian National Institution

Specialist Groups of the IUCN

Species 2000 ITIS

Terra Human

The Nature Conservancy

The Wildlife Trust

The World Parrot Trust

UK Nature and Wildlife

UNEP United Nations Environment Programme

UNEP World Conservation Monitoring Centre

U.S. Shorebird Conservation

Verein Jordsand zum Schutze der Seevögel und der Natur

Vista Verde

Vogelwarte Sempach

WCMC Species Database

Weltarbeitsgruppe für Greifvögel und Eulen

Western Hemisphere Shorebird Reserve Network

Whale and Dolphin Conservation Society

Wildfowl & Wetlands Trust Slimbridge

World Association of Zoos and Aquariums

World Database on Protected Areas

WWF (World Wildlife Fund)

Worldwildlife Wildfinder

Yaqu Pacha

Zentralverband Zoologischer Fachbetriebe Deutschlands

Zoo-AG Bielefeld

Zoodatenbank Germany

Zoodatenbank France

Zoodatenbank Switzerland

Zoologische Gesellschaft Frankfurt

Zoologische Gesellschaft für Arten- und Populationsschutz

PICTURE CREDITS

(left = l., right = r., bottom = b., bottom left = b.l., bottom right = b.r., top = t., top left = t.l., top right = t.r., center = c.,
bottom center = b.c., top center = t.c., center left = c.l., center right = c.r.)

Arco
NPL 13 b., NPL 15 t.l., NPL 20 b.r., NPL 22 r., Delpho 23 b., Schneider 27 t.c., NPL 27 t.r., Frei 28 b.r., Frei 29 t., b.r., Sutter 30 t.r., Henry 31 t., NPL 32 t., NPL 32 b., Philips 33 t., Schneider 34 t.r., Discherl 34 b., Frei 34 c., NPL 35, NPL 65 b., Bahr 105 b.l., NPL 119 c.l., NPL 128 b.r., Weyers 152 large, NPL 166, NPL 170 t.c., Denne 182 t.l., Frei 183 l., NPL 183 c.r., b.l., NPL 184, NPL 189 c.r., 189 b., Tuns 202 b., Tuns 219 t.r., Therin-Weise 229 t.r., Wegner 229 b., NPL 232 t.r., 233 t.r., Weimann 231 b.

Arndt, Ingo
38 b., 53 t., 53 b., 78, 87 t.l., 91 b.r., 113, 114, 115 large, 118, 126 b., 127 t., 132, 136 t.l., 138, 141, 195, 199 b.r., 210 t.

Brehm, Hermann
79 t.l., 142 b.r.

Corbis
NASA 9 t.r., Louie Psihoyos 16 t., Kevin Schafer 18 b., 19 t., John Carnemolla 21 b., Martin Harvey 22 l., Richard Wear/Design Pics 24, Anders Ryman 51, Jonathan Blair 64, Arthur Morris 99 b.r., Karl Ammann 126 c.r., Jeffrey L. Rotman 145 b.r., Anthony Bannister 147 c.r., David Turnley 158 b.l., Sharna Balfour 181 c.l., Theo Allofs 198, Theo Allofs/zefa 201, Paul Darrow/Reuters 214, Tom Brakefield 225 b.l., Gavriel Jecan 225

ditterightbild
Stempell 33 b.

Dolder, Willi
8, 9 t.l., 9 c.l., 9 b., 10, 12 b., 13 t., 14 t.l., 14 t.c., 14 t.r., 15 t.c., 15 large, 17 b.l., 17 r., 19 c., 19 b., 20 b.l., 21 t., 23 t., 25 t., 25 c., 26 t.l., 26 t.r., 27 t.l., 27 large, 31 b., 36 t.c., 37 t.c., 37 t.r., 37 large, 40 b.r., 41 t., 41 c.r., 42 b., 43 t.l., 43 t.r., 43 b., 44 t.l., 44 t.c., 44 t.r., 45 t.l., 45 t.c., 45 t.r., 45 large, 46/47 large, 47 t.r., 48 t., 48 b., 49, 50 b.c., 50 b.r., 52 t.r., 53 c.r., 54 t., 54 b., 55 t., 55 b.l., 55 b.r., 56 t.l., 56 t.c., 56 t.r., 57 t.c., 57 large, 59 c., 59 b., 60 t.r., 60 b., 61 t., 62 t.r., 62 c.r., 62 b., 63 t.r., 63 b., 65 t., 66 b.l., 68 t.l., 68 b.l., 69 t.r., 69 b.r., 70, 73 t., 73 c., 74 b.l., 75 b.l., 75 t.r., 76 b.l., 76/77, 77 t.r., 79 large, 80 c.l., 82 t.l., 83 c.l., 83 c.r., 85 t.r., 85 c.r., 86 t.r., 87 large, 87 b.r., 88 b.r., 89 t., 90/91 t., 91 t.r., 94, 95 t., 97 b.r., 102 b.l., 102 b.r., 106 t.l., 106 t.r., 107 t.l., 107 t.r., 111 c.r., 117 t.r., 121 t.r., 121 b.r., 134, 135 b.l., 140 t.r., 140 b., 143 t., 144 t.r., 144 b., 145 t., 146 t.r., 146 c.r., 146 b.r., 147 large, 148 c.r., 149 b.r., 150 b.l., 150 b.r., 151 t.r., 152 inset, 153, 156 t.l., 157 b., 158 t.l., 158 b.r., 160 t.l., 160 b., 161 b., 165 t.l., 165 b., 167 t.c., 167 c., 168 t.l., 168 b.l., 168 b.c., 168 b.r., 170 b., 171, 172/173, 173 t.l., 174 t., 175 b., 176 b., 177 t.r., 178, 179, 180, 181 b., 181 c.r., 183 c., 184, 185 t.l., 185 t.r., 186, 187 t.l., 187 c.r., 192 l., 192 r., 193 t., 193 b.r., 196 t., 196 b., 199 b.l., 202 t.l., 203, 209 b.l., 213 t.r., 213 c.l., 213 b., 214/215, 216, 217 t., 220 t.r., 220 b., 221, 222, 223 l., 224, 225 t., 226 b.l., 226 t.c., 226 t.r., 226 large, 227, 228, 230, 231 t.r., 232 t.l., 232 t.c., 233 t.l., 233 t.c., 234 t.c., 234 t.r., 235 t.l., 236 t.l., 236 t.c., 236 t.r., 237 t.l., 237 t.c., 237 t.r., 238 t.r., 239 t.c., 241 t.r., 242 t.l., 242 t.c., 242 t.r., 243 t.r.

Dossenbach, Hans
37 t.l., 38 c.l., 39 t.r., 47 t.c., 86 b., 116/117, 117 c.r., 172 t.r., 177 t.l., 210 b.

Friedhuber, Sepp
106 t.c., 205 t.r., 212 small

Gerth, Stefan
169

Getty Images
Keren Su/China Span RM 72 b., Tui De Roy/Minden Pictures RM 95 b.l., Timothy G. Laman/National Geographic 95 b.r., James L. Stanfield/National Geographic 143

Grunwald, Harald
93 t.r., 93 3rd from t.r., 197 t., 208, 209 c.l.

Güttinger, René
115 b.l., 115 b.r., 238 t.r.

Held, Andreas
42 t.r., 65 c., 75 b.r., 104 b., 110 t.r., 110 b., 149 t.r., 150 t., 151 large, 152, 163, 173 t.r., 174 b.r., 200 t., 239 t.l.

Hoogervorst, Fred
148 c.l.

Kaphahn
Ladygin 89 b., Medvedev 93 2nd from t.r., Gudkov 123, 124 b., 130 t., Medvedev 167 b., Kochnev 193 b.r., Chernyavski 194 c., Gudkov 240 t.r.

Kreinz, Robert
99 l., 194 b.

Layer, Werner and Kerstin
71 c., 111 t.r., 119 large, 120, 121 t.l., 128, 128/129, 130 b.l., 135 c.l., 135 r., 156 b., 159, 162, 187 b.r., 199 large, 240 t.c.

Marent, Thomas
11 b., 40 t., 50 b.l., 71 t., 84/85, 90 b.r., 107 large, 112, 122 t.r., 127 b., 131, 136 large, 200 b., 219 b.r., 235 t.c., 240 t.l., 243 t.l.

Pohl, Gernot
52 b., 111 large, 165 t.r., 175 t.r.

Pölking, Fritz
67 t., 80 c.r., 80 large, 88 l., 126 t.r., 128 b.l., 203 c.r., 205 2nd from t.r., 205 large, 207 t.l., 207 t.c., 207 t.r., 207 large, 215 b.r., 231 t.r., 243 t.c.

Pum, Eva and Helmut
57 t.r., 58 t.r., 59 t., 67 b., 96 b.l., 154, 161 t.r., 164/165, 205 large, 218, 234 t.l., 235 t.r.

Rogl, Manfred
92/93, 100 c. large

Sailer, Alexandra and Steffen
77 c.r., 100 b., 103, 133 t., 137, 155 t., 241 t.l.

Schulz, Gerhard
30 b., 130 b.r., 194 t.c.

Skorski, Dirk
96 b.r., 217 b.

Stefan, Josef
66 t.r., 98 b.r.

Sutter
Wendler 20 t., Lacz 26 t.c., Heulcin 90 l., Lacz 109 b.r., Jeske 139, Dragesco 172/173, Rao 173 t.c., Lacz 188, Gohier 189 t.r., Lacz 190 t., Heulcin 191 t.c., Walker 217 t.r., Lacz 219 c.r., Heulcin 238 t.c.

Trunk, Alfred and Annaliese
197 b.

Volz, Andreas
96/97, 98 l., 108 c.r., 108 b.

Wothe, Konrad
11 t., 28 l., 28 c.r., 36 t.l., 36 t.r., 39 large, 41 b.r., 47 t.l., 50/51, 57 t.l., 58 large, 61 b., 67 t., 68/69, 73 b.r., 74 b.r., 79 large, 80 c., 82 b., 83 b., 86 t.l., 93 b.r., 101 large, 104 t.l., 105 b.r., 109 large, 111 t., 117 b.r., 122 t.c., 124 t.l., 125 b.l., 125 r., 133 b.r., 142 t.l., 148 b., 155 b.r., 167 t.r., 181 b.r., 191 t.l., 204 b., 205 3rd from t.r., 212/213, 238 t.l., 241 t.c.

Ziesler, Günter
119 c.l.

INDEX